D0004892

Katie —

**At Least in the City
Someone Would Hear Me
Scream**

Perhaps the cutest
dress Ever....
Aren't you glad
you were coerced
into buying?
Enjoy!
XX
Wesley.

Also by Wade Rouse

Confessions of a Prep School Mommy Handler: A Memoir

America's Boy: A Memoir

At Least in the City Someone Would Hear Me Scream

[Misadventures in Search of the Simple Life]

Wade Rouse

Harmony Books · New York

Copyright © 2009 by Wade Rouse

All rights reserved.

Published in the United States by Harmony Books, an imprint of the Crown Publishing Group, a division of Random House, Inc., New York.
www.crownpublishing.com

HARMONY BOOKS is a registered trademark and the Harmony Books colophon is a trademark of Random House, Inc.

Library of Congress Cataloging-in-Publication Data

Rouse, Wade.
    At least in the city someone would hear me scream / Wade Rouse.—1st ed.
        p.   cm.
    1. Rouse, Wade.   2. Gay men—Michigan—Biography.   I. Title.
    HQ75.8.R677A3   2009
    977.4'14044092–dc22
    [B]   2008050592

ISBN 978-0-307-45190-3

Printed in the United States of America

Design by Lauren Dong

10   9   8   7   6   5   4   3   2

First Edition

To MY PARENTS and GRANDPARENTS

You taught me that tires on gravel roads, and locusts, and whip-poor-wills singing after a thunderstorm were really the voice of God. And you were right. It just took me a few decades to realize it.

To GARY, Who Taught Me

Do not go where the path may lead,
Go instead where there is no path
And leave a trail.
—Ralph Waldo Emerson

Contents

Author's Note

Readers need to know that names (besides me, Gary, and a few of our family and friends) and identifying characteristics have been changed, and, in some instances, characters were composited, locations and details recast, and time compressed. This was done to protect anonymity and streamline the narrative, and also out of a sincere desire to remain in the cottage and county I now love and call home.

Green acres is the place to be.

Farm livin' is the life for me.

Part One

Wade's Walden

As I came home through the woods with my string of fish, trailing my pole, it being now quite dark, I caught a glimpse of a woodchuck stealing across my path, and felt a strange thrill of savage delight, and was strongly tempted to seize and devour him raw; not that I was hungry then, except for that wildness which he represented. Once or twice, however, while I lived at the pond, I found myself ranging the woods, like a half-starved hound, with a strange abandonment, seeking some kind of venison which I might devour, and no morsel could have been too savage for me. The wildest scenes had become unaccountably familiar.

—HENRY DAVID THOREAU, *Walden*

Of all the wonders of nature, a tree in summer is perhaps the most remarkable; with the possible exception of a moose singing "Embraceable You" in spats.

—WOODY ALLEN

Coonskin Cap

There's a raccoon on my head.

And I don't particularly look good in hats.

Especially when they're still moving.

I certainly wish this were one of those "Hey, look at me standing here on vacation in Wall Drug wearing a fifteen-dollar coonskin cap pretending to be Daniel Boone, so hurry up and take the goddamn picture!" moments, but it's not.

No, my cap is very much alive, very much pissed off, and very much sporting a bad stink, a head filled with razor fangs, and a lot of painfully sharp claws.

But I guess I'd be pissed off, too, if someone interrupted my late-night dinner reservation.

Who knew that in the woods you simply can't shove a forgotten bag of trash into your garbage can?

I didn't.

That's because I'm a city boy, a self-obsessed gay man who intentionally bedazzled himself in roughly $1,000 worth of trendy clothing just to walk the trash out *in the middle of fucking nowhere*!

I honestly believe, deep down, that I am like K-Fed in Vegas, or some pseudocelebrity on vacation who just might be ambushed by the paparazzi at any moment.

But I'm really just a lost soul, in every possible way.

Not long ago, I moved to the woods of Michigan from the city, because I wanted to be a modern-day Henry David Thoreau.

My goal? To find myself, to find my modern-day Walden Pond, by stripping away superfluous luxuries and living a plainer, simpler life.

Thoreau famously wrote: "I went to the woods because I wished to live deliberately, to front only the essential facts of life, and see if I could not learn what it had to teach, and not, when I came to die, discover that I had not lived."

And he is right. The woods have already taught me something of great value: I *am* going to die. Specifically, I am going to die after being disfigured by a raccoon.

But at least I have had a life-changing epiphany, albeit a bit too late. The epiphany "Never go to a place that doesn't have a Starbucks within arm's reach or you might find a wild animal clinging to your scalp" has already edged out my all-time favorite epiphany, the one I had in eighth grade: "My God, my thingy doesn't seem to work when I kiss girls!"

The raccoon digs its claws into the side of my head and begins to burrow, like it's trying to bury the apple core it still has in its mouth into the middle of my brain.

My hair! I think. *You're jacking up my hair!*

Which is another reason why I shouldn't be living in the woods. I care more about how my profile will look when I'm found dead than about actually trying to stay alive.

The raccoon locates an artery, and I begin screaming, like any man who is truly scared for his life.

And then I pee on myself.

I admit it. There is no shame.

I scream again, yelling, "Help! Help! There's a raccoon on my head! Can somebody, anybody, help me?"

But I sadly realize this is a rhetorical question, that it doesn't matter what I yell, because no one can hear me in the woods. My closest neighbor is a "holler" away, or whatever the hell they say out here in the country.

In fact, my yells simply echo off the surrounding pines, the voice coming back to me sounding a whole lot like Drew Barrymore right before she gets offed at the beginning of *Scream*.

I do have enough wherewithal, however, to scrunch my eyes shut, in order to protect my vision, and to begin spinning like a top, twirling like a drunken, crazed ballerina, to jostle the beast free. Unfortunately, the coon is along for the ride.

I can feel blood beginning to trickle down my face.

I will later read on Wikipedia, the online encyclopedia: "Raccoons are unusual for their thumbs, which (though not opposable) enable them to open many closed containers (such as garbage cans) and doors. The raccoon is most distinguishable by the black 'mask' of fur around its eyes and the long, bushy tail. They are intelligent omnivores with a reputation for being clever, sly, and mischievous. Raccoons range from 20 to 40 inches in length (including the tail) and weigh between 10 and 35 pounds. As city dwellers in the United States and Canada increasingly move into primary or second homes in former rural areas, raccoons are often considered pests because they forage in trash receptacles."

I, of course, read this too late, like I do everything in my life: the nutrition chart on Little Debbie boxes, the prescription for my Xanax, the size 4 tag in the back of my "men's" jeans.

However, I am a child of the '70s, which means I didn't really have to read to learn anything; I just had to watch TV. And that I did.

That's when it hits me. The solution to my problems.

What would Lucy do? I ask myself.

Lucy would fight back, in some wacky-chocolate-factory, grape-stompin', Vitameatavegamin way!

So I grab the garbage can lid, and the flashlight I am holding, and begin to wield them like shields, like Brad Pitt in *Troy,* and whack the raccoon, taking part of my temple along with it. But the coon doesn't budge. It screeches and digs its claws more deeply into my skull.

It's those damn thumbs. They may not be opposable, but I swear this thing could hitchhike.

The coon's tail swings over my shoulder, and, for a second, I resemble Madonna on her Blonde Ambition tour. And then I realize this is my payback. Just a couple of weeks ago in the city I was making fun of a woman with hideous hair extensions in Walgreens. I mean, I had to: The color and texture didn't even match her real hair. And I could see where she had clipped them in.

The raccoon scratches my temple, and I release more urine down the pant legs of the dark jeans I love so much.

I drop the flashlight and the garbage can lid and desperately try to grab the raccoon with both hands. It latches onto my left arm, which is layered in a brand-new $500 Banana Republic leather coat.

I pull an armful of fur out of the frightened beast, and it hisses at me.

"Let go, you stinky little bastard!"

These words sober me instantly as I remember the night in the city not so long ago when I yelled exactly the same phrase at a hairy, stinky man who tried to snatch the Longchamp handbag off the arm of one of my best girlfriends as we left a downtown nightclub. That night, in desperation, begging for Lucy's guidance, I had yanked from my True Religion jeans pocket the only two items I had to thwart the would-be criminal: my tube of Burt's Bees Lip Shimmer, to use as a mock knife, and my spearmint breath freshener, to use as my gay-boy Mace pepper spray. And, believe it or not, this ad hoc city survival plan had worked.

I *never* left the house, no matter where or when, even at night in the country, without these two items: breath freshener to keep me minty and lip balm to provide a pop of color and shimmery shine. A fella never knows who he might run into . . . an old boyfriend, a purse snatcher, the paparazzi, a raccoon.

Instinctively, my right hand goes deep into the pocket of my dark jeans to yank out my Sephora artillery.

My furry nemesis suddenly grabs my upper lip—growing bored by this drama—and the pain shocks me back into reality. I manage to simultaneously poke at the animal with my lip balm and square up the breath spray as best I can in the dark, just as if I were going to snap a picture of myself with a cell phone camera, a tactic I have perfected. I take aim at the whites of the raccoon's beady eyes, just like I had done at the purse snatcher.

And then I spray.

Twice.

Because that's what I always do to ensure freshness.

The coon squeals, bites me on the hand, and then grabs my super-shimmery lip balm. I release the breath spray, the raccoon releases my arm, and it sprints into the deep, dark woods, the little bandit blinded temporarily, I'm sure, but now sporting surprisingly minty breath.

Thank you, Lucy. Thank you.

And just like her, I start to cry—weep, really, like only Lucy can weep—out of panic and terror, of course, but mostly out of an overwhelming sense of reality.

What would Lucy do?

Well, right now, the director would yell, "Cut!" and she would go off to her trailer and start reading tomorrow's script. I am not so lucky.

As I stand in the dark, in the north woods, with no cameras or TV lights, no new script waiting for me, I realize that I brought all of this on myself.

I moved to the country intentionally, because I wanted to follow my dream of being a writer. I wanted to face down my rural childhood. I wanted to create "Wade's Walden."

I wanted to live simply, like Thoreau.

I wanted peace and serenity.

But I think I got rabies instead.

Signs, Signs, Everywhere There's Signs

Let's get one very obvious thing straight from the beginning.

I am not Mr. Nature.

I am not Grizzly Adams.

I am not Yul Gibbons.

I am "manly" in the sort of way that Isaac Mizrahi is manly.

I cannot live off the land like a Pilgrim, although I did rather admire their buckle shoes and penchant for wearing black.

I am not one of those bullshit macho guys who thinks he can go on *Survivor* and then cracks two days in because he's out of hair gel. I *need* my hair gel. Specifically, I need my Dirt from Jonathan Antin.

I *need* my stuff.

Which, typically, comes from Sephora and not Bass Pro.

I should not be living in the woods of Michigan. I grew up in the Ozarks, in the woods, and it was not the best place for a chubby gay child to live. It was beyond surreal, like finding David Gest shopping at Big Lots.

The closest I now come to the rural roots of my childhood is eating my beloved Kashi Go Lean cereal, which tastes akin to the sassafras bark I used to pluck and chew as a kid, and watching episodes of *Reba,* which has taken the place of my old *Hee Haw* fascination.

I purposely transformed myself from a country rube into a sophisticated city boy, a Starbucks-swilling, pashima-wearing, catch-a-Parker-Posey-independent-movie kind of guy.

I now wear jeans so tight that when I sit down with a cell phone in my pocket I accidentally ass-dial one of my friends.

It takes me at least an hour in the bathroom before I go anywhere, an hour and a half if I'm shaving. I get ready to my favorite music while trying to perfect dance moves. My all-time favorites are: "Genie in a Bottle" by Christina Aguilera; "Respect Yourself" by Madonna; "Freedom" by George Michael; "Toxic" by Britney Spears; and "Fergalicious" and "Glamorous" by Fergie.

I consider Kenneth Cole to be on par with Gandhi for his contributions to the world.

I eat the same specialized low-fat, high-protein, low-sodium, low-sugar foods every single day. I ship extra luggage ahead for a three-day weekend somewhere. I work out two hours a day. I highlight my hair so it looks "sun kissed" but never highlighted. I tan. I whiten my teeth. I like to wear chokers and anklets and rings and watches and bracelets.

All of which is why I am the world's most unlikely Henry David Thoreau.

All of which is why I'm the last person you would expect to find living in the middle of the Michigan woods, within walking distance of a country store that sells turkey hunting licenses and camouflage instead of in the city within walking distance of a good Thai restaurant or a Crate & Barrel.

Remember that episode of *Sex and the City* when Carrie goes to the country and has no idea what to do with herself? That's me. Except in slides instead of stilettos.

I like the rush, the frenzy, the insanity of city living and getting a thousand things done in a day. I love mainlining quad-shot lattes, running twelve miles in the city park, heading to dinner with friends at a hip new restaurant, and slurping a couple of mojitos shaken by a guy who looks like a Zac Posen model.

I like to look pretty. I like to get my hair cut at salons by beautiful, bored men who only go by an initial—"Yes, I have an appointment with *Z*!"

I like to buy feta-stuffed chicken breasts and ahi tuna at Whole Foods.

I like to buy retro Froot Loop T-shirts for $50 at Anthropologie.

I get microdermabrasions and tint my eyelashes.

I may be the only man in the United States to buy Mary Kay and swipe lotion and bronzer onto his bare legs in the supermarket while he thumps kiwi.

I'm proud of that.

But this doesn't necessarily mean I was fulfilled. It doesn't mean that I was happy.

I may sound about as deep as a Slip 'n Slide, but I'm not.

Like so many creative, driven types—gay or straight—who were raised in the country, I fled to the closest city, as quickly as I could, to escape my rural upbringing. And I just kept on running: to new jobs, to bigger promotions, to better places.

Or so I thought.

But then, I turned forty.

Four. Oh!

I am the ultimate cliché.

But, truly, that's when it hit me: I had always been running from my childhood, and I was tired. Mentally and physically exhausted. I hated my job. I hated that my dreams of being a writer hadn't been fulfilled. And (insert maniacal laugh of my parents here) I was beginning to believe that there was a void in my life that the city and its incessant, nonstop activity and noise could no longer fill.

But I kept ignoring the signs.

In reality, I don't know why I, or my partner, Gary, would ever have wanted to return to rural life.

We already fled the cornfields, and endless baseball diamonds, and dirty IGAs, in our knockoff Cole Haans, because our memories of teenage rural life were mostly of getting spit on in high school for pinch-rolling our jeans, or for nabbing the lead in *Pirates of Penzance*, or, more honestly, for secretly hoping to make out with the captain of the football team in the bench seat of his pickup.

We fled to the city, any city, to be enveloped in enormity and anonymity. We wanted to be both individuals and invisible, to be accepted but left alone. And we wanted, more than anything else, to reinvent ourselves. But reinvent ourselves as what?

I grew up worshipping Erma Bombeck instead of George Brett, Joe Montana, or Buck Owens. When boys from school would come to my house they would inevitably make fun of her books—*The Grass Is Always Greener over the Septic Tank* and *If Life Is a Bowl of Cherries, What Am I Doing in the Pits?*—which I had sitting on my nightstand, and the photos of her I had pinned to my corkboard wall.

"What's *wrong* with you?" they would often ask.

Which is why I ran and ran, and kept running, from rural America, until I found myself in the city doing everything but what I had initially set out to do.

Write.

I was making great money, I was traveling, I was eating at the best restaurants.

But was I happy?

My parents often say that many city people like me are "full of nonsense," meaning we urbanites become so used to being surrounded by meaningless things and misguided people that we have lost sight of what's truly valuable in life.

I thought they were full of shit.

And then I had one of those life-changing days, the really big, super-shocking kind, the kind, perhaps, that Mary had when she learned she was a pregnant virgin or Jennifer Grey experienced when the bandages came off her nose.

I had been waking up at four A.M. to write my first memoir, *America's Boy.* I had been consumed with writing about my childhood— the beauty, the horror, the unconditional and transformational love of family—and could not sleep any longer without getting it all out. One morning, when it came time for me to go to my job as a PR director at a prep school—a position that entailed mucho schmoozing and dwindling self-esteem—I had to force myself to stop writing by turning on the TV as loudly as possible to distract myself.

Today was blaring as I raced around our tiny city bungalow, leap-frogging our mutt, Marge, in the hallway. Matt Lauer was interviewing a couple who had quit their jobs to run a B&B in Bali.

"We have discovered the secret to happiness. Follow your obsession," they told Matt.

"You freaks!" I yelled at the TV as I dry-swallowed a vitamin, aspirated Kashi, lint-brushed my suit, reviewed my meeting notes, and tossed a Bonz down the basement stairs for Marge to follow. "I'm happy!"

I found myself in my car, already late to work for another day of insanity and stupidity—already preoccupied about meaningless meetings, preoccupied about what I was wearing, preoccupied about the fact that I didn't have enough time to write, preoccupied about the last thing I'd yelled.

I was happy, damn it!

Or was I happy in the way that sheep or lobotomy patients are happy, mindlessly bleating and going through the motions? Was I just one of the "sheeple" (part sheep, part people), a term a friend of mine used when referring to many Americans who seem to sleepwalk through their lives?

I was so preoccupied that I didn't realize, until it was nearly too late, that I was almost out of gas. So I beelined across two lanes of highway traffic to hit an exit and chug into a gas station.

I started filling my tank when a man's voice confidently boomed out through the pump to remind me that by starting a Value Rewards Program I could be earning bonus points for every gallon of gas and large Pepsi I purchased. I angrily finger-punched the Mute button, but it didn't work. The man continued to tell me, in excruciating detail, how I was basically a fucking idiot for not taking advantage of this incredible promotion.

I smacked Mute again.

Nothing.

So I grabbed the window washer sitting on the side of the pump and used the handle to "poke" the Mute button.

The man's voice stopped.

But then a woman's voice came over the intercom: "Ummm, baby, yeah . . . you gunna stop whackin' our pump, or I'll have to call the po-lice, mmmkaay, baby?"

I glanced over at the window.

A woman who looked like Mo'Nique was staring at me with her hands on her hips.

The intercom popped on one more time: "We all have bad days, baby. Hell, I'm havin' a bad life."

I got in my car, gripped the wheel, and saw that my hands were shaking.

I eased my way back into an all-out traffic jam and instantly came to a complete stop.

"Goddamn it! No! No! No! Move, traffic! I'm late!"

And, for one moment in my life, I couldn't go anywhere. I couldn't rush ahead.

So I started thinking of my morning, of my life.

Was I having a bad *morning*?

Or a bad *life*?

I asked myself again: *Wade, are you happy?*

And then I became emotional. So emotional, in fact, that I lowered my head on my steering wheel and began to sob as Christina Aguilera told me I was beautiful.

When a car honked to knock me from my stupor, to let me know I could inch ahead a few feet, I lifted my head from the wheel in time to see a man holding a sign on an overpass above the highway. The man, who looked like a greasy, heavily medicated version of Jesus, held aloft a cardboard sign that read in poorly scrawled letters: WHAT WOULD YOU DO IF YOU COULD NOT FAIL?

He was backlit by the morning sun, rays splaying from behind his body, and the image looked like one of those religious paintings, in black velvet perhaps, or color-by-numbers, that you find buried under other crap in a cluttered antiques store. I was stunned to see this phrase: This was the mantra that our friend John Fletcher had been chanting at me for years as he encouraged me to pounce on my writing dreams *without* fear.

As my car inched toward the overpass, the man simply reached over and, as if on cue, dropped his sign, which flitted and fluttered and floated like a butterfly caught in a crosswind before landing *directly* over my windshield.

All I could see, in close-up 3-D, my eyes crossing to make sure I was still reading it correctly, was its message: WHAT WOULD YOU DO IF YOU COULD NOT FAIL?

I braked immediately, panicked, unable to see, and fetched the sign off my window, ignoring the angry honks of the drivers. I shoved the sign, which was covered in grimy fingerprints and smelled like gas and motor oil, into my backseat. As I came out from under the overpass, I glanced in my rearview mirror, and Jesus was waving at me—alternately blowing kisses and doing the sign of the cross, like a mix of the Pope and Liza. The sun had obliterated his face into an explosion of white. As my eyes turned toward the road again, it was then I caught a glimpse of the backside of Jesus' cardboard sign reflected in the driver's mirror. It was the outside of a packing box, with an address that read: WALDEN'S AUTOMOTIVE.

I took this, pardon the obvious pun, as a sign.

It was, in fact, the millionth sign in my sign-filled morning, but it was the most obvious and the one to which I finally paid attention.

I took this final sign with the same seriousness as if God Himself had vaporized into my passenger seat, turned off the Christina Aguilera CD I was listening to, and said, "Pay attention, dumb ass!"

So, for once in my life, I did.

Wade's Walden

Early in the spring of 1845—some 160 years before I would make my way into the middle of the Michigan woods—Henry David Thoreau, then twenty-seven years old, first began to chop down tall pines to build the foundation of his home on the shores of Walden Pond in Massachusetts.

According to the *Encyclopaedia Britannica,* Thoreau was disillusioned and bored by working in his family's business, making pencils and grinding graphite, and decided in early 1845 to take up an idea of a Harvard classmate who had once built a waterside hut in which "one could loaf or read." In the spring Thoreau picked a spot by Walden Pond, a small glacial lake located two miles south of Concord on land that his mentor Ralph Waldo Emerson owned.

From the very beginning, says *Britannica,* this move gave him profound satisfaction.

Once settled, Thoreau restricted his diet for the most part to the fruit and vegetables he found growing wild and the beans he planted. When not busy weeding his bean rows and trying to protect them from hungry woodchucks or occupied with fishing, swimming, or rowing, he spent long hours observing and recording the local flora and fauna, reading, and making entries in his journals, which he later polished and included in *Walden.* Much time, too, was spent simply in meditation.

Out of such activity and thought, continues *Britannica,* came

Walden, a series of eighteen essays describing Thoreau's experiment in basic living and his effort to set his time free for leisure.

So how does this parallel my own life?

My Ozarks grandmother was a secret *Walden* devotee.

She used to tell me that she attempted to make sense of her life—a life she felt had gone too quickly, a life she felt she had too often squandered—through two books: the Bible and Henry David Thoreau's *Walden.*

In our "coffee chats"—the morning talks we had at our old Ozarks log cabin as we sat swinging away the summers of my youth and the final summers of her life on a barn-red glider that sat atop a sand-colored bluff overlooking a vast expanse of Sugar Creek—my grandma Rouse told me, quietly, confidentially, in a whisper that I could barely distinguish over the distant rushing of the creek, that the Bible gave her *afterlife* meaning but that *Walden* gave her *here-life* meaning.

She passed this wisdom along only to me, knowing that in the Ozarks, such crazy talk was considered heresy. To publicly put any book on the same level as the Bible, or to mention anyone in the same breath as Jesus, meant you were next in line to get the "Cuckoo whistle" at the IGA.

My grandma had an old hardbound edition of *Walden* she had "borrowed" from the library. For about seventeen years.

The book was akin to the delicate little flower arrangements she kept too long on her bedside table: While *Walden* began to smell a bit moldy and look a bit past its prime, it continued to hold a mesmerizing power.

My grandma would read to me from *Walden,* which she kept hidden in the center of her oversize Bible lest someone should walk up unexpectedly. She would read and then explain what each passage meant to her.

She had so many favorite passages from *Walden* that I remember them vividly to this day, passages she recited at every single coffee chat, no matter where we were in the book.

Live each season as it passes; breathe the air, drink the drink, taste the fruit, and resign yourself to the influence of each.

This line, said my grandmother, a notorious penny-pincher who had survived the Depression, was a prime reason why—one day on a whim, after a lifetime of saving and folding used tinfoil—she bought our log cabin on Sugar Creek.

"Live!" she would exclaim to me, giving the word more power and gusto than that with which she had probably lived much of her life. "Live!"

And then, as a contrast, she would whisper, "Resign yourself to the influence of nature," and gesture dramatically toward the creek, into the sky, pointing at the sandy-colored bluffs in the distance, her Avon bracelet like a hawk in flight.

As if on cue, the wind would carry the scent of the surrounding woods, and my mind would stop wandering. I would stop thinking about running away to search for shale or go inner-tubing, and I would listen to the creek. To the wind. To my grandmother's breath.

I succumbed to nature.

But then I grew up, and time flew along diligently, like the geese headed south, and I could only think of how much I hated being gay, and creative, and trapped in the country. I dreamed of running away to buildings, to masses of people, to anonymity. I begged for time to fly. I prayed for ten, twenty years to pass.

And fate, like it always does, granted my wish.

In her final years, my grandmother began to write me long letters, reminding me of *Walden,* asking if I was reading Thoreau. "Are you on the right/write path?" she would scribble, the letters smearing as she dragged her aging palm against the wet ink.

Then my grandmother passed, and I—like we all do—begged to have that lost time back, to be next to her, to succumb to nature.

Still, her voice resonated in me, and passages from *Walden* would just pop into my head at odd times, like while I was driving or sitting in a meeting at work, and I would think, *Have I lived? How did I get to this point right here, right now? Is this my life's destiny?*

This popped into my head that fateful morning, and it was then I knew: My grandmother wasn't crazy. She was trying to tell me to chart my own course, one she hadn't been able to chart as a woman born in the early 1900s, who had children and no schooling but a head full of dreams, including that her grandson would not simply, as Thoreau famously said, "fall into a particular route."

So, initially, I did what my grandmother had done: I went a little bit off my rocker.

My partner, Gary, and I meandered, purely by chance, to Michigan for a vacation. I needed to leave my lumbar-perfect office chair, scrape the mollusks off my ass. I needed to breathe and take stock of my life. I needed quiet and time to think.

I had never been to Saugatuck, Michigan, touted as the "Fire Island of the Midwest" and the "Art Coast of Michigan." In fact, I had never been to Michigan. But, as soon as we arrived, I became "smitten with the Mitten."

Like my grandma, I believe that everyone has a place they dream of living, a nirvana, a heaven on earth, a place where—when you reach it—you feel it resonate in your soul: *I have arrived. This is where I am supposed to be.* For some, it might well be a lodge in the mountains, a hut snuggled next to the Caribbean, a loft in Manhattan, a country house in Tuscany, or a log cabin in the Ozarks. And yet, the majority of us maybe hit such dream spots only a few times in our lives, during a week's vacation.

The first time I arrived in Saugatuck, Michigan (after being directed here when on vacation the previous year in P-town), I instantly knew my question had been answered, because the answer resonated in my soul: *I have arrived. This is where I am supposed to be.*

Where I found myself was a small town—with a big asterisk.

I found myself in Gayberry.

That's what I instantly termed this little area, this mix of Mayberry RFD, Martha's Vineyard, and San Francisco. It wasn't the small towns I was familiar with or similar to the ones Gary knew. In the summer, Saugatuck has a Hamptons feel, resorters flocking from nearby cities to the nostalgic little beach town to soak up its charm, shop in its outstanding art galleries, and load up with blueberries and strawberries and peaches and apples at its picturesque U-Pick farms.

And yet, at its heart, Saugatuck is isolated rural living.

It's both the sound of coyotes in the winter and million-dollar yachts in the summer.

If there's a place with a Jekyll-and-Hyde complex, this would be it.

Saugatuck-Douglas is an artists' colony located among Lake Michigan's towering sand dunes. The neighboring towns of Saugatuck and Douglas sit along the Kalamazoo River and the waters of Lake Michigan.

The beaches are among the most stunning in the United States, the summer air humidity-free, the vistas breathtaking. The towns are a throwback, complete with quaint, window-boxed cottages and whitewashed Victorianesque storefronts that bustle with activity, art galleries on par with the big cities' best, and top-notch restaurants. It has survived modernization and thwarted the flirtations of big chains, like McDonald's, to remain a Midwestern Martha's Vineyard, a resort area without strip malls and billboards and tackiness.

Smitten with Saugatuck-Douglas, Gary and I immediately began to look at homes in the quaint townships, because that's what gay men do between shopping and tanning: They look at real estate. But between housing costs, property taxes, and my Rouse Depression-era stinginess gene, we couldn't afford a second home here, much less property.

And then someone "suggested" we look *outside* town.

An agent drove us roughly ten miles out of town, where we rediscovered rural America. Away from the expensive resort homes and cute shops and tanned city tourists riding bikes, carrying Louis Vuitton bags, and sipping lattes, we found farms, horses, gorgeous wine vineyards, little lakes, and our dream house, a knotty pine cottage sitting next to an overgrown lot with a single-wide trailer on it.

The presence of the trailer and our lack of cash meant we weren't really "looking" to buy. But then we made the mistake of innocently wandering inside this quaint cottage perched in the woods—a "classic Michigan cottage," it was termed—a gut-rehabbed home angled just so against a backdrop of swaying pines and sugar maples so heavily draped with leaves they looked as if they were bending down to give us a hug.

The moment I walked up the curving flagstone pathway, inhaled the smell of wood walls and then smoke from the dry-stack stone fireplace, saw the retro sink that was big enough to hold a cupboard full of dishes, looked up at the sleeping loft, I knew I had rediscovered the essence of my grandparents' old log cabin on Sugar Creek.

Gary and I walked out onto the screen porch and watched the sun shimmer through the swaying trees. Through our sweep of woods, we saw a burst of blue. We were a mile or so from the lake, so I knew it couldn't be the water. When we asked the Realtor, she told us our neighbors owned a hobby farm, including a fairly large blueberry field.

"They'd probably let you pick your hearts out, if they like you," she said.

I looked at Gary. He looked at me. We looked at this unblemished spot of land. It was so simple and yet so spectacular. It was roughly a million times bigger than our postage-stamp-size yard in the city.

"It's next to a trailer," Gary said, preempting me.

"It'll change," I coaxed. "It's called gentrification. Look what's happened to our neighborhood in St. Louis. Nasty houses replaced by huge homes. Things change. People change. Places change."

Gary didn't look convinced. And I didn't really sound that convincing.

And then we heard what we thought was the sound of thunder, though the sky was cloudless, deep blue. The surrounding pines began to shake and quake, like a dog after a bath, and in them we spotted a virtual swarm of gigantic, prehistoric birds rumbling and squawking. Eventually, they began to flap very unglamorously down from the pines to the ground outside the screen porch to feed on corn that had been scattered for them.

"Wild turkeys," the agent said.

They were the most hideously beautiful creatures I had ever seen: wobbly red necks, creepy eyes, thin legs.

We watched—standing silently and rigidly on the porch—as the turkeys ate for nearly an hour, the three toms protecting their ladies by fanning their feathers like ostriches and then strutting around proudly. And then we moved and the porch creaked, and the turkeys began to run, if you can call it running—strut, strut, strut—until they were hidden in the woods.

The next morning, we were drawn to look again at the cottage, and the turkeys were back. And, along with them, an assortment of finches and indigo buntings. I noticed the unfurling ferns and wild-flowers in the woods.

"This land used to be a nursery," the agent told us.

Gary, a gifted gardener, gasped.

I instantly thought of my grandmother, and of Thoreau, who famously wrote in *Walden:* "Our life is frittered away by detail . . . Simplify, simplify."

And so we did.

By adding a big second mortgage to our lives.

As we signed our names on the loan documents, Gary and I looked at each other, and he asked, "What should we name the place?"

"Writer's Block," I said. "No, Whispering Pines."

"That sounds like the name of a nursing home," Gary said.

"Wait . . . How about Turkey Run?"

"Isn't that what Martha Stewart named her place?"

"No. Turkey Hill. But we can copy," I said. "If Martha likes it, what more do we need?"

And so we had Turkey Run. And I had an even bigger dilemma, an irrational inability to get this place out of my mind when we returned to the city.

On the evening I saw God/Liza disguised as a homeless man on the overpass, I blew off my evening workout and instead went to a local bookstore, where I grabbed a quad-shot white mocha and sat cross-legged in the middle of the aisle, skimming a paperback version of *Walden.*

And then I got to the following passage:

How vain it is to sit down to write when you have not stood up to live.

That's when it finally, *finally* hit me: Was I truly *living*?

There is a difference, I then realized, between being alive and living.

"Live!" my grandmother had told me. "Live!"

I reread the introduction to *Walden*.

Thoreau didn't just write *Walden* to write a book. He set out to conduct an experiment with his own life.

"Could he survive, possibly even thrive, by stripping away all superfluous luxuries, living a plain, simple life in radically reduced conditions?" asks Jonathan Levin in an intoduction to the book.

Besides building his own shelter and chopping his own firewood, he would grow and catch his own food, even provide his own entertainment, writes Levin. It was, as Thoreau delighted to point out, an experiment in basic home economics; but, in truth, his aim was to investigate the larger moral and spiritual economy of such a life. If, as he notes in the book's first chapter, the "mass of men lead lives of quiet desperation," perhaps by leaving it all behind and starting over on the relatively isolated shores of Walden Pond, he could restore some of life's seemingly diminished vigor.

Could I?

Could I uproot my life and wander into the woods to find myself, my happiness?

Who has the balls to do that?

My vigor was certainly diminished. I catered to wealthy women. Most mornings, I already wanted to gouge my eyes out with a plastic fork at breakfast meetings. And, let's be honest, my spirit was being squashed every single day by a president and government who condemned my life and equated my existence with evil.

I grabbed a stack of coffeehouse napkins and began to do some math, never my strong point. I figured if the average male life span was just a hair over 75 years, that gave me a total of 900 months to live. So, right this instant, I had spent 504 months from my life's checking account, leaving me some 396 months to live.

Three hundred and ninety-six months!

But how could I leave my life, my job, my friends?

Who follows their heart? It's insane.

And then I read the following passage, near the beginning of *Walden*:

So thoroughly and sincerely are we compelled to live, reverencing our life, and denying the possibility of change. This is the only way, we say; but there are as many ways as there can be drawn radii from one centre. All change is a miracle to contemplate; but it is a miracle which is taking place every instant.

I looked up, blinking, as if I'd just had water thrown in my face, and I knew in this nanosecond, I knew holding the book: I would return to my rural roots. I would return to the woods. More specifically, I would be a full-time writer in Michigan. I would set out to embrace the simplicity in life, to discover the essential facts of life, a complicated man striving to lead an uncomplicated life.

I would be a modern-day Thoreau.

Moreover, I would move back to the country with the intention of not only making myself a better person but also righting some wrongs. I wanted to be myself in a rural area, not the wannabe straight boy I had pretended to be. I wanted to be unafraid of the wild animals of the woods, not cry when I touched a frog. I wanted to stand in the rain and let it drench me, not scream out damnation at the skies above for ruining my hair. I wanted to slow down and breathe.

Fueled by enough caffeine to power a large generator, I wrote "WADE'S WALDEN" across the top of another coffeehouse napkin and began to scribble down my new life goals, one per napkin, that would match the tenets and principles that Thoreau set forth in *Walden*.

I wrote:

LESSON ONE
Devote my life to writing full-time and embrace the
"solitary life"
(Commune with nature; enjoy peace and quiet; savor serenity; nature walks instead of malls; write, write, write!)

LESSON TWO
Eschew the latest entertainment and fashion for simpler
pursuits
*(No cable! No magazine subscriptions! No shopping in boutiques! No
new shoes! Play games! Read! Get to know Gary again!)*

LESSON THREE
Learn to love the snow
(Face my fear. Embrace the powder!)

LESSON FOUR
Embrace my rural brethren
*(Toss out my country stereotypes and stop flinching from my youth.
Love thy neighbor!)*

LESSON FIVE
Participate in country customs
*(Just because I hated gigging frogs as a kid doesn't mean I can't enjoy
some rural traditions! Break out of your snotty city rut!)*

LESSON SIX
Live off the land
*(Thoreau tended to a seven-acre bean garden. We can and will nur-
ture a vegetable garden, and live off it for the summer!)*

LESSON SEVEN
Nurture our country critters
*(There is no need to scream when I see spiders. They are just as afraid
of me. Feed the birds, romp with the deer . . . remember, I am en-
croaching on their world, not the other way around.)*

LESSON EIGHT
Rediscover religion
*(Can I rediscover my spirituality in a part of the world where I feel I
still don't belong?)*

LESSON NINE
Let go of my city cynicism
(Enough said . . .)

LESSON TEN
Redefine the meaning of life and my relationship with
Gary
(Who am I? Who are we? *What do we want out of life? Can our relationship chart new ground in uncharted territory?)*

I walked out of the bookstore, head high, heart racing. I looked back at the mall, the Crate & Barrel, the PF Chang's, and mentally said, "Good-bye."

"Give me two years and two months," I told Gary when I got home. "That's how long it took Thoreau to write *Walden* in the woods. Give me two years, two months. Either we accomplish these goals, or we fail, or we go crazy, but let's redefine our lives. We can always move back to the city. We only live once, right?"

I handed Gary my napkins.

"This is old school, girl!" he laughed. But then he turned serious. "Are you sure about this? It's not just the fact you don't like to get your hands dirty, but you don't like to be more than walking distance away from a Starbucks. I know we're close to a resort town, but we'll be living miles out in the woods. This is rural America you're talking about. This is a part of the country we *left intentionally* to begin with, remember? It may be fun on vacation, but we always get to come back to the city. You won't have a job. Think about that. You cherish structure and a monthly paycheck. And I'll have to see if I can transfer my sales job with my company. This will be like jumping off a tall building and possibly going *splat!*"

I nodded.

I didn't know what I was doing.

"Let's do it, Thoreau!" Gary said, shocking me. "Let's do it!"

Buoyed by faith, stupidity, and a partner who was willing to jump off that very tall building with me, two neurotic urbanites and one neurotic mutt walked out of the city, thumbed their noses at their lives, and set off into the woods, just like Thoreau.

Or, more appropriately, Little Red Riding Hood.

Thankfully, I didn't know at the time that this move to rural America would end up testing our spirit, our manhood, our faith, our sanity, our prejudices, and our relationship. We would weather blizzards and ice-fishing, goose festivals and raccoon attacks. We would live without magazines and malls, Trader Joe's and HGTV.

But would we survive our return to the country?

All I knew on the day we moved from St. Louis and waved goodbye to the Arch and the city life I loved was that this would either be the bravest thing I had ever done in my life or the worst mistake I had made since I gave myself an Ogilvie home perm in high school.

Part Two

Life Lessons

When we are unhurried and wise, we perceive that only great and worthy things have any permanent and absolute existence, that petty fears and petty pleasures are but the shadow of the reality . . . By closing the eyes and slumbering, and consenting to be deceived by shows, men establish and confirm their daily life of routine and habit everywhere, which still is built on purely illusory foundations. Children, who play life, discern its true law and relations more clearly than men, who fail to live it worthily, but who think that they are wiser by experience, that is, by failure.

—HENRY DAVID THOREAU, *Walden*

We came to Redbud filled with hopes and dreams of a better life. And basically, we've seen those hopes and dreams crushed and battered before our very eyes.

—ANDY FARMER (CHEVY CHASE), *Funny Farm*

LESSON ONE

Devote My Life to Writing Full-Time and Embrace the "Solitary Life"

I have never felt lonesome, or in the least oppressed by a sense of solitude, but once, and that was a few weeks after I came to the woods, when, for an hour, I doubted if the near neighborhood of man was not essential to a serene and healthy life. To be alone was something unpleasant. But I was at the same time conscious of a slight insanity in my mood, and seemed to foresee my recovery.

—Henry David Thoreau, *Walden*

A Sticky Situation

Gary and I move on what would turn out to be the coldest day of the year, a prison-gray early winter's morning with a wind chill of fifteen below zero. Our hands ache even in thick gloves.

We drive north, winding our way through Chicago, passing under the GREAT LAKES, GREAT TIMES! sign welcoming us to Michigan, and then, finally, we arrive at our new home.

In the middle of a frozen wasteland.

Leading our U-Haul processional down our long driveway, I encounter two deer—looking rather bored, as if they had just snuffed out cigarettes after gossiping about the possums. I slam on my brakes, forgetting that the driveway is a solid sheet of ice, and promptly slide into a ditch.

"Nice driving!" Gary yells out of his window. "We can still go home, Thoreau! Trucks are still packed."

I get out to survey the damage—nothing more than a dented bumper and badly damaged ego—before slipping and falling in my Kenneth Cole boots.

And then, like me, night falls.

Suddenly.

Around four in the afternoon.

And though I already feel lost, I now feel shipwrecked, scared.

I fall asleep that night, exhausted, before waking in a panic—drenched in sweat, chills running up my spine—to the lonely, tormented howls of coyotes.

I was having a nightmare that we moved to the country, and I got lost in our woods—the ones right outside Turkey Run—looking for a Starbucks, before surprising a pack of coyotes who were drinking Folgers and chewing Skoal. They chased me directly to the single-wide trailer that sits in the overgrown lot next to us. I knocked on the trailer's front door, which is emblazoned with plastic red roses the color of rotting meat, and it just popped open, where I was greeted by a group that included a trio of gap-toothed, banjo-plucking inbreds from *Deliverance;* Floyd the Barber, who gave me a mullet; and Gomer Pyle, who whittled and worked on a carburetor. I sprinted out of the trailer and ran a mile down to our country store, where I wanted to purchase an issue of *People* and a Pumpkin Spice latte, but instead I ran into a redneck who was buying ammo and rope and beer, all the tools necessary for me to be dragged behind his pickup.

That's when the coyotes woke me up.

This is my vision of rural America, a place I have populated with hideous stereotypes. And although I did know a couple of people who fit these descriptions, I know better than this.

But there is just something creepy about being this isolated, something spooky about living in an area with people who prefer to be this isolated. And we are definitely alone out here, on 3.5 acres of land, in the middle of the woods, a large swath of lakeshore land inhabited by fewer people than the spinning class I used to attend.

I look over at Gary and our eighty-pound salvage mutt, Marge, who are sleeping. We are all exhausted from unpacking. Gary and I had both fallen asleep after eating a DiGiorno's pizza. Marge's head is now resting on the pizza stone, a ring of crumbs outlining her mouth.

I get out of bed. I trip over a box and stub my toe.

It is so dark I must feel my way around the room.

In the city, there was light, a lot of light, from streetlamps, and neighbors' homes, and motion-sensor garage lights, and passing cars. Here, there is nothing. It is beyond black; it is womb dark.

Gary has yet to install the endless brigade of night-lights he has brought with him. His penchant for night-lights (in a myriad of forms, like lighthouses, birds, butterflies) along with seasonal candles and dish towels is part of a defective gene he inherited from his mother, along with nut allergies and an overwhelming desire to use way too much fabric softener. I now realize it was a mistake for me to mock him for wanting to unpack the box with the twenty or so decorative little lights first.

And where the hell are the three thousand scented candles we own? We should at least have those out and burning when we need them the most, considering we opted to invest our retirement funds in Yankee Candles instead of a Roth IRA.

I stub my toe again on our dresser. I deserve my new hammertoe.

Gary does not like it dark. He prefers to sleep in a virtual airport landing strip. In the dark, you see, he might stub a toe, like I just did, or accidentally miss the toilet when he pees, or, worse, he may not be able to see the murderer's face right before he is stabbed to death.

After growing up in the country, it took me years to adjust to the constant dull glow of a city. And then it took me years to adjust to Gary's added indoor night lighting. Finally, I became desensitized to light. Now, I can fall asleep in a tanning bed and don't know if I can sleep without the extra wattage.

I fumble around, grab a flashlight sitting on top of some towels, and shine it on my copy of *Walden,* the first thing I have placed on my nightstand. This book has become my baby blanket now, my safety net, my Xanax.

I have nervously underlined passages, and I find the following in the perfectly round glow of my flashlight: "It is darker in the woods, even in common nights, than most suppose. I frequently had to look up at the opening between the trees in order to learn my route . . . I believe that men are generally still a little afraid of the dark, though the witches are all hung, and Christianity and candles have been introduced."

Witches! I hadn't even thought of witches.

I flick off the flashlight and get back in bed, pulling the covers over me. I think of the episode of *I Love Lucy* when the Ricardos moved to the country and couldn't sleep because it was so quiet.

I listen to the wind roaring off Lake Michigan.

We will die before morning.

How can it be this dark?

It's so damn dark I can't even see my hand in front of my face.

And I am doing just that. Holding my hand in front of my face. *Where in the hell am I?*

I stare at my hand. It tells me everything I need to know.

All you need to do in Michigan in order to show folks where you live is to hold your hand directly in front of their faces, palm facing out, like you're going to slap them.

But instead, you point to a part of your hand.

The state is shaped like a mitten.

For instance, a Detroit native will point to the bottom part of their thumb, while a Grand Rapids native will direct you more toward the outside of his palm. Traverse City–ites will point to the top of their pinky.

I live on the outer, lower left edge of my palm, where my love line begins to trail off into nothingness. In my case that vast nothingness is Lake Michigan, which I can hear roaring in the distance, the winter wind engulfing our little cottage in its chilly howl.

I get up again, thinking about witches, and try to maneuver my way around our new bedroom in the pitch black.

There is not a single shaft of light. But despite this fact, Gary has gone ahead and closed the curtains, which I didn't want up in the first place, in order to prevent, and I quote, "country killers from seeing our silhouettes."

I make my way over to the bedroom window and slide the curtain open. Our windows are frosted over.

It is cold, very cold outside—the kind of cold where you can hear the trees crack and moan in agony, like their bones are breaking.

Gary's mother has made us little cottage curtains for the bedroom. Like mother, like son. Gary's mother's home, I am convinced, is the first home built entirely out of curtains. She has thick, dark burlap curtains backed by thick, dark plastic liners in every window of her house. I am still unsure if the house is painted, since it's a nonstop circle of fabric. Which is why she has to keep her night-lights on during the day. We celebrate Christmas in the dark. I never know if it is sunny or raining or the world is being attacked by aliens.

I squint my eyes and peer out at our new landscape. There are no billboards, or office towers, or condos. There are no next-door neighbors. There are trees, and trees, and more trees.

My bare feet ache from cold and fear. I stare into blackness. Slowly, the wind begins to die down, and it gets very quiet. The sky quickly begins to clear, and the moon shifts just enough to shine brightly through our bedroom window. It sits in the sky, soaring above the pines. Suddenly, it is bright as day.

Marge snores, turns over, stretches, and kicks Gary in the face. He gets out of bed and stares out the window with me.

"What are you doing!" he says, alarmed. "People might see us."

"Who?" I ask. "Who is going to see us? There is no one around."

"It's beautiful," he finally says. "It's so . . . clear."

We have forgotten how tired Mother Nature gets in the city, her stars, her moon, her sun covered in a haze, their rays softly filtered through a film, everything in need of a good shower. Here, in the country, there is no layer, no pollution, no haze, no dull, no vaseline on the camera lens to make Gene Hackman look like Ashley Judd. You see what you see. And tonight we see a moon as bright as a floodlight, illuminating our woods, our pines glowing green, the ice on the yard a virtual Rockefeller Center skating rink at night.

We are lost for a few seconds in this new world, feeling, for an instant, at home. But then, out of nowhere, in the near distance, something scrambles by, suddenly, quickly. It is something big but amorphous, like that gritty footage of Bigfoot they always show on cable, where you can't tell if it was something horrifying and real or simply some drunk guy laughing his ass off in a rented monkey costume.

Gary yelps as if Josh Duhamel from *Las Vegas* has unexpectedly shown up shirtless and kissed him on the lips.

"Oh, my God! The Melon Heads, the Melon Heads, the Melon Heads!"

Ahhh, the Melon Heads. Here we go again.

Just the night before, my evening had unfolded like an episode of *Entourage*. Albeit for a significantly older and gayer group of guys all still trying to look and act like they were twenty-five-year-old actors and hangers-on in Hollywood.

This was our farewell dinner, our swan song from the city. We were scared shitless but didn't want anyone to know it.

So our close friends took us to a new restaurant in St. Louis, the kind where the buzz is actually bigger and better than the food, there are snaking lines just to get into the bar, and dollar bills featuring important presidents are exchanged with the too-tan, too-thin gay maître d' sporting eye makeup and Day-Glo teeth.

We ordered tapas and Spanish-Caribbean-American-European fusion dishes, and I drank sangria, and then we went to a hip new bar where everyone looked like a well-rested Abercrombie model.

"Wait, wait!" said our friends, who then presented us with an assortment of gag gifts, the kind you laugh at, then immediately throw away when you get home.

Like the calendar of Michigan facts that says something depressing on each new day, like:

"Did you know Michigan receives 200 inches of snow per year?"

"Did you know the average winter temperature in Michigan is 21 degrees?"

"Did you know black bears and mountain lions are now being spotted in the woods of southwestern Michigan?"

I had laughed. Gary had winced, visibly.

And then we opened a gift, another book, entitled *Weird Michigan*. The tome was a goofy coffee table book described as "Your Travel Guide to Michigan's Local Legends and Best-Kept Secrets."

The book sported an array of Post-its designed to guide us to pages that pertained to legends about Saugatuck and the surrounding area.

The first spread we turned to in the book was entitled, in giant, creepy letters, "The Legend of the Melon Heads." According to this legend, a strange race of subhuman creatures still resides in the woods outside the town of Saugatuck, in the forest near where we now live. These mutated beings, it stated, were known as Melon Heads because of their small bodies and "disproportionately bulbous craniums." It goes on to say that local children are warned not to wander into the woods lest they be attacked by these vicious monsters, which are said to kill and even eat anyone unlucky enough to venture onto their turf.

Like us.

According to legend, the Melon Heads despise normal people because they were once treated at a local insane asylum for a rare condition called hydrocephalus, which causes large pockets of fluid to form on the brain. The Melon Heads suffered severe physical and mental retardation because of this, and, to make matters worse, were experimented on by staff at the asylum. When the facility was eventually shut down, the Melon Heads were simply released into the local woods, where they continued to mutate, becoming little more than wild animals filled with hatred toward normal-looking people.

Of course, I laughed, like any normal-headed person would, but Gary had already turned downright moribund. For Gary, such entertainment presents doom. Such gifts embody the apocalypse; they represent reality, truth, the way things actually are in the world. After seeing *Legally Blonde,* for instance, Gary honestly believed he was a video essay away from getting into Harvard Law.

Right now, staring out into the yard, I could try to reason with Gary. I could try to present him with the facts. I could tell him the chances of getting hurt in the country are statistically insignificant compared to those of getting hurt in the city, due simply to the sheer number of people. I could remind him that, in our relatively safe city neighborhood, we had carjackings, a murder, and a string of burglaries not far from our home. I could tell him all this, but it would be fruitless, like trying to talk Star Jones into shopping at Tuesday Morning for her penthouse.

So I try to humor him instead. "Your head's not much bigger than theirs. They'll just think you're family."

He looks very seriously at me and says, "I uprooted my life for you, Thoreau."

Suddenly, Marge wakes up and begins baying and pacing. Her barks cause "the thing" outside to scamper quickly through our woods, back and forth, like it is showing off, and then it begins running full speed.

Toward our bedroom window.

Gary and I are both screaming now and watching this unfold through our fingers, like we do when we watch horror movies. The Melon Head approaches, Marge barking, us yelling, and then, at the last second, it crests the hill of our lawn and veers back into the woods. Gary clamps the curtains shut.

"What have we done? What have we done?"

He is crying.

Real tears.

He is shaking.

The dog, I notice, has peed a little pool on the wood floor next to the window.

"We are installing bear traps around the perimeter of the house, we are installing a security system, we are covering the basement windows and sealing them shut, and we're turning the basement into a panic room, like Miss Jodie Foster had."

Gary is rambling without taking a breath. He has a crazed look in his eyes.

"The thing didn't look like it had a gigantic head," I say. "It looked pointier."

"Exactly!" Gary says. "That's even worse. Someone could barge right in and poke us to death with sticks they found in *our* woods. Can you imagine?"

I can't.

I may be scared, but I cannot imagine this.

I know I should let it go, that Gary is upset, but I can't.

"Why would someone break into our home and then poke us to death with sticks?"

"*Because* they can," he says.

"Don't you think that would be time-prohibitive for a killer?"

"I don't know what that question means, Mr. Smarty Pants. But killing with sticks seems like an authentic country way to commit a crime. It's very *Dateline NBC*. They'd title it 'A Sticky Situation' or something."

"Why wouldn't they use a gun?"

"Is it hunting season? I don't think soooo. Sticks seem logical."

"Sooo, would they sharpen the sticks first? Or just leave them dull, so they could only bruise our kidneys?"

"They'd sharpen them. With their knives."

"OK, OK. Now we're getting somewhere. Then why wouldn't

they just go ahead and use their knives to kill us? Why would they stand in our woods and take time to sharpen their sticks into a deadly point? Are you telling me our killers have waited until we got here so they could consciously decide to pick sticks from our woods in the pitch black, wait for the skies to clear, and then sharpen the sticks into points? Why would they do this?"

"Because it's fuckin' creepy. They can do whatever they want, torture us—sloooowly—because, out here, there's nobody around to hear what's going on. At least in the city someone would hear me scream!"

And he's right.

It does make perfect sense, in a John Carpenter sort of way. Killers standing in our woods, sharpening *our* sticks. Us screaming, them laughing.

I get up, double-check all the locks on our house, and then crawl back into bed.

"Good night, Ricky," I say to Gary. "Go to bed."

"Good night, Lucy," Gary whispers.

The next morning Lucy and Ricky will find deer tracks—not footprints or pointy sticks—dotting the snow in their yard.

And yet we still price out bear traps, finally ruling them out for Marge's safety. But we do buy and install new deadbolts on all the doors and then plug in roughly fifty night-lights and set out four hundred scented candles.

We may be killed in the country, but at least we'll see the Melon Heads coming at us with pointy sticks.

Thoreau Has a Beer with Norm and Cliffy

My dream starts today.

I am a writer in the woods.

I am embracing solitude.

I will conquer my first Life Lesson in Wade's Walden.

I am Thoreau.

In tight-fitting loungewear.

Three days after unpacking and getting settled, Gary starts his first day of his new-old sales job in a brand-new territory. He is miserable leaving this morning; I am selfish. I am happy to see him go and leave me alone with my dream.

I had sprinted out of bed, excited to begin my day. And now I find myself sitting totally alone, surrounded by pines and barren trees, wrapped in blankets on our screen porch, in front of an electric fireplace, my PowerBook open.

There is snow on the ground, but our outdoor thermometer registers 42 degrees. The sun is shining, and its filtered rays splay and splinter through the swaying pines. The light dances across an ancient pine picnic table I now use as my desk. I sit on an old bench that shows the years of butt imprints like fossils in lake stones. This is where I feel I need to write. I must work in the woods, no matter the temperature.

This is my first day of my new job in my new life.

I smile.

I inhale deeply, the crisp air burning my lungs.

It smells, well, like shit.

I sniff again, following the lead of Marge. And then I hear whinnying. And then I hear a jackass cackling. Our cottage sits a couple of miles from a horse farm, and they have obviously done something manure related, because it smells like I'm living in a PortaPotty.

I retrieve a firewood-scented Henri Bendel candle and light it, which makes the screen porch instantly smell like S'mores and diarrhea.

I hold my latte, which I have personally and proudly made, up to my nose. I have promised myself—in an attempt to simplify—that I will not drive into town every morning for a latte at the cute little coffee shop that looks like it was built in 1870. They make "Caramel Silks," a mix of white chocolate, caramel, and three shots of coffee. It is legalized crack. But who needs that, right? I don't even need Starbucks anymore.

I sip.

My homemade white chocolate latte tastes like sweetened dirt, reminding me of the time when I was a chubby kid who tried to mix sugar and mud together because I thought it would taste exactly like chocolate.

I shake my head, clearing the negativity.

I smile again.

The screen porch is now my office, the critters my coworkers. It is quiet. I look out at five cardinals chattering on ice-covered, low-hanging sugar maple branches. Three, the males, are bright red, and their color is shocking, like blood on snow. The two females are dull gray, and they fade into the branches. *No wonder I'm gay,* I think.

I have brought *Walden* onto the porch with me. So far, I have flipped through it, found passages that have meaning to me, underlined them, and then seat the book back down. Now that I am officially here, I need to reread it, I realize, to juxtapose Thoreau's life in the woods a century and a half ago with mine today.

I turn the cover and begin to read.

Page one. Opening paragraph. *Walden.*

Let my dream commence.

When I wrote the following pages, or rather the bulk of them, I lived alone, in the woods, a mile from any neighbor, in a house which I had built myself, on the shore of Walden Pond, in Con-cord, Massachusetts, and earned my living by the labor of my hands only. I lived there two years and two months. At present I am a sojourner in civilized life again.

"What?!" I scream. "Are you fucking kidding me?"

The cardinals scatter, and two chipmunks that had been sitting on a stump filling their cheeks with corn Gary had placed on it dash into the center of our backyard. They stand on their hind legs looking around, half-surprised, half-pissed.

Even the dog has raised her head and is staring at me, confused.

Sorry, Marge, but I have been duped.

"Thoreau only lived in the woods for twenty-six months before hightailing it back to Boston?"

I am talking to myself.

Out loud.

I picture Thoreau sitting at Cheers with Norm and Cliff, having a Sam Adams, laughing about his short stay in the woods.

I thought he *wrote Walden* in two years and two months but then continued to live at the pond. I didn't think he left after two years and two months. I thought he actually died at Walden Pond when he was like 110. He returned to civilized life? I thought he had chosen simplicity forever. How did I miss this critically important part of the book?

I write the first words to my new memoir. They are, simply: *"I am fucked!"*

I smile at my honesty but quickly panic.

Oh, God, Thoreau would never have written "fucked" in *Walden*. What am I thinking?

I can see it now. All the effete, intellectual reviewers who revere *Walden* will write, "That's why Thoreau was Thoreau and Rouse is just another whiny half-price-bin author who prefers using profanity over nuanced language."

Why didn't I read this whole book before I moved? We already put our house on the market and moved to nowhere. I have no friends. I have no mall. I have no job. I have chipmunks and birds and trees.

I do, however, have yet another epiphany—this one coming like a car slamming into a guardrail, an "Oh, my God, what have I just done?" moment that comes a millisecond too late: I have deluded myself into believing this is what I wanted; I have ruined my life.

I stand up and press my face against the chilly screen on the porch, seeking clarity. I look up, and a hawk is circling, back and forth, and back and forth, like the old-time gliders I flew as a kid. Suddenly, the hawk dives straight down, five feet in front of me, and picks up in its talons one of the chipmunks I had scared moments earlier. Alvin stares at me as he is lifted skyward, kernels of corn spewing from his now open mouth. My heart is racing. *My God, what is going on?* I think. This is why I hate those dog rescue shows, exactly why I don't watch Animal Planet, where an eerily similar and serene scene begins with a calm voice-over that says, "The rural Michigan woodside is a seemingly safe place for this furry fella to raise a family . . . better watch out, little guy!"

I look out in the yard and see his little friend, Simon, staring upward. And then he looks over at me, stares at me really, challenging me. He is alone, inconsolable and furious. We are one.

Simon chatters something, turns, and skitters away. I stand shivering on the screen porch. It's not the cold that's making me shiver anymore, though. It's the fact that I am all alone in the woods, away from a life in the city that I had wanted since I was a child. And now I'm back, in so many ways, from where I came.

Simon chatters again at me as he runs to safety, and I shiver again, this time because I can actually translate what he has just uttered.

Simon says: "You're just like my friend Alvin. You are not only screwed. You're dead."

I'm Going Knots

Thoreau wrote eloquently about solitude, his days out of the city and immersed in the countryside. He loved everything about it, including the quiet.

> *I find it wholesome to be alone the greater part of the time. To be in company, even with the best, is soon wearisome and dissipating. I love to be alone. I never found the companion that was so companionable as solitude . . .*

On the other hand, I have quickly come to believe that solitude is highly overrated.

Silence sucks as a companion.

First of all, it doesn't talk back.

Or gossip.

I would much rather have my city friends here, right now, to talk about the hot guys on *So You Think You Can Dance?* while we eat pizza and drink wine.

Solitude is a ringing in the ears, a silence so loud you can hear madness buzzing, like a summer mosquito.

I have grown accustomed to noise. Lots of noise: car alarms, police sirens, traffic, neighbors, church bells. I have grown accustomed to soft noise and loud noise and noisy noise. I have grown accustomed to everyone sleeping with the help of white noise machines, the faux sounds of silence, the chirps of crickets, the splashing of waves necessary to drown out the traffic, to help bring serenity and sleep.

Now I only need to crack a window to achieve this.

Our rural home is silent, which should be conducive to writing. This is one of the aspects that appealed most to me about Turkey Run: no neighbors. No noise.

I should be producing no less than ten book-ready pages a day. I read that David Sedaris once said that he accomplishes this when he's in a groove. But he writes in Paris, where he can see berets from his apartment window and hear funny police sirens and run down to the corner to retrieve coffee and baguettes.

Here, in the middle of nowhere, it is eerily, creepily, lose-your-mind silent. There are no city sounds. There are no sirens, no neighbors, no helicopters, no loud radios, no car alarms, nobody yelling on cell phones, no kids shuffling down the sidewalk to school. There is . . . nothing. It is too quiet to work. Too quiet to write. Too quiet to do anything except think about how quiet it is. There are no resorters within 150 miles. They are all in Chicago, or Detroit, or Indianapolis, doing city things.

There aren't even the city smells with which I have grown familiar: car exhaust, the smoky burger smell from the neighborhood bar, the melange of beans and expensive perfumes at the local coffeehouse, the smell of asphalt and urine and lots of human skin.

It is like waking up on Mars.

This morning, I cracked the door of our screen porch and heard only the sounds of a woodpecker whacking at a frozen tree and the whinnies of some horses and the hee-haw of a jackass. Sound carries a great distance in the country, where there is nothing to dilute it, no buildings for it to bounce off of, no concrete for it to dissolve into, only open land extending all the way to open water.

I close the screen door. It is too cold to work outside now.

So I'm standing inside Turkey Run, completely alone, staring at our wood walls, when I am suddenly stunned to discover just how knotty "knotty pine" really is.

I run my hand over the walls and get a splinter.

Jesus. I even miss drywall.

For the next few days, I pretend to work but instead sit in our cottage and stare catatonically at the pine walls, creating images out of the knots, actually naming them—"Alien," or "Frog," or "Pam Anderson"—based on their little knotty patterns, and then I hang Post-its underneath them with these monikers, like they are paintings on display at the Louvre.

Gary comes home late one evening and notices my handiwork. "Nice," he says. "I see the writing is going well, Thoreau."

But I am jealous of Gary. He is not here. He is "out there." And while he may not be in a big city, he still sees Pizza Huts and strip malls, some concrete signs that the state of Michigan has, at least, been colonized.

The next day, I stand in the bathroom mirror and tweeze the majority of my eyebrows. It is amazing how, once you start, you cannot stop. You pluck one, and then its neighbor seems unnecessary, huge, like a redwood. So I pluck and I pluck, until I look like Mr. Clean, and then, alarmed, I try to fill them back in with an eyebrow pencil I stole from a friend. I do a very bad job and end up looking surprised, nearly crazed, a male version of Bette Davis in *Whatever Happened to Baby Jane?*

I make a pot of regular coffee. I don't drink normal black coffee, so I don't know how much is too much, until I drink six, eight cups, so much coffee that my pupils dilate and then spin like pinwheels. Crazed from the caffeine, I write short, manic, nutty, two-sentence letters to friends in the city that state:

"I think I saw a Yeti today."

"Please send me a Henri Bendel candle."

"I ate four cans of soup by two P.M."

I show Gary my letters.

"At least you're writing," he says sarcastically.

I spend a day dressing Marge up in different outfits. In the tea towel pulled down over her ears and forehead, she is Sasha, the poor Russian woman begging for bread crumbs. In white Gap underwear that I pull tight around her midsection like a tennis skirt, and with a tennis ball in her mouth, she is Mandy, who is here for lessons at the club. And by tying a red bandana around her waist and adding a touch of sparkly lip gloss, she is Trixie, the town whore.

"You need help," Gary says.

And then he sees Trixie.

"How much does she charge for a hand job?"

To make some sort of noise, I eat. I like the sound my jaw makes when it moves and crunches stuff. I head to the little country store and buy the only staples they have in stock: sleeves of chocolate chip cookie dough, Orville Redenbacher microwavable kettle corn (sweet *and* salty), Funyons, French onion dip, and wine.

Basically, two weeks into my new life, I've become Johnny Depp in *Secret Window.*

Actually, I've gained six pounds since we've moved. At this rate, medics will have to remove the roof and airlift me out in the spring. I'll be on one of those cable shows called *The 918-Pound Man!* and Richard Simmons will come sit with me and try to roll me over.

To combat my loneliness, I finally decide to shower and put on something one wouldn't wear in either a hospital or a nursing home.

I pull on my Banana Republic jeans, the dark ones with cool pockets, the ones that make me look like I've just sneaked out for a latte with Julia Roberts. I cannot button them. I grunt and groan and pull and tug, but . . . the . . . tiny . . . fucking . . . button . . . will . . . not . . . go . . . into . . . the . . . tiny . . . fucking . . . hole.

I rip them off, roll them into a ball, and throw them into the corner.

"I'm pregnant!" I yell.

Marge comes over and nervously wags her tail. I usually only yell like this when I learn Gary has charged a new car on his credit card.

"It's not you, sweetie, it's me."

I stand naked in front of the mirror and look at myself. The indentation that the jeans button has left in my midsection makes it look as if I have recently taken a bullet to the gut.

Still, I feel like I want to make some sort of an effort, so I pull on some loose-fitting khakis and a loose-fitting tan sweater.

I look like a Schwan's man.

By the end of my third week in the country, I see no point in even trying to dress or look cute and instead opt for the following outfit every single day: pajama bottoms with dancing pine trees, a Northwestern hooded sweatshirt, tube socks, a *Survivor* Australia baseball cap, smudged eyeglasses, and a pilled, royal-blue, coffee-stained robe. A FedEx man asks me one afternoon if I need, and I quote, "any help." I am eating popcorn out of the bag when he asks me this, and I cram some more in my mouth and tell him, in no uncertain terms, "Mmfff#&!mmffmm!"

Finally, Gary begins to get concerned. "What's going on?" he asks. "This is what you wanted."

"It's soooo quiet. I can hear our pine trees creak in the wind. I can hear coyotes howl in our woods, just yards from our house. I can hear raccoons criminalizing our bird feeders. I can hear static in my head. I'm freaking out."

"You are blessed," Gary says to me. "*You . . . are . . . blessed.* You have what you always dreamed. Slow down. Deep breaths. This is a huge adjustment. Look around at what you have, not what you're missing."

And then he stops himself and walks away. He doesn't tell me he is miserable, and I know not to ask.

Well, Well, Well

The doorbell rings one morning.

I am so excited to have a visitor that I spray on Dolce & Gabbana cologne before I answer the door.

"Well, hello, sir!" I say cheerily.

"Is the man of the house around?"

This is, seriously, what this man, who looks very much like Jack Palance, asks me.

"He's at work."

This is, seriously, what I reply.

"Yep, well, I'm here to double-check on your well and septic, make sure everything is OK. Some of us locals get worried about city folk who move here permanently, especially in the winter. Just wanted you to know that everything's fine. Everything's brand-new. Septic won't need to be drained for probably eight, ten years, and your well looks fine."

Are you speaking Portuguese?

I thought we were on public utilities. I thought everyone in the twenty-first century was on public utilities. Though I am the more practical and pragmatic person in the relationship, Gary is the more logical one. He can fix things. He can put together things like TV trays without using directions. I thought north was "up" until I went to college. Still, I thought I knew about our utilities.

"Is this normal?" I ask Jack Palance.

"Most folks here in the country have well and septic. Do you know how much it would cost to run public utilities all the way out here?"

I don't. I don't care.

What I do care about, however, is where our magic water comes from and where our shit goes.

So I ask.

Jack Palance begins to explain—excitedly and in great detail. I have a feeling I am the first person ever to have shown interest in his line of work, except when there's an emergency. What I am able to cull from the exquisite explanation is that we are very much like pioneers. Gary and I are responsible for our own shit, and we are responsible for our own water, just like the pioneers, except we don't have to bury our doodie to hide it from the bears or haul up our water in pails.

I learn that our water comes from deep within the surrounding ground and is not transported to us, like I used to believe, from some magical place like San Pellegrino or pumped from a nearby mountain spring by cute elves.

What I find particularly troublesome is that our poo doesn't simply go away, like it did in the city, to some faraway place, like Wichita. It merely travels a few feet away, to our backyard, like it's going to a family picnic, where it will sit bubbling right under our firepit and badminton set. I find this highly discomforting, in a we-live-on-a-fault-line sort of way. I will share the mysteries of what I've learned when Gary returns home, as though I was the very first reader of *The Da Vinci Code,* but he, of course, already knows all of this. He will tell me that I should look at our situation positively, that it allows us to say "See you later" to our poop, but never "Farewell forever, old friend."

Now that I know our situation, I am even more deeply disturbed, mostly because I don't think that shit should be that close to drinking and bathing water.

"Your waste is in a tank. It's very safe and sanitary," Mr. Palance tells me.

Still, the truth remains that my poop hangs out by the house, long-term, like a friend who doesn't get the hint to leave when you're yawning.

My family used to have well water at our old cabin on Sugar Creek. We didn't, at first, even have septic. We just sat on an elevated toilet—"the Throne," we used to call it, because you had to walk a narrow set of steps and twirl-jump to sit on the seat—and then pooped into a hole in the ground far below. Occasionally, my grandmother would dump something down in the hole, but you usually had to keep the lid shut so flies wouldn't come into the cabin.

I felt very removed from society at the cabin, and this feels rather the same way, which terrifies but emboldens me. I will be plucky Laura Ingalls, leaving Gary to be pretty but sickly Mary. He will go blind. And I will bring him water to cool his parched throat, water I have gotten from our very own ground.

OK, it will most likely be the other way around, but I like my version better.

In trying to be neighborly, I escort Jack Palance down our front steps, which are covered in a thin layer of snow. I make it down two stairs before I slip—a comic on a banana peel—my tractionless Kenneth Cole shoes looking pretty but pointless in front of my face.

"You need some waders," he tells me. "Good luck out here this winter."

"Thank you, sir," I say as he helps me up and out of the drift.

"And it's 'ma'am,' by the way," Jack Palance tells me, lowering the hood of her jacket to reveal a tuft of long, wiry hair. "Why do we lesbians always have to take care of you gay boys?"

Shin City

I head into Saugatuck early this morning to hit the town, see if I can simulate the life I led in the city, inject my loneliness with a shot of small-town companionship and civic pride.

I live in Mayberry. My life should be like a never-ending episode of *Evening Shade*.

A resort town is always bustling, right?

Yes.

In the summer.

Today, the village is a ghost town, a wind tunnel, cold and isolated, just like me.

I head into the coffee shop, order a latte, and see that there are two tables of elderly locals, one filled with women, the other men.

I take a seat with the women, introduce myself, and tell them I am lonely and looking for friends.

Their bewildered looks make it clear that they have mistaken me for a man-whore.

"No," I explain. "I just want to know what there is to do around here. How do you keep busy?"

I learn from these windburned women in stocking caps that I have many options:

I can knit.

Join Curves.

Check on shut-ins.

Deliver meals-on-wheels.

Shovel sidewalks for the handicapped.

Sing with a church choir.

Write for the paper's police blotter.

"Or kill myself," I offer.

No one laughs.

I drive home, tuning into static-y NPR, trying to discern if I'm listening to Diane Rehm or John Madden.

I head inside Turkey Run and carry the spit remnants of my now-cold latte onto the screen porch.

"Hey, Tom! How's it goin' this morning? Can you believe that traffic jam on the interstate?"

The turkey in our side yard, just beyond the screen porch, looks up at me and gobbles, his neck swaying from side to side.

"I know, I know," I say. "Coffee tastes just like tea, am I right? Judy, huh?" I whisper. "She always makes it weak."

The turkey tires of my conversation, needing to get back to his cubicle in the woods, and struts away from me.

I walk inside and Swiffer everything but the toilet. Then I feather-dust every surface, including Marge's head. I eat three bowls of Kashi and go ahead and throw the ingredients for a rustic stew in the Crock Pot.

I then make slice-and-bake cookies, nervously watching the oven until they are done, and then eat a dozen while they sizzle-burn the roof of my mouth.

I turn to look at the clock on the microwave: It is 9:15 A.M.

I walk up a flight of stairs to the carriage house over the garage that we have transformed into my official office, the retreat where I am supposed to write when it's too cold to write outside.

I stare at my laptop.

I've dreamed of this moment my whole life, and I'm paralyzed.

What is wrong with me?

Like many childhood bedrooms, mine seemed much bigger than its twelve-by-twelve size.

That's because I tended to live inside my head as much as my bedroom, and my imagination had no boundaries.

My room had a corkboard wall, where I posted photos of Erma Bombeck along with my poems, which were decorated with little flowers and hearts and suns in the margins.

Alone in my bedroom, I used to talk into my hairbrush—which could rip through my thick hair and leave a perfect feather from forehead to nape—thanking the academy for its generosity, before reading the grateful audience one of my poems about a tree.

Every night before I would fall asleep, I would stare at posters of Farrah Fawcett and Raquel Welch that I had placed on the wall directly in front of my bed, my hope being that these women would somehow, via osmosis in my sleep, capture my emerging manhood, make me love them, desire them, desire all girls.

And then I would wake up and go to school, wholly unchanged, and stand by the monkey bars reading *Where the Red Fern Grows.*

OK, I wasn't just reading, I was bawling. Convulsing, really, something boys in the Ozarks aren't ever supposed to do, especially on the playground.

I remember the day—when I was finishing *Where the Red Fern Grows,* absolutely hysterical over the outcome—when two mean boys, the stereotypical kind in dusty jeans, dingo boots, and uncombed hair, ran up to tell me that they *really* had something for me to cry about.

And then they kicked me.

Hard.

In the shin.

Which is one of the worst places to get kicked, because, even on a fat kid like me, there is no fat.

So I did this thing I used to do whenever I felt alone, like I was going to explode from not being understood: I would clamp my eyes shut, clamp out the external world, and wait until I could hear my heart beat and then slow, until I could hear the minute noises of my world.

Not my screaming classmates playing dodgeball or the school bell, but a robin mining for a worm, the wind rustling through a creaky old elm branch.

And then I would pop my eyes open and things would seem OK again.

At least for a little while.

It was pre-meditation, pre-yoga, pre-Zen. It was my solitary survival guide.

I remember thinking that day, as I rubbed my shin, breathing normally again, *You know, I should never be alone. Especially here.*

I even told my grandma about my new life philosophy, and she replied, "It's better to be alone than with bad company."

But I knew that couldn't be true.

I was alone all the time—at school, at home, during the summer at our cabin—and it wasn't particularly good. Yes, I had my family. But that doesn't count when you're a kid.

Over time, I attached a stigma to being alone in rural America. Being alone meant I was different, odd, friendless.

My solitude was magnified. There were very few people, and I was unlike any of them.

Writing poems was odd.

Liking Erma Bombeck was weird.

Reading *Where the Red Fern Grows* was strange.

So I ended up surrounding myself with people, feeling that, intrinsically, that made me popular and, thus, normal.

As I grew older, I sought to do the "normal" things that "normal" people did. I got "normal" jobs.

I searched for myself externally, lived outside my head, where it seemed safer.

I worried about what everyone thought of me and my life—my job, my career path, my sexuality, my clothes, my friends.

Being alone seemed so wrong that I would rather have dined with Hitler and Mussolini than eat by myself at a restaurant, the waiter condescendingly inquiring, "Just one?" because I was constantly consumed with the belief that everyone was thinking, *Why is that freak all by himself? Doesn't he have friends? What's wrong with him?*

Being alone in my head was even worse: It seemed odd, stupid, a waste of time.

I guess I was always anticipating that kick in the shin.

I still feel as though I am twelve and back in my bedroom, afraid to get lost in my own head, because it's not normal.

Bored, I pop open my desk planner and calendar, which still occupies a space of great importance on my brand-new desk. It sits prominently in the center, an island of white in a sea of shiny wood.

My calendar is empty.

Every little square, marking each and every day of my month, is empty.

Only the "Notes" section in the lower corner contains one word, written in red: *Write!*

I flip my calendar back exactly six months to this day and look at my former life. Every fifteen-minute allotment of time is filled with a meeting, a task, a conference call, a lunch, a strategic planning session, an event walk-through, an errand for someone.

Beside each task I have jotted an intricate series of secret codes that only I could decipher.

I learned to write in my own shorthand, almost a journalistic pig Latin, when I was in graduate school at Northwestern and had to jot interview notes in a hurry or scribble secrets I ascertained from reading a memo upside down on a subject's desk.

I brought that to my former career in PR, using a language of secret codes—a combination of personal SOS signals and the Mayan lexicon, if you will—to help me navigate through every situation and person, codes that could never be deciphered should someone flip through my planner or should I lose it. For instance:

"GHC1" meant "Get her coffee first" before starting a
    meeting.
"2xM" meant "Double-space the memo."
"M^2" meant "Mean Mommy."
"NT," or "No talk," meant "Don't talk unless called upon."

"Cabs?" meant "Do we need additional cabaret tables?"
"LDT" meant "Lunch downtown."
"P ✔" meant "Press check."
"CP" meant "Carpool."

Six months ago this morning, my day in my old life started at five A.M. and ended at seven P.M.

I squint at something that catches my eye and hold the calendar in front of my face.

It is then I notice the single letter I have written, minutely, in red, between every meeting, every conference call, whenever I had a few seconds of downtime.

"W!"

I am momentarily baffled. I immediately think of George Bush, but realize I would never have written his name unless forced to at gunpoint.

Then I think it means "Wedding," or "Wedding gift," since I had an upcoming wedding scheduled in my day planner for a woman with whom I worked and despised. She used to sneer at me, for God's sake, something I hadn't seen anyone do since Alexis Carrington, and she always asked me condescendingly to "tidy the mess" after a staff luncheon.

But then it hits me: *"W!"* means "Write!"

I sandwiched the most important thing in my life into infinitesimal time slots between endless activities that consumed me.

And the only thing on my to-do list today?

Write.

And all the time in the world to do it.

I stand up, march to the screen porch with Marge following, and challenge myself to do something I haven't done since I was a kid, since I felt out of place and like I was going to explode.

Since I got kicked in the shin.

My goal? To reach a moment of absolute stillness at least twice a week, to reach a place that complements this place. I vow to do this no matter my mood, no matter my mental state.

Just look at Marge now, staring off the screen porch, serenely inhaling what surrounds her, watching the turkeys, listening to the chipmunk fill his cheeks with corn off the stump by the edge of the woods.

So I clamp my eyes shut, clamp out the external world, and wait until I can hear my heart beat and then slow, until I can hear the minute noises of my world. And then, I can. I can hear what Marge hears: the little breaths and gravelly thunk of corn as Chipper fills his mouth; his footsteps as he scampers back home along the logs we have stacked as a border around the yard.

"Let us spend one day as deliberately as Nature, and not be thrown off the track by every nutshell and mosquito's wing that falls on the rails," writes Thoreau.

So today, I am with myself again, the only sound the dog's breathing.

And then I hear it: a gobble, another gobble, a succession of gobbles. I pop open my eyes, and a group of turkeys—two giant toms and about six hens—have wandered into the side of our woods to eat corn that Gary has scattered. Though it is sunny right now, in the distance, over the lake, I can hear thunder—Michigan has thundersnow on occasion, storms that literally rain snow—and the toms lift their heads and return the call, mistaking the storm for a friend. I shut my eyes again and can hear the turkeys talk to one another, feed on the corn. I open my eyes, and the toms are spreading their wings, strutting for their ladies, and then they are off for a leisurely walk through the woods.

I look at Marge. She exhales contentedly and smiles at me.

With this as my example, I head back upstairs to my office.

A double window on the east side of the space overlooks the back of our woods, our neighbor's pond and creek, the edge of their blueberry fields. When the clouds are held at bay by the lake, the sun rises quickly over the trees, an orange globe turning into a yellow spotlight. I squint at my laptop. I do not have curtains up here. I did not want curtains. I did not want anything blocking my view of the morning commuters—the birds, squirrels, chipmunks, rabbits, deer—already engrossed in their daily routines.

There is a new, natural order to my life. I have never had a "natural order" before. I have had routine, constant routine, controlled chaos.

This time, I can define myself, my life, on my own terms.

My heart is suddenly racing, my mind filled with so many thoughts that I am unsure if my fingers can move across the keyboard fast enough to capture them all. I haven't felt this way since I was young, when I believed the world was full of possibility and that it was mine for the taking, a boy writing poems about trees, talking into his hairbrush, and worshipping Erma Bombeck.

I write for hours today, not looking at my desk calendar, or even the clock, for once in my life. The sun simply moves across my window, the extended shadow that is cast by my desk lamp serving as my sundial.

I may be alone but I am not lonely. And there is a profound difference.

Thoreau writes: "Not till we are lost, in other words not till we have lost the world, do we begin to find ourselves, and realize where we are and the infinite extent of our relations."

Today—a too bright winter's day—the woods seem to glow yellow and red from the light illuminating the trunks and branches of enormous weeping willows and pines.

Later in the day, when Gary returns home, we take a walk in our woods, me following Gary, who follows Marge, the leader of our pack. Though it is bitterly cold, the filtered sunshine is warm on my face. It is a Wednesday, and this is our lunch break. I am not sprinting off to a meeting, or to PF Chang's, or gagging down a yogurt while on a conference call. No, I am simply walking through our woods on a winter Wednesday. This is the way it is now. And this is the way it is meant to be, I have to believe. This is the natural order of things. Marge charges ahead, her feet stirring up frozen leaves stiff with winter rigor mortis, and then she is off . . . after a chipmunk sunning on a log. Gary chases after her, calling her name, laughing.

It is at that moment I know I have won Lesson One. So I decide to keep an official scorecard of my life lessons, to keep tally of how I am doing in my rural boxing match.

Wade's Walden—1. Modern Society—0.

"I think we're lost," Gary yells back at me.

I smile.

"But I guess we're in no hurry, right?" he says.

LESSON TWO

Eschew the Latest Entertainment and Fashion for Simpler Pursuits

I had this advantage, at least, in my mode of life, over those who were obliged to look abroad for amusement, to society and the theatre, that my life itself was become my amusement and never ceased to be novel.

—Henry David Thoreau, *Walden*

My Life on the D List

It starts snowing in February with all the seriousness and severity of Dick Cheney. By Valentine's Day, my heart becomes icy, and I can't see the top of our front porch railing. By the end of February, my face is frozen into a perma–Cheney grimace, and meteorologists report that it has already snowed nearly as much this year in this part of the state as it has in any of the 111 years since they've been keeping records.

It will not stop until April.

See, I don't yet comprehend that while I may be isolated, a Michigan whiteout actually transforms you into a castaway, left alone in the middle of nowhere with only your wits to protect you.

And I don't have wits.

Nada.

I was born without them.

I was born with qualities that don't really matter in my rural new world, superpowers that won't save my ass at times like this, when you need wits and gumption and pluck, all the stuff that farmers and Eagle Scouts and avalanche survivors have. I was born with the innate ability to detect quality leather goods and to despise people who wear fanny packs and write checks and give clerks exact change.

But now, as part of my and Gary's misguided goal to live simpler, richer lives, we don't even have cable to make up for our lack of wits, to help us make it through this winter.

As part of Lesson Two, we have voluntarily opted—at least for a little while—*not* to install cable TV, thus removing our cultural breathing tube, our connection to entertainment and the world at large. When we moved, we opted to give up not only cable, but also magazine subscriptions and shopping in malls and boutiques in order to let go of the "city nonsense," although we did install a dish for wireless Internet because I needed it to make a living.

"It is the luxurious and dissipated who set the fashions which the herd so diligently follow," Thoreau wrote.

But how can I live outside the herd mentality when Paula Deen is my shepherdess? How can I reach spiritual enlightenment when Hannah Montana is my Buddha, Kathy Griffin my high priestess? It's impossible to turn myself over to a higher power, like *Walden*, considering my spiritual guides have always been Patty Duke, Melissa Gilbert, and Judith Light.

I want my MTV.

I have quickly learned that without cable I am a boring human being, and that Gary and I have little to talk about besides our hair and weight and his tendency to get fever blisters.

Without cable, we are able to receive only two channels in the woods, and everyone looks like they're walking around in the same blizzard we are.

Living without cable is what I believe living with an inverted penis to be like: a constant search for something you know is there but just can't locate. I become panicky and uncomfortable. I constantly hyperventilate. I have never gone more than a few hours without Suzanne Somers.

I can't even ask Lucy for help, because I can't locate her on TV.

I miss *The Real World*. I miss *The Dog Whisperer*. I miss Joan and Melissa. Who is on *American Idol*? Is *The L Word* still about lesbians, or is there a spinoff now about lemurs?

Thoreau didn't have cable. But, then again, I remember too late, he didn't have TV. Or radio. Or cell phones.

Thoreau didn't grow up with *Charlie's Angels* and *Fantasy Island* and Joan Collins and Pizza Hut. It was much, much easier to philosophize about nature and life's simple beauties when you rode around on a horse, and went to minstrel shows, and had wooden teeth, when your mind hadn't been branded and brainwashed from early childhood into believing you are only good and worthy if you have Gloria Vanderbilt jeans, Lip Smackers, and Tommy Hilfiger.

But now, I find myself in the woods, alone as an adult, stranded in the snow, like James Caan in *Misery,* socially and culturally hobbled.

Which is why my snow-drenched solitude—my first winter in the woods—is so miserable and my detox from the shallowness of today's culture so blindingly painful.

I honestly thought it would be easy.

"Just go cold turkey," I used to tell friends who were tattooed in nicotine patches or trying to diet. "It's easy."

I am a disciplined sort. I had lost weight. I had changed my life. I thought it would be a snap. I truly thought I would be endlessly entertained out here in the woods, amused by endearing woodchucks and singing cardinals and tap-dancing deer, that my life in the country would be some charming Disney cartoon.

But I don't have cartoons. Instead, I am sweating through my cable-free detox like a crack whore without, well, crack or sex. Instead of *Nip/Tuck* and *Project Runway,* Gary and I play board games at night.

Every . . . single . . . night.

Gary and I plot our evenings around specific games, just like we used to plan our schedule around TV. Mondays we play Monopoly; Tuesdays, Scattergories; Wednesdays, Cranium; Thursdays, Trivial Pursuit; Fridays, Candy Land; and the weekends center around dominoes or Hearts, a card game.

Right now, it is Friday, 15 degrees, and snowing. So we play Candy Land. Again.

At least Candy Land is my favorite board game because it is the gayest game of all time. What's most fun about Candy Land is the fantasy part. It's how, sitting here in the woods, I dream my life to be rather than how it actually is: Gary and I in search of the lost king of Candy Land, wandering around a rainbow-colored, sugarcoated forest and encountering nymphs and magical creatures, instead of being trapped in a whiteout wearing yellow sweats—the ones that make me look like I have scurvy—sporting greasy hair and eating anything in sight that has salt or sugar in it.

Or that can have salt or sugar added to it.

Gary loves Candy Land, too, mostly because—since it's made for children four and under—it requires no ability to read and only minimal counting skills. Though he absolutely adores games, Gary is not a good board game player. In fact, he's horrific. Playing games with Gary is like playing with a stroke victim.

I am dozing off while sipping a cup of Sleepytime tea that I'm convinced Gary has laced with a date-rape drug, because it's been nearly ten minutes since I made my last move. Gary, who must actually believe that he is Garry Kasparov, is still contemplating his next maneuver—*even though there is no brain function required in Candy Land, even though every move is based on the color of your card!*

I am screaming all of this in my mind, my boredom at this game, my frustration at Gary, my depression over living in the middle of nowhere, doing nothing, playing games every night like one of the Little Rascals, my weight ballooning faster than Kirstie Alley's, swelling into an internal rage like the undertow in Lake Michigan. I have the desire to explode, to witness carnage. I have an overwhelming desire to slap Gary, but I'm too sleepy.

This is my chance to work on our relationship. This is our chance to talk. We spent years not talking, sitting in front of a TV, exhausted from working late, having others entertain us, while we ate popcorn and then fell asleep, drooling on each other.

Growing up, my family used to play games every night during the summers at our log cabin in the Ozarks. This is how I got to know my grandparents as people and not just grandparents. I *need* to get to know Gary again. So I ask, "If Candy Land were real, which character would you be and why?"

Gary looks up at me and scrunches his face into his "I'm thinking deeply!" expression, which is very close to his "I've just burned my hand!" expression.

"Well, I couldn't be Gramma Nutt, because I'm allergic to peanuts, and she runs a peanut farm. Lord Licorice is mean and grumpy, and—girl!—I'm a hella good time!"

This response would typically strike me as very cute, but I only want to scream, "Jesus Christ, make a move! You're not decoding the cancer gene."

"I think I'd be Princess Frostine," he answers. "Yep, that's me to a tee!"

Now, Princess Frostine is who I want to be. I had my answer fifteen minutes ago. He cannot take my answer, because it doesn't fit him. According to Candy Land, "Princess Frostine is said to be the sweetest in all Candy Land. She is the perfect picture of grace and beauty; she is everything you would want a princess to be. Wherever she goes, her Snowflake Scepter spins a trail of sparkling sugar snowflakes. She spends her day ice-skating, or having tea with visitors in her gazebo."

Even though I can't ice-skate, I can drink date-rape tea with the best of them, and I am the picture of grace and beauty, although not right now in my scurvy sweats.

"Who are you?" Gary asks.

"Princess Frostine!"

"We can't be the same person! Pick someone else!"

This is where my undertow explodes into a death tide.

"No, you pick someone else, because *I am Princess fuckin' Frostine! I am the picture of grace and beauty!*"

Gary stares at me like I'm nuts. And I am. I have been spitting hunks of Pringles and French onion dip (and what is a *French* onion, by the way?) and now have potato spittle in the corners of my mouth.

I back down quickly, like a wild elephant that gets hit by a tranquilizer dart.

How can I ruin our time together? I think.

So I respond nicely, "Why don't you be Lolly? She's fun. She's . . ."

"Ditzy! Say it!" Gary screams. "Lolly's ditzy! Dancing around to her own music, in a cloud of twinkling lights. Hey, it says on the box that she is easily distracted . . . that's not me."

The oven timer buzzes. The Tollhouse cookies are ready.

"Oooh, cookies!" Gary sings, sprinting to the oven. "Nothin' says lovin' like cookies in the oven!"

And despite the overwhelming odds that Gary should, at some point in his life, win a single game of Candy Land—I mean, a monkey would eventually win a game—he loses again, which makes me very, very happy, an emotion I desperately need right now since I don't have television to tell me how I should feel.

Chicken Little

The only thing I get in the mail anymore are bills and flyers to attend monster truck derbies. I walk a quarter mile up our gravel driveway for nothing. I raise the little red flag on our mailbox—even though I have no mail to send—just to "show activity." I stand at the end of our drive and actually wait for the mail truck, like crazy old men do, only to watch it sputter on by.

When Gary and I moved to Wade's Walden, we decided to stop *InStyle,* live without *Out,* and survive sans *Men's Health, Men's Vogue,* Pottery Barn catalogs, pretty much any publication that featured pretty men, pretty women, pretty celebrities, pretty clothes, and pretty home accessories.

And now my mailbox—and the cultural guideposts to a world I once knew existed outside this swath of fifty-foot pine trees—is empty.

I did it because of Thoreau, who wrote, "For my part, I could easily do without the post-office. I think that there are very few important communications made through it."

Well, he was wrong.

I mean, didn't he ever read *Transcendentalist Vogue,* or *Betsy Ross Living,* or whatever was popular back then?

Canceling my connection to the celebrity world is like asking André Leon Talley to wear Wranglers to the Oscars. It simply goes against the natural order of the world. It throws on the planetary parking brake midorbit.

Which is what happened to me. I was lost when I lost touch with the celebrity world, with the Oscar buzz, and Paris Hilton, and Cameron Diaz, and Justin Timberlake, and Jessica Alba.

See, they are my friends. My true friends, who are there with me every week, photographed on their way to a club or a Starbucks, or on a yacht, wearing or holding or drinking something I might very well be wearing or holding or drinking by tomorrow, depending on availability and shipping.

Worse, I have nothing to read on the toilet, no paparazzi swimsuit shots of Ryan Phillippe to ogle, no "What Was She Thinking?" gown shots of Paula Abdul.

This is the main reason why when our neighbors, who live directly behind us on a large swath of acreage that includes a blueberry field, go out of town and ask—out of genuineness or, perhaps, sheer desperation—if we can pick up their mail, I jump at the chance.

I agree to help them out, largely because I want to appear neighborly but mostly because I'm nosy and I hope I might stumble across an issue of *People*.

But our neighbors are—proudly—not *People* people. They do not buy into mainstream culture or the latest fads. They make trails throughout their woods. They feed the animals every day.

Basically, they do what I should be doing with my life in the woods.

Our neighbors were among the first to welcome us with open arms to the country. I remember them trudging sturdily onto our front porch unannounced, an older man and woman in waders and heavy coats. When they knocked, Gary and I had stared at each other in a panic, neither of us wanting to open the door. We assumed they came here, in the middle of the winter and woods, to kill the fags.

When we opened the door, a woman with short, steel-gray hair pulled off a cute knit cap and exclaimed, "Oh, thank goodness! A gay couple bought this house!"

They have lived in this area most of their lives. Their world is these woods. Their world, in fact, is wood. Their devotion now belongs to the lost art of fan carving, and they have a burning desire to keep alive this old-world folk art.

"As artists, we are so thankful you're here," they said to us after we'd exchanged backgrounds. "You understand the true beauty of this place. You understand!"

And I'm really trying.

But the only thing I really understand right now is that I don't even know who's been nominated for an Academy Award, and I'm worried if I don't find out soon my well-honed critical radar will begin to rust and I'll start to think that *Patch Adams* is Oscar-worthy.

To retrieve our neighbors' mail, Marge and I wind through our woods, meander down the trails in their forested property, pick our way across their creek, zigzag through their blueberry fields, and then walk up their long gravel driveway and across the main road to their mailbox.

I nab their mail, which is mainly purchase orders for their art, and rifle through their bills, letters, and assorted junk mail.

Nothing.

Ahh, but then, there, stuffed in the middle of the pile, is a magazine, the first I've seen in a long time. It is glossy and slick, shiny and reflective in the daylight. I stop cold in the middle of their driveway and look at the cover.

It is a copy of *Backyard Poultry*, a magazine dedicated to, and I quote, "more and better small-flock poultry."

I didn't even realize that there was an entire magazine dedicated only to poultry, much less a subset focused on more and better small-flock poultry.

I mean, I think *Real Simple* is a conceptual stretch as a magazine.

Yet I have to admit this cover of *Backyard Poultry* is eye-catching.

It features a colorful enough character, a goldeny-yellow-feathered chicken with a bright red neck and big plume, which looks like an equal mix of a bored runway model and chicken Cher, in the Bob Mackie outfit she wore to the Oscars that featured the mammoth headdress.

Standing in a gravel driveway in the middle of the woods, not having seen a paparazzi shot of Reese much less a gay-themed ad in *The Advocate,* for weeks, I instantly admire this famous chicken, this bored poultry Paris Hilton, looking pretty and thin but a bit hungover. I picture it entering a Kimora Lee Simmons KLS fashion show with a Starbucks.

I wonder if the chicken is booked months in advance for shoots like this, and flown to nice stockyards all across the country, and specifies—like J.Lo does in her contracts—the kind of corn it wants waiting when it arrives in the luxury pen that doubles as its dressing room.

Fascinated, I begin thumbing through the issue and stop to read an article entitled "Working with the Cock(s) in the Flock."

I mean, how could a gay man pass that up?

I finish it and continue on, reading pieces like "Hatched in a Skillet" and "The World's Smallest Chickens." Really, it's a lot like reading a farm version of *OK!*, tidbits of bizarro information disseminated in titillating doses. Thirty minutes later I have devoured the entire magazine and feel very up-to-date on everything poultry.

This newly acquired knowledge actually inspires me, until I place the mail on their dining room table and remember they have given us a list of chores they would like us to perform while they are out of town.

I reach into my pocket and retrieve the "Farm Checklist":

- Feed ducks
- Water ducks . . . add wheat to water.
- Fill grit and oyster shell containers in duck pen.
- Let ducks out at 7 A.M. in the morning; lock ducks in pen at 7 P.M.
- Gather eggs daily
- Feed wild birds (spread corn in driveway and along forest paths)
- Feed critters in woods

I look up, blinking exaggeratedly.
Is this written in Sanskrit?
Critters? Grit? Oyster shell? Ducks? Eggs?
Hello? I need a translator!

And a wardrobe change.

I am not *dressed* for *"chores."*

Instead, since I was venturing outside Turkey Run—actually crossing a street, no less, where someone might finally drive by and see me—I have crammed my fat ass into ill-fitting flat-front cords, rather sexy pointed leather cowboy boots with just the slightest lift, and a paisley, bedazzled shirt I bought in Palm Springs.

I look like a disco ball.

And then I realize that this marks the first time I have done anything farm-related since I attempted to bale hay as a teenager but instead nearly got hung from a barn loft after leering at the hot, shirtless boys.

Our neighbors have eight ducks, which they adore. They provide not only eggs to our neighbors but companionship as well. They are cute things, really, and look and act much like a fleet of neurotic, uptight butlers to the queen.

As soon as the ducks see me and Marge approach the pen, they begin to quack loudly, lining up single file and ambling up the gangplank to their safe house, an old garage-cum-barn whose back half has been transformed into their home and nesting quarters.

I unlock the door to the pen, holding it open with a crate, and the ducks disappear, the leader peeking out nervously from the barn to watch my actions. I pour their feed into large bins on the ground, drag the hose into the pen and fill their water containers, and then add a little wheat to the water, which creates a pre-microwave Malt-O-Meal concoction. I let water run for a few minutes at the base of the pen, which, finally, melts the snow and turns the area into a swimming hole, and then I make my way into the barn. When I open the door to their inside pen, the ducks flap their wings and scream, and then line up single file again and march down the gangplank. The door now open, they excitedly half-fly, half-run into the surrounding blueberry fields, eventually marching through the snow toward the creek that rings the farm.

Their indoor dorm is filled with hay and little crates that have been turned on their side. This is where they sleep and lay their eggs. I gag at the smell, that farm stench of fresh hay and fresh shit.

I walk up to a crate and look into the hay.

I don't see an egg.

And then I remember Gary telling me slowly, cautiously, "You will have to dig through the hay with your hands. Ducks bury their eggs. This will be the hard part for you."

Gary had told me this like I had been involved in a plane crash in the Himalayas and he was a doctor instructing me over a cell phone how to perform a tracheotomy with a Bic pen.

I skim my hand over the top of the hay.

Nothing.

I take a deep breath and dig my hand deep into the hay, pushing it back and forth. My hand hits something warm and runny.

I feel like a midwife.

I lift my hand up to my face to inspect it, and my fingers are covered in greenish shit dappled with blue and black, like a kid's finger-painting portrait.

I gag.

I rub my hand against the crate, try to clean it with hay, but everything sticks to it, as if my hand is covered in syrup.

I then search the pen for some kind of digging instrument. I retrieve a coat hanger, which our neighbors have nearby and Gary suggested I use, and begin combing through the hay. I try to think of this as a game—to keep from getting sick—like I do when I pick up dog shit in the yard. I pretend it's Easter and I'm searching for candy-filled plastic eggs.

I begin finding an egg or two hidden in each crate and use my hanger to move the crap-coated orbs into a plastic bucket.

At the very last crate, I crouch down, stick my hanger into the hay, and poke something hard.

"*Quack!*"

I peer into the dark crate, and one duck is still nestled in it, kind of scooting around uncomfortably on her behind in the hay. She is trying to lay an egg and seems panicked to have a viewing audience.

I scooch back on the heels of my boots and wait for her to finish.

"*Quack.*"

Rustle.

"Quack."

Rustle.

"Quack!"

Rustle.

The duck, it seems, is in no hurry.

I am, however.

In addition to not wanting to inhale the stench any longer, I still have remnants of my city past. I still want things to happen at lightning-quick speed; I expect prompt service. I demand only the best. I still haven't lost that urban zip, that ability to veer across three lanes of traffic at 85 miles per hour and hit an exit ramp at the very last second on two wheels.

I still have little tolerance for the slow and deliberate pace of the country: me stuck behind a farmer on a tractor; me trapped behind a woman at the country store telling the clerk about a horse that just gave birth; me waiting for a duck to lay an egg.

So I yell at the duck: "Get it out . . . *now!*"

My voice—in the silence of the barn—scares even me. I scooch forward and poke at the duck's ass with my hanger. It quacks but spreads its little legs even wider.

Lay the egg now, I'm thinking, *or I'm comin' in for it.*

The duck turns and looks at me, and then—*plop!*—drops its egg and waddles down the gangplank to join the others.

That's more like it, Quackers.

I collect about eight or so eggs and leave the pen feeling very victorious. I wash my hands under the hose and then run the hose over the crap-covered eggs. The eggs come partially clean and reveal beautifully colored shells in shades of blue and pink.

But then I look down to see that my beautiful man boots are now covered in duck excrement, too.

It looks like I've been in a paintball fight.

I curse, tossing some corn in the driveway, onto some stumps, and into the edges of the woods, and make my way home along our trails, Little Red Riding Hood and her basket of eggs.

The first thing I do is call my parents and tell them—proudly—about my big day with the ducks.

My dad ends up relating a story about a friend of his who ate duck eggs during the Korean War, and I believe, though I could be wrong, that his friend ended up either hospitalized, pregnant, or growing a beak.

This panics me to the core of my soul, considering the whole bird flu epidemic thing, so I begin Lysol-ing and Purell-ing and bleaching everything in sight. And then I do what any normal person would do: I place the dirty eggs in the dishwasher, pour in some Cascade, turn it on, and then completely forget about them.

"Idiot!" is the first thing I hear Gary say when he calls home and I detail my triumphant day. "You can't put duck eggs in the dishwasher."

I open the dishwasher and survey the apocalypse: broken shells; egg remnants crammed in the metal thingy at the base of the washer. I remove the trays, get on my hands and knees, and begin cleaning it out and relaying my father's duck egg story.

Gary says we're not in Korea.

That evening, he heads back to our neighbors' barn, returns with four more eggs, and promptly makes chocolate chip cookies with them, to prove his point.

"Eat one!" he demands.

I take a bite.

"Swallow!" he demands.

I swallow loudly and then chase it with a huge gulp of milk.

"Tastes just the same, doesn't it? They're better than chicken eggs. They're organic. They don't have hormones, they haven't been processed. It's natural. We're going to use them from now on to cook with. This is why you say you moved, isn't it, Thoreau?"

He's 100 percent right.

I smile.

And gag internally.

After crawling into bed and wishing my own Ricky Ricardo a bitter "Good night!" I dream I marry the cover model from *Backyard Poultry* and we fly all over the world together. I am featured in magazine articles in *People* and *US Weekly* and *Esquire,* whose headlines scream, "I Love My Cock!"

My mate happily produces zillions of eggs, which I am forced to eat.

I wake up in the early morning hours, drenched in sweat, and go to the bathroom to pee. Standing in front of the mirror, the moonlight angled on my face just right, I swear that I have grown a beak.

Welcome, Wal-Mart Shoppers!

In rural America, you really only need a few stores for shopping: a country store, a feed store, a hardware store, and a Wal-Mart.

You learn to do more with less in the country because there is less in the country. And this fits with my goal to *want* less, to *have* less.

The rural shopping philosophy flies in the face of urban planning.

In the city, I shopped at roughly fifty stores a week. A typical week would involve scurrying to Home Depot, then Lowe's, then Target, then a mall or two, then buzzing through Whole Foods, Trader Joe's, and the city grocery before making stops at Walgreens, World Market, Pier One, Borders, and Barnes & Noble. I would buy at least two coffees a day, one from a drive-through Starbucks and another from a local coffeehouse. I felt I needed more because there was more. I was surrounded by everything anyone could ever want. And, thus, I wanted it all as soon as I saw it.

Now I have winnowed my marathon shopping down to a precious few "stores" that perform multiple duties, much like a surgeon who can style hair or a spinning instructor who can fill a tooth.

You want a gallon of milk and some ammo? A pizza and a hunting license? No problem. Walk to the country store.

Two feet of rope and mole killer? Hardware store. Aisles two and eight.

Work gloves, birdseed, whole corn to feed the deer and wild turkey, rock salt, and even a nice paperback? Feed store.

Now, let me be honest, the shops in the resort towns of Saugatuck and Douglas are not only downright adorable, but many carry fabulous high-end home accessories and fun clothing. But many are closed in the winter, and, truth be told, it's difficult to live every day off of $3,000 oil paintings, $200 Teva sandals, and T-shirts of sunsets.

Which is why Gary and I break the ethical pact we made long ago and head to a Wal-Mart a distance away that sits on a secondary road paralleling the highway. We, for once, want to get everything purchased in one fell swoop before the snow comes again.

Shopping at Wal-Mart is a fairly schizophrenic act for both of us. I grew up in Wal-Mart country—literally the Ozarks stomping grounds where the first store was built. And while Wal-Mart was undoubtedly a genius concept—providing tiny towns with a superstore that offered nearly everything under one roof at drastically reduced rates—it also undoubtedly helped gut many little burgs, drawing townsfolk from town squares until the family-owned stores were empty. Saugatuck-Douglas fought the chains, and, as a result, is the better for it. The towns are small but thriving.

Yet while we love our nearby resort town with its unique, independently owned shops, we don't always love the time it takes to shop.

And shopping at a Wal-Mart does fit into our desire to live less frivolously, to shop outside of boutiques and specialty food shops, to stop buying name brands. So we give Wal-Mart a try and compare this act to kissing a woman, after a few shots of tequila, on a dare.

The parking lot of the particular Wal-Mart we venture to is filled with trucks. Not just regular pickups, mind you, but those giant-wheeled, jacked-up, need-a-stepladder-to-climb-in type trucks, many of which, I notice, feature rebel flags.

"Note to drivers," I say to Gary in the parking lot. "We're in Michigan, next door to Canada. Not really rebel-yell territory."

The first thing we smell in Wal-Mart is doughnuts and Big Macs. To the left is a McDonald's; straight ahead is a bakery. The next thing we notice is mullets. Lots of 'em. And families with packs of children. Not just two or three, or even—like in St. Louis's staunchly Catholic families—four or five, but hordes of kids, like an entire elementary class that's gone on a school trip to study bad hair and fried food.

In his desire to help me live a more Walden-esque life, Gary has become a rapid coupon clipper. He now organizes hundreds of coupons in his red Velcro Hannah Hansen coupon organizer, which divides and subdivides coupons by category: breads, cereals, soups, dairy, meat, etc.

From a distance, he looks like a flapper carrying a red clutch.

We start our Wal-Mart shopping experience by heading first to the dairy aisle.

Milk?

Scrrriiiiiiitchhh!

I grab two gallons of fat-free milk, and Gary un-Velcros the Hannah Hansen coupon holder, which elicits a sound similar to squeegeeing a window that has been covered in rubber cement.

Gary yanks out a coupon and yells, "Score! Fifty cents off mama's milk!"

Butter?

Scrrriiiiiiitchhh!

Bread?

Scrrriiiiiiitchhh!

Cereal?

Scrrriiiiiiitchhh!

Toothpaste?

Scrrriiiiiiitchhh!

We perform this scritch-and-sniff tango for nearly an hour, meandering Wal-Mart in yoga pants (me) and he-capris (Gary), until we notice two men circling us in produce like sharks, both of whom look very much like their goal in life is to be featured on *America's Most Wanted*.

"I think I saw them in dairy," I whisper to Gary, who replies, "Snap! Crackle! Pop!"

"Snap! Crackle! Pop!" is what Gary always says to me when he cannot understand my whispers. He says it's because I have too much spit and too low of a voice to be understood in a whisper. I say it's because he is going deaf and needs an ear horn.

"I saw them in dairy casing us," I now say too loudly, so Gary can hear.

The men stare and laugh.

The two men—both of them, of course—have mullets.

Anytime Gary and I see a mullet, the hairs on our heads—the ones that have been styled to spike and curl instead of cultivated to climb down our necks—stand on end even more.

One of the men is wearing a camouflage hat, and the other is wearing a camouflage hunting suit.

"I can't see them," Gary says to me. "They're camouflaged."

I start to laugh, like I always do in tense, inappropriate situations— weddings, baptisms, job reviews. I am laughing so hard, in fact, that I fart. Which makes Gary laugh so hard that we double over the shopping cart.

When I look up, the boys are huddled around us, fake-looking at a head of iceberg lettuce like they've just discovered the Hope Diamond in a bin.

"Can we help you fellas find sumpun?"

I don't know what to say, so I whisper, "Are we being Punk'd?"

Gary doesn't hear this, of course, but the hunters do.

"You callin' us punks?"

This is very much how people end up being dragged behind pickups, I think to myself.

Although I do wonder, as jacked up as the trucks are in the parking lot outside, if our heads would even drag on the ground.

Still, this is exactly how every country fight I was ever in growing up started: pure stupidity. Pure intolerance.

"No, sir . . . sirs," Gary says.

"You fellas from around here?" the one in full-on *Apocalypse Now* camouflage asks.

"Yep," I say, trying to sound like a local.

"You fellas own a summer place or sumpun?"

"Nope. Full-time residents."

"All right, then. Just seein' if you was from around here or needed directions or sumpun."

They walk away, tossing the head of lettuce into the bin, which causes the other heads to roll onto the floor.

Gary and I run, hurdling heads of iceberg like they're land mines. "Are you an Ameri-can, or an Ameri-can't?"

Gary says this to me by the green peppers, and I start laughing again. This is what Gary says every time we are confronted by someone who looks as though they would kill just to impress George W. Bush.

"Well, are ya, son?"

I start laughing.

Whenever I start laughing, Gary views it as a green light, his sole goal to get me to cause a scene. "Do ya have gumption? Get-up-and-go? Don't need the government to lift ya up by yer bootstraps, do ya? Or are ya one of those Democratic faggoty fags who wants to get married and ruin our country?"

I am doubled over the cart. I fart again.

"You fellas OK?"

It's our friends, juggling yellow peppers. We didn't even see them approach us.

Now is about when Gary starts to get pissed. He was spit on growing up. Country-fuck bullies scare him for only so long, and then all his inner rage builds and explodes. He would rather die fighting.

"We're just fine," he says primly. "We're quite enjoying our Wal-Mart experience."

The boys eye him up and down, stopping on his he-capris.

I doubt very much these two country rubes have ever seen a man in three-quarter-length drawstring cargo pants featuring a giant flower on the ass, much less in the winter.

They are about to say something, something stupid and stereotypical and vicious, but when their mouths open, all I hear is:

Scrrriiiiiitchhh!

"Do you fellas"—and Gary says *fellas* very emphatically—"need a coupon or sumpun?"

Sumpun sounds, well, like *sumpun*.

I'm unsure if these camouflaged gentlemen have ever been challenged by two fags, but they stare at each other in complete and utter shock, grunt "No," and stalk away.

"There is an eighty-twenty chance," Gary says, now very serious, "that one of us is going to get killed."

We save, according to our Wal-Mart receipt, roughly $16 thanks to our coupons, which, we both agree, seems a fair price to pay for re-claiming rural America, our country childhoods, as well as our lives.

The Other White Meat

Shopping at the feed store every Saturday morning has replaced my former Saturday routine of shopping at Banana Republic, Aldo, Kenneth Cole, and the Gap.

This is like replacing meth with Bubble Yum.

We shop at this aluminum-sided feed store with a wide, old-planked front porch—like the ones they have on Southern plantation homes—because it has become our responsibility to feed every bird, squirrel, chipmunk, and woodland creature in southwestern Michigan. The feed store just north of town has stolen the heart of my debit card.

While Gary buys corn, millet, sunflower seeds, and an assortment of sprays and hoses to euthanize me, a clerk asks if I need any help.

I cannot come up with anything to say, so I ask, "Have you seen *Babe*?"

She is wearing a burlap apron and has an assortment of tools and gloves and feed bulging out of the kangaroo pouch. "Excuse me?"

"You know, that little pink pig that talks?"

"Darryl, have we seen *Babe*?" she screams.

I hear "Jesus!" from behind an aisle of farm equipment, and Gary rushes over. "Why are you such an ass?"

"I'm *being* friendly."

"No, you're not. You're being an ass. You think you're too good to be in a feed store."

I hate it when he's right.

"Go load two bags of whole corn into the back of the SUV," Gary solemnly instructs me, "while I'm checking out."

I back the SUV up to the loading dock and wait for someone to help. A man in overalls passes by, and I honk at him. "Can I get two bags of corn, please? Oh . . . *whole* kernel."

"I don't work here. And customers load their own feed."

I audibly groan and say, "You've got to be kidding me," and then haul my ass up to the dock. I try to lift a bag of corn, which weighs roughly seven hundred pounds.

"How much fucking corn is in this?" I scream at a Loretta Lynn look-alike wearing a gold cross the size of the real cross, who is having no trouble doing exactly the same thing.

I drag the feed bag to the edge of the dock, go back down the stairs, and back the SUV up even more, until the gate is scraping against the dock. I head back up to the dock, try to lift the entire bag into my arms, and grunt-scream, stumbling a bit to stay upright, just like those weight lifters do on the ESPN's *The World's Strongest Man* specials when they're trying to lift a locomotive. I don't do as well, since the bag weighs considerably more than me. I try to heave the corn off the dock and into the back of the SUV, but it goes, oh, maybe four inches, bounces off the dock, and hits the gate, bending it backward.

I miss the car entirely with the next bag.

"What are you doing?" Gary asks. He's been watching my handiwork. "How could you do this?"

"They're heavy!" I whine.

Gary lifts the bags into the trunk and says he has a gift for me for being such a good sport. Gary always rewards bad behavior. He gives Marge a treat when she bites a stranger.

I open the bag, all excited. I love a gift.

Gary has gotten me a hat that says something. I pull it out, expecting—for some reason—the hat to say VON DUTCH, but instead it says, simply, THE BEST VITAMIN-ENRICHED FOOD FOR SWINES.

He got me a pig hat. It has a silhouette of a pig. They didn't even go to the effort of screen-printing on a little Porky tail.

I glare at Gary.

"It was free. They were giving them away. And I know how much you love Babe."

He's right. I love that little pig. And he did get me a gift, which it seems in the country is as rare as finding gold doubloons in the sand.

I put on my hat and wear it all day with the same pride with which Babe would have worn a bow tie.

Tanorexic

Gary and I pass a mirror in Turkey Run one morning and are startled to see something faint, pale, and ghastly.

We jump, backpedal, and realize the reflection is of us.

We haven't tanned or worked out in nearly six weeks, an act of will that is incomprehensible among most gays, and—with us—an act deserving of sainthood. Gary, who is typically the color of George Hamilton in the summer and Babyface in the winter, is probably the closest he has come to his natural color since he left his mother's womb. I usually take on a coppery glow, considering I have a drop of Cherokee Indian blood in me, but am now the pallor of the snow falling outside.

Out of depression, Gary pops open a bag of chocolate chips, which we mainline.

If we could snort them, we would.

When you stop tanning and working out, you no longer care what you eat, because you no longer care what you look like.

When you wear only sweat pants and tube socks and hoodies, you no longer can tell what your body looks like.

Until you shower.

And then you just make sure to keep your eyes up.

Not tanning and working out has opened up vast holes in our daily schedules. I have gained roughly three hours of daylight, something I would devote to my children if I had any. Marge now hides from us. She has "benefitted" from this extra time by being preened and cleaned and dressed up more than a virgin being offered for sacrifice.

Not working out was perhaps my greatest sacrifice when we moved. I originally thought that hard, outdoor labor—like prisoners perform—would keep my body toned and my skin brown. But it's winter in Michigan, and if I did hard labor outside, I would lose a limb.

I came to Michigan to gain solitude, to gain clarity, to make up for all the hours I have lost. By focusing solely on writing—for even a short period of time—and not on myself, I thought I might change myself internally for once, and not externally.

A large part of my adulthood has been focused on making myself attractive, on making up for my lost youth—when I wore Husky jeans and shirts with darts my grandmothers made to fit around my boy-boobs, when I ballooned to nearly 260 pounds. Slowly, I transformed my body into a Jude Law work of wonder; I became a gay man all gay men would envy: slim, sleek, firm, muscled, blond, tan. I made money. I spent money. And hear this clearly: I do not regret a single moment it took me to get there. Because, in a way, that helped me get here. But I do regret the time I now spend to stay at this personally and societally induced state of perfection.

I have lost perspective. I admit that. And I am growing older. I hate to admit that. But even the amount of time I now spend on myself cannot reclaim my youth, cannot make me look like the buff twenty-one-year-olds who populated my gym in the city.

"I never knew, and never shall know," said Thoreau, who wrote extensively about vanity, "a worse man than myself."

But am I a bad man or just a misguided one?

I receive a sign.

I notice that something strange begins to happen at the end of every month: I not only am writing more, but Gary and I also begin to have a larger surplus of money, even though we are making less.

I arrive at the shocking fact that we are saving hundreds of dollars a month by not having cable, by not tanning, by not eating out four times a week, by not buying a new pair of shoes, or jeans, or a watch, or a choker every week.

Gary even lights fires in our ancient woodstove morning and night, keeping our house toasty warm—although my skin begins to crack from the dryness—and I watch our utility bills descend lower than a limbo dancer.

I pull out old check ledgers.

Jesus, Mother Mary, the Apostles, and the donkeys who brought them all to Bethlehem!

Not even counting our second mortgage and utilities, we spent well over $1,000 a month simply watching TV, fake-baking, doing squats, eating out, reading magazines, and buying stemware and tank tops.

Over the past five years, we've spent some $60,000 on sushi, slides, workout gloves, and *Esquire*!

Minus the crack, Gary and I were basically Bobby and Whitney.

It seems outrageous, ludicrous, but I am shocked that that was such a huge part of our lives, and, strangely, I still miss it: the new restaurants, the new boutiques, the latest fashion and home accessories. We're not living in Iceland, mind you. The cute shops in Saugatuck will reopen and showcase the latest, the resorters will return in the trendiest cars and garb, but it's shocking what happens when you voluntarily remove yourself from society and trends, even for a short while.

And I don't like it at all, because these external things do have significant meaning to me. Clothes are my reward for all the hard work, for every minute of sweat and effort I still put into myself and my health. They are now the chocolate topping on my life sundae.

And new furniture and cute lamps and fall dinner plates are my thank-you for years of doing well in school, for challenging myself to do better and to do more.

Or am I just lying to myself? Am I just so shallow and so insecure that I feel I need this stuff to make people like and respect me?

Could Suze Orman be right?

Is it necessary to have two homes, three cars, a new Razr, blond highlights, a swimming pool, and Zoom!-whitened teeth?

For me, the answer has always been "Yes!" and I fear it still is.

So, at what point exactly did I lose myself while thinking I had found myself in a Pied Piper society? When did my connection to culture, and to trends and technology and sex and scandal, overtake reason?

Or, rather, am I even lost at all, or simply happy with all my stuff?

I get this message loud and clear one morning from Marge.

To clear my head, I take her for a walk on a frigid morning. I have not taken Marge for an "official walk" in the woods yet. I have been too preoccupied with myself, have only let her out to potty and then let her right back inside the cottage.

Today, when I grab her leash, head out the back door, and say the magic words—"Wanna go for a walk?"—she whines excitedly and then stops, paralyzed, at the edge of our woods, takes one paw, lifts it in the air, and then timidly touches the snow-covered path before quickly pulling it back, much like I do when I touch manmade fabrics. She paws again at the ground, sniffs it, timidly touches the earth again with her paw, and whines. She begins to turn in a circle, looking around and around, whining loudly. Marge looks ready to go, seems excited to go for a walk like she always does, but now she is scared, paralyzed.

I am baffled. Marge has romped in these woods before, sprinted after chipmunks and squirrels and rabbits. She has watched leaves fall onto her back, chomped at deer flies that buzz by her head.

And then it hits me.

There are no sidewalks in the country.

And Marge has never gone for a walk out here on a leash.

Marge is a city dog. She has lived her whole life enveloped in concrete. She equates walks with the city, with a leash and endless concrete. In the city, Marge was scolded for walking on a lawn; she had to be encouraged to run on the grass in the dog park, spent her whole dog-walking career beelining to the nearest cement, be it a sidewalk, or street, or driveway, just like a pedestrian. We are in a concrete-free zone here in the country, and it's like she has to be trained all over again.

Just like me.

We have both been conditioned by our former environment, trained to behave in a certain way. And when we are removed from our comfort zones, we both panic. Marge needs concrete. I need my stuff. It's what makes us feel safe.

Each little step forward Marge and I make is like conquering new territory.

But can an old dog learn new tricks?

"Come on, sweetie," I encourage her. "It's OK. See?"

She tenderly steps forward, like she's walking on coals, crying the whole way.

This is what I must do, too.

I don't want to lose who I am or what I love, but I don't want my love affair with consumerism and image to overwhelm me either.

I end up walking Marge all the way to the lakeshore. It is still cold—mid-30s, maybe—but I run with Marge along the edge of the lake, stopping long enough for her to slide along the ice-laden shoreline, nip at frozen waves she mistakenly believes will lap toward her at any time.

The views of the lake—the steely blueness, the mini ice caps—are breathtaking. Marge and I inhale, the wind stinging our throats.

The lakeshore road is dotted with birds and animals darting back and forth in front of me, beside me. I nearly trip over a chipmunk, nearly run into an errant seagull caught in the stiff wind.

We head back toward the cottage and then down our road, which leads to a winery and horse stables and farmland.

The landscape in Michigan is filled with every terrain, every natural nuance. It's like God was really caffeinated when he got to the northern U.S. and decided to throw a little bit of everything into the state. From the lake and its undeveloped sandy shoreline, I head inland, snow dotting the rolling hillsides filled with cows, and then horses, and then grapes.

Marge and I trot past those prepubescent grapes, which are sucking up the wetness from all the winter's snow. This area is perfect for growing grapes. "The Banana Belt," it is called, because temperatures around the lake typically keep the surrounding land from getting extremely cold or extremely hot. Lots of lake moisture, a temperate climate—it's Napa Valley gone rural.

The vineyards look like kaleidoscopes as we trot along, the miles of rows of twisted vines interconnecting and spinning, forming an earthy helix mural. A bit farther down, a few horses and a couple of jackasses take a stand at the fence and watch Marge and me zip past. The horses, even just standing, are pure muscle, living statues, every vein popping and twitching.

I have yet to see a person running today. Not even a car. It is me and my dog.

When I used to work out in the city after work, I headed to a giant gym crammed with people and benches and machines. I would change into $300 worth of adorable workout clothes, pick a treadmill in the mass of humanity, turn on my iPod, and tune out the world, my feet flying across the rubbery belt, my goal to be so exhausted that I could not think, that I could forget my job, my life. And then I would rush home to walk Marge on the city concrete, both of us rushing, sniffing, but not really bothering to look around.

When I return to Turkey Run, I pass the very same mirror I passed earlier and see that I am smiling like some kind of freakin' idiot. I look down at Marge, who is panting, and I can swear that she is smiling, too. My thighs burn, and I can feel my body again, for the first time in weeks. Marge laps her water, and I bypass the chocolate chips, opting to make a protein smoothie.

My eighty-pound mutt walks over, jumps into my arms—such a no-no to the Dog Whisperer—and licks my face. I hold her closely, and we dance a little salsa, back and forth and back and forth, and I realize that both of us, at least for one day, are finally enjoying what's around us, finally beginning to conquer our fears.

We may never completely lose our love affair with concrete and consumerism, but Marge and I are richer in so many ways, because we are learning—one step at a time—to live without city sidewalks.

Wade's Waders

rip open the birthday gift that Gary's mother has sent me, with a little help from Marge, who is adept at gingerly removing wrapping paper and bows and ribbon and tissue with her giant jaw.

No matter what I feel or believe, or the flashes of incredible clarity I receive, I *need* and *want* a nice gift right now, a useless city gift, a shirt with sequins, or low-riderjeans, or something in suede or leather. I desperately want to embrace my second Life Lesson—to eschew the latest entertainment and fashion for simpler pursuits—but I'd prefer to do it with an asterisk.

Gary's mother, second only to Mrs. Claus, perhaps, is the single best gift buyer in the universe. She could find Hitler the perfect mustache trimmer.

Over the past decade Gary and I have been together, she has always bought me the perfect clothes, in the right style, size, and color.

She is my personal Isaac Mizrahi.

In a dickey.

Gary's mom buys me Hollister tank tops, Gap T-shirts, and Banana Republic jackets, along with Justin Timberlake and Kelly Clarkson CDs. She truly thinks, I have become convinced, that I am a thirteen-year-old girl. Which is why I adore her.

In fact, one of my closets right now—of the four separate closets scattered throughout our cottage—is filled with some one hundred pairs of shoes she has purchased for me and Gary at Christmas, on birthdays, at Valentine's, over Memorial Day, on girls' shopping week-ends.

I have running shoes and cross-trainers. I have trendy, pointy shoes that look like leather canoes and ankle-length suede zip-up boots. I have Uggs and Timberlands and more black, buckled Kenneth Cole Reactions than a whole town of Pilgrims. And there will be more. Gary and I are the *Sex and the City* girls. We have just as many coats and jackets, too. We have more leather than an S&M bar.

Despite this, I am in need of a fashion fix. I can't buy it myself, so I need someone to do it. I need some fabulosity. Between feed stores and Wal-Mart, I am camouflaged out. I open the gift, half expecting to find that space suits or corsets are now in style.

My heart is racing.

The box is big.

I rattle it.

My God, it's shoes.

Heavy shoes.

They're the hand-tooled Kenneth Cole boots I requested that look like the ones I saw on *Entourage* before we moved.

I rip the lid off the box.

I cannot look.

My hand hits something cool and thick.

I smell rubber.

Did she get me a set of Goodyears?

Waders?

Waders!

Are you kidding me?

It seems that since there are no sidewalks in the country, Wade needs waders to navigate.

Without falling.

Or ruining his nice shoes.

So he won't have to shovel in suede or slides.

But, unfortunately, waders are the Toyota Corollas of shoes.

Devoid of style or personality.

Purely functional. Indestructible. Impenetrable. Dull.

Waders are condoms for the feet.

No wetness or dirt can penetrate their two-foot-high, four-inch-thick rubber wizardry.

I am not a fan of functional.

I prefer items that look good and feel bad, items that are expensive and pretty but are pretty much useless. Like me.

I buy shoes based solely on appearance. The insoles could be made of glass shards and barbed wire, and I would not only purchase them but also wear them to a dance-a-thon if they were a perfect match with my jeans or made someone, anyone—even a blind man—look twice.

I buy sofas based on the impression they make and not on the comfort they provide. I would rather lie on a couch alone with an aching back for 350 days a year just for the great joy those remaining 15 days provide when guests arrive and go, "Oh, my God, look at that fabric. I love the lines!"

But there is absolutely no way to make a wader look good. You cannot make a giant, lace-up, army-green rubber boot look stylish.

"What do you think?" Gary asks sheepishly. "You need them. You cannot wear suede boots and slides in the woods. You're going to kill yourself."

I glare at him.

But he has a point.

I have fallen so many times this winter my back looks like a Baltimore Ravens jersey. I went to a doctor someone recommended—who I swear was a horse vet—and he gave me a pill, one pill the size of a toaster, and told me not to fall anymore, or he'd have to shoot me.

"They don't even have any holes in them—like Crocs—so I can bedazzle them with cute seasonal clips," I say to Gary.

He smiles. He knows that's a better response than "I'm going to rip the fucking adenoids out of you and your mom's throats."

"Try them on!" Gary encourages me.

Waders are too thick to force a pair of jeans over, so pant legs must be tucked inside, which gives me the look of a flamboyant marine. Worse, there is simply no possible way to color-coordinate when vomit green is serving as your base.

Gary tells me—politely, softly, like he's woken me up at midnight for an intervention—that waders are necessary for living in the woods, like handbags are necessary for urban women.

He lists the reasons why:

- Waders *never* get dirty. "You simply hose them down or spray them with Windex and give 'em a wipe."
- "They're indestructible!"
- "They will never lose their shape."
- "Above all else, they're safe."

And, honestly, they will eventually save my life. I will be outside cleaning up the winter debris and I will kill a Michigan rattler sunning in our yard.

OK, so it is a garden hose that I will whack in half with a hoe, but still, I comfort myself with the knowledge that a rattler's fangs could never penetrate this impenetrable rubber.

My waders become my rural baby blanket, providing comfort and safety. And I begin wearing them everywhere, every day, in the rain, sleet, snow, sun, honestly believing that they are like women's high-fashion rain boots and that I can make my army-green waders *the* new fashion statement, like the Olsen twins did with giant sunglasses and Martha did with her poncho.

I walk to our country store in my waders one nice winter day to buy rock salt and some mole killer, forgetting that it is a national holiday and resorters could be around. Of course, a group of gay men whiz by, whistle at me, and then stop and hop out of dueling Mercedes convertibles, looking as if they just finished a Dolce & Gabbana photo shoot.

They are very pretty men. *Very* pretty men. And they are wearing very pretty shoes. Shoes that I have not seen. I walk in and grab my rock salt and then head to the back of the country store, where they keep stuff like ammo and arrows and mole killer.

I return to the front of the store, where the pretty men in pretty shoes are buying vodka.

Suddenly, they start laughing.

At me.

I look down. I am wearing my waders with tube socks and ripped sweats. I am sporting a heavy green poncho.

I look like the fashion-challenged child of Don Knotts and Bat Girl.

I tip my hat—my pig feed cap, thank you very much—right at them, very politely.

I try to back up, to disappear into the aisle filled with mouse traps and poison, but my waders mock me, squeaking with each and every mini-step.

The pretty boys laugh and turn to leave.

Channel Thoreau, I think. *Wade's Walden! Wade's Walden!*

My hands are shaking. My head is going white with anger and embarrassment.

What would Lucy do?

"Waders are . . . so . . . next year!" I yell after them. "You just wait! You just wait!"

And then one of my rubber waders, like the stop on a pair of old skates, drags the floor in the country store, and I fall forward, throwing my items onto and over the counter.

The door chimes, signaling the exit of the Backstreet Boys in laugh-filled hysterics. I pull myself off the floor with as much dignity as possible, and yank my tube socks up to my knees, so the waders won't rub a blister.

"Just the rock salt and mole killer?" the clerk says to me.

Do You Have These in a Size 2 . . . to Go?

OK, the pig hat just isn't cutting it.

And the waders? Not so much.

I can't take it any longer.

Screw Thoreau.

I have been dreaming of this day for weeks. I am fake-asleep, fake-hugging a pillow, acting all content.

And then our snow-covered gravel driveway goes silent. Gary is gone for the day. The whole day. I jump out of bed, like a kid at Christmas, and run excitedly to the window. All clear. Thirty minutes later—after I've showered—I am out the door.

I am sneaking to an outlet mall roughly an hour from our cottage. I might as well be having an affair, considering the amount of secrecy and desire involved. I cannot take the woods any longer. I cannot take the isolation. I cannot pretend to be content with playing games, and feeding ducks, and watching chipmunks. I cannot take the fact that I haven't bought a single item of clothing in weeks. I now dream about jeans. I have nightmares that I am running barefoot after new Kenneth Cole shoes, and they are always just a step ahead.

I have told Gary that today is "a focused writing day," that I will not answer the phone. "I do not have time for such idleness," I think I said to him. And I don't. I don't even stop for a latte on the way; I am on a mission.

Of course, I have shopped online and have spent hours perusing clothing. But that's just not the same as being in a store, rifling through racks of new clothes, feeling fabrics, trying on jeans and shirts in full-length mirrors, monopolizing the time of gay clerks with too many highlights and too much attitude.

Still, this is a risky move: How will I hide the bills and the clothes? What if Gary comes home early? There is more risk involved than making homemade meth in the bathtub while smoking a cigarette and lighting candles.

So I am driving far away to get my fix, already overwhelmed by the highway, the traffic, seeing other people who are dressed in something other than a robe.

I am worried about what I will find when I get there, almost as if I have been frozen in time and came out expecting dinosaurs, or an ice age, or flappers.

What have I missed?

After being alone so long, the outlet mall resembles what I picture heaven to be like: hundreds of fabulous retail stores with clothes 50 percent off or more. The outlet mall actually resembles Michigan's little resort towns, all whitewashed and filled with lighthouses.

Lord knows, I can't shop in town. Someone would see me and say something to Gary. I can't ruin my Thoreau-esque reputation this early on in the contest.

I am one of the first cars in the outlet mall lot. I check my hair and then beeline into Banana, fill my arms with merchandise, and spend the next hour making more costume changes than Celine. I buy nearly $300 worth of clothes . . . with cash. The clerk looks at me with a mix of envy and fear, like I'm 50 Cent. I feel sick. I feel guilty. And then I buy a quad-shot latte and I feel much, much better. Energized, really. So I buy a casual summer men's dress jacket from Guess ("You look *so* European," the sales clerk, who looks like a chubby Jessica Alba, tells me. And I believe her.) I buy a pair of what I'm pretty sure are ladies' jeans, just because the oversize pockets hug my ass like a pair of Slenderalls, and then cute Ts from J. Crew. I gorge in the Gap outlet, simply because I can buy ten items for $50, and then I liberate Lancôme from the remainder of its stock.

I am trying on a watch at Fossil when my cell phone rings. It's Gary.

I don't want to answer. Should I answer?

"Hello?" I say weakly. And then I cough. For some reason.

"Are you OK?"

"Yeah. Just cranking on my writing. I think I might be coming down with something, though."

"What do you think of the watch? Hot, right?"

This is the sales clerk, who, naturally, has a voice like Harvey Fierstein's.

"Who is that?" Gary asks.

"I have classical music on in the background."

"Oh. I just wanted you to know I'll be home in about an hour. All my afternoon appointments got canceled. I'll see you soon. Hope you feel better. Keep writing, Thoreau!"

Noooo!

I rip the watch off my wrist, toss it at Harvey, saying, "It's a little too feminine for me," and sprint out of the outlet mall wearing my new women's jeans.

I drive like Jeff Gordon, sweating, coffee oozing out of my pores, my jeans tearing into my skin. Since they are women's, they ride too high and lift and separate where they shouldn't be lifting or separating. I have to pee so badly, my stomach aches. I remember what my mother, the nurse, has always said: "The bladder just bursts in a car wreck. Shatters like glass. People never think about this, but it's one of the most common medical emergencies in a car accident."

I don't want my bladder to burst. I love my bladder. But I'd rather suture it up myself and keep driving than have Gary discover I've been sleeping with Eddie Bauer.

Please don't be home, please don't be home, I pray the whole drive. I go 90 miles per hour in my Honda Element and make it back to our cottage in under an hour. I hit the garage-door opener. My moment of truth. The door opens. His stall is empty.

I made it! Thank you, God!

I grab my ten shopping bags and carry them all up to our sleeping loft, which we rarely venture up to unless we want to have sex somewhere different. I cram my shorts, T-shirts, jackets, and shoes into an old trunk we have sitting at the foot of the bed, covering them with a quilt. I run outside and cram the shopping bags into the bottom of our trash barrel. Just as I head back inside, I hear Gary's car bumping down the gravel drive.

I try to catch my breath but instead catch my reflection in a mirror we have that is ringed with pine trees and jumping fish: I'm still wearing my new women's jeans.

I hear the back door slam. I run to the bathroom, kick off my jeans, wad them up, and toss them in the cabinet under the sink. Gary walks in.

"You poor thing. You didn't even get to put on pants today."

He hugs me. And then it hits me: When am I ever going to be able to wear any of this stuff with him around?

I officially forfeit Lesson Two—*I need my stuff, I admit it*—and do it big-time, joining a local gym and tanning salon and looking into a trip to Palm Springs.

This evens my scorecard: Wade's Walden—1; Modern Society—1.

LESSON THREE
Learn to Love the Snow

I weathered some merry snow-storms, and spent some cheerful winter evenings by my fireside, while the snow whirled wildly without, and even the hooting of the owl was hushed.

—Henry David Thoreau, *Walden*

Let It Snow, Let It Snow, Let It Snow!

t is late February, deep into winter in the North Country, and this is—count 'em—the fifteenth straight day we have had measurable snow. There will be roughly forty more. I'm glad I don't know this yet, or I would walk out into the storm, open my mouth, and inhale snow until my lungs are filled.

How many seasons does Michigan have? Two. Winter and construction.

An Eskimo visited Michigan during the winter and complained about the weather.

You know you're from Michigan when you have more miles on your snow blower than your car . . . when you find 0 degrees "a little chilly" . . . when you begin to define summer as three months of bad sledding.

Michiganders joke about the snow.

It's the only way they know how to survive.

It can begin to snow in the Mitten starting around Thanksgiving, a few heavy, wet, puffy flakes that melt your heart and then, quickly, just melt. There is often enough snow to provide a fairy-tale white Christmas without being an inconvenience. And the pictures are storybook: pines dusted with snow, Victorian storefronts twinkling with lights that reflect off the powder, carolers and horse-drawn carriages in Saugatuck, a coating of pure white to cover the dull, colorless nothingness of the winter ground. Everything looks freshly painted.

A Michigan winter shows early but not tellingly, much like a woman's pregnancy. It is sweet and romantic, a little blip of cuteness.

And then the big guns come out.

By the end of February, it's an apocalypse.

I have a new favorite phrase, which has replaced my former favorite, "Do you have this in an extra-small?" My new phrase goes something like this: *"Stop snowing, damn it! Stop snowing right now! Oh, God, oh, God, oh, God, please make it stop!"*

We have about two feet of snow on the ground—enough to cover Marge to her midsection—but this is mere Cool Whip compared to the gigantic meringue that will soon be heaped upon my humble pie.

What started today as a lake-effect snow warning has morphed into a blizzard watch. I do not know about blizzards, whiteouts, or gale-force winds. We never had much of a winter in the Ozarks, where it would ice, knock some power lines down every few years, or simply "snow and go," as we liked to say. And then the weather would break, temperatures would climb to 60 degrees, and it would be briefly warm enough to smell the earth once again.

In St. Louis, the Arch seemingly closed if the city received more than three inches. It was pure panic when meteorologists predicted a dusting, urbanites swarming the grocery stores for milk, eggs, and bread, a list of staples I've never really understood unless everyone is planning to survive for a week on French toast.

In Michigan, you have to pay attention to the weather. Three inches is just a hiccup.

Gary and I continue to break Lesson Two like cheap stemware and opt to have a satellite dish installed. We rationalize our failure by saying we need to have the Weather Channel at our disposal, to stay on top of the changing climate, especially since Gary must still drive in sketchy weather for his sales calls.

Still, we go ahead and get the premium package, which includes 1,682 channels, along with HBO and Showtime. In the midst of a snow squall, a man who calls himself Li'l Jim arrives to install our dish. Li'l Jim is a four-hundred-pound mountain of a man who is taken with wearing a curiously tiny conductor's cap, which is like putting a peanut on an elephant's head.

"So is there a Big Jim?" I ask Li'l Jim, wondering just how big you have to be to move up from Li'l to Big.

I would be Amoeba Jim in that family.

Gary cuts me off, asking the other question I was wondering about. "So . . . how are . . . you . . . you know, going . . . to, umm, get . . . like . . . on the roof?"

I picture Li'l Jim falling and being airlifted off our property. Or, worse, losing his hat, which I really think is a cork to keep his fat from spewing out the top of his noggin.

"Oh, you fellas don't want no dish up'n this'yere roof," he laughs. "I'm installin' a pole in your yard and settin' the dish on it. Michigan snow sticks to a dish like entrails on an arrow . . . you don't wanna have to crawl up on your roof every half hour to broom it off, now, do ya? Oh, and the pole costs an extra two hundred and fifty dollars."

As soon as Li'l Jim is done, we write him a ransom check and then immediately watch twelve episodes of *Saved by the Bell* before turning to the Weather Channel, where we begin learning our new, northern weather vernacular from Jim Cantore, who Gary strongly believes should only report the weather in tank tops.

Weather Lesson Number One: A heavy snow warning means it *may* snow, even though it is already snowing outside.

Weather Lesson Number Two: A heavy snow watch means it *will* snow, even though it is already snowing outside.

Weather Lesson Number Three: A lake-effect snow warning is the equivalent of a virtual whiteout.

Weather Lesson Number Four: A blizzard is certain death.

"Do you think he's a good kisser?" Gary asks about Jim Cantore, who looks like he spends more time at Gold's Gym than in front of the satellite radar.

I could care less if Jim Cantore started stripping right now, because my face is pressed to our window.

I have never seen this kind of snow, this blinding Irwin Allen–movie-esque-disaster snow.

And yet this snow doesn't seem to affect the locals. I find it fascinating to watch the local news, the footage of drivers defiantly flying down and then, ultimately, off the highway, many laughing as they emerge, mouthing, "Oh, that's Michigan."

I am not so amused.

I become addicted to watching the regional radar on the Weather Channel and then on my laptop, the lake-effect snow rotating in heavy, thick bands along the lakeshore counties, Lake Michigan a literal fuel tank of moisture. It snows with the same heaviness of a spring thunderstorm, sheets of snow that accumulate so quickly I find myself blinded by white, like I'm living on an endless sheet of computer paper.

"Move! Move, you blob!" I blow at my computer screen, secretly believing my breath might miraculously budge the storm.

I become an amateur Al Roker, learning everything I possibly can about meteorology. A low-pressure system that has moved on toward Buffalo should mean our snow is over by now. But that is not so, with the temperature of the lake and the direction of the wind. It's like living on the wrong end of a snow blower.

Our cottage sits roughly a mile or so from the lake, and while this is dreamy in the summer, it is nightmarish in the winter.

This is my first blizzard warning. And it's a doozy. It's been a whiteout for forty-eight straight hours. It was awe inspiring the first four hours, and then I thought it was pretty. After that, I began to shovel, and shovel, and shovel, and I began to find the snow annoying. Now, I pray for it to get dark so I can't watch it snow anymore.

I'm about to have a stroke.

By day two, I become obsessed with the fact that the snow simply cannot, or will not, stop. So I watch the radar on my computer, the lake magically regenerating snow that should be in Paris by now.

How is this possible?

I venture outside and stick an old yardstick into the snow. I begin going out every hour, like clockwork, until finally my yardstick disappears in a drift.

Yardstick!

Disappears!

Hello?

I start drinking a bottle of wine on day three at exactly five P.M. to bring on some sort of mental and physical relaxation. I take a bath and drink and drink and drink, and, right before I am about to drown, I think of Stephen King, whose creativity would be heightened by this weather. I think of him sitting in his writing studio on Maine's coastline, writing and writing and writing, laughing evilly, knowing he has another bestseller, even if it's about a possum with ESP and a desire to drink human blood.

This storm has made me appreciate King's brilliance, though. I mean, he got *The Shining* right on. I have written nothing the past few days but "Stop fucking snowing . . . stop fucking snowing . . . stop fucking snowing . . ."

My nostrils are inching under the bathwater, and I blow bubbles, wondering if Brad Pitt would play me in this movie. It has Oscar written all over it. Except the movie version would undoubtedly have Brad-Wade save a family of orphans from falling through the ice on a frozen lake.

I am so drunk that I can clearly envision Brad and me in Hollywood discussing the script: two Missouri boys laughing over beers about our Ozarks childhoods. And then Brad would kiss me, and he'd leave Angelina, and we'd adopt four children and talk about carbs and ab work and live in Malibu when we're not in Rio.

Suddenly, I sober up, realizing I don't want to die carrying around an extra ten pounds. They'll show me bloated on TV, and someone will make a joke about why I wasn't on *Celebrity Fit Club*.

Yes, a blizzard can make you slowly go nuts.

Unless you're Gary, who's already there. He wants more snow, as much as God can possibly rain down on our heads. He wants to build snow forts and make snow angels and snowmen and snow ice cream and anything that can utilize snow as a primary ingredient.

He shovels in his sweater-socks, hideous throwbacks to the 1970s that are part shoe (leather insole) and part sock (knee-high flannelesque material). He looks like a Dr. Seuss character.

On day four, the snow slows to a natural disaster. Since I'm hungover, Gary relieves me and begins shoveling. He doesn't wear gloves.

He yells at me as I stare at him out our front door, "My hands are numb!"

I mouth, "You're a moron!"

Later, he will tell me that I hurt his feelings, that the snow is romantic, that we are tucked away where we belong—in a cottage in the woods by the lake.

"Where do you have to go?" he asks, lighting a fire in the ancient wood-burning stove, the glow illuminating the knotty pine, the shadows from our carved wooden bears and lodge-inspired deco dancing in the flickering glow. "Where do you have to be? Just be still and enjoy this."

I know he is right. Our house is adorable, a throwback, a one of a kind, a cabin quaint enough to be in *Midwest Living*. Gary's innocence inspires me, so I give him a blow job—a "snow job," I call it— knowing that when it's over he will quickly fall asleep (every man is the same, gay or straight) and I can return to doing the only thing that makes me happy right now.

When I hear Ricky begin to snore, Lucy pulls her laptop from underneath the bed and boots it up. It is pitch-black, but the embers from the fire, the white of the snow, and the light from my screen illuminate my world.

I finally fall asleep at two in the morning, staring at the radar on my computer, the snow magically regenerating over us like a mushroom cloud.

Oh, the Weather Outside
Is Frightful . . .

How bad is the snow our first winter?

Lest you think I exaggerate, let me put it in very simple terms: I can't walk through it.

Yes, I know I have a tiny torso, short legs; think dachshund, not greyhound. Still, the snow is too high to step up and over, so I have to trudge right through it. Even Marge, a real dog, can't even leap over the top anymore unless she was riding a pogo stick. She makes it near the top and then—*whack!*—she hits the never-ending snowbank. Marge can barely even take a shit. And she *does* have the legs of a greyhound. She has to hike her ass abnormally, like she's getting a colonoscopy, and then her poop just disappears, magically, like in an airplane toilet, never to be seen again, a point of great consternation for Marge, since she can't see it, sniff it, check the evidence to make sure she really did something.

How bad is the snow?

I now have to clear our satellite dishes for TV and wireless Internet every thirty minutes, or I lose reception. The heavy wet snow pelts the dishes, coats the trees, like soap suds in a car wash.

The only real winter gear I have is a wool peacoat I bought during a shopping trip in the East Village. It was a great deal at $500, and looks great with the only other winter wear I own: gray wool slacks with oversize pockets and a bright red cashmere turtleneck. I have squeezed into these, defying the odds and the sleeves of cookie dough, like I'm dressed up and waiting in the green room to appear on *Regis and Kelly.* But no one calls for me, no one comes to get me for my appearance, or even for lunch.

I fear for Gary's safety, driving around the coast in the winter, but I fear for my sanity even more. I am here, alone in the woods, in the dark of winter—where day looks like night, and night looks like day.

I can no longer get warm, no matter how high I crank the furnace, so I try to light a fire in our wood-burning stove—like Gary just did—but nearly set myself on fire. I am truly the son of my father. My mother did *not* have an affair with a postman who looked a little like Cliff Robertson, I am now convinced. My father sets himself on fire, and I do the same. Case closed.

To brighten Turkey Run and my mood, I turn on every single light—and we have literally hundreds—little lamps and big lamps, chandeliers and spotlights, overheads and night-lights, bright hundred-watts and fluorescents in the pantries. I stare into them, my pupils burning, like a poor man's shock therapy, to make myself more alert, more sane, but I catch a glimpse of myself in a mirror, and I look more Norma Desmond than Dr. Phil.

I grab a broom to go sweep off our satellite dishes yet again and fall down our front stoop.

The snow is hissing and swirling around my head, like a sky full of cobras. Suddenly, Marge startles me. She is barking. I turn, and she is yelping at Turkey Run, which is glowing like a UFO. It has an eerie, otherworldly brightness, and it scares me a little, too. It scares me because I do not see myself living here. It is all wrong.

"It's our house, girl. It's OK," I tell Marge, trying to convince myself more than her.

Marge barks at me.

"What's wrong, girl?" I ask.

In my head, I see her mouth moving, like those skits on *Conan,* and she is saying, "Take me back to the city, jackass."

I shake my head back and forth and up and down, trying to clear the image. It doesn't work, but the northerly wind picks up and scoots across my body, quickly giving me clarity. I am muttering something, I realize.

"I want to go home. I want to go home."

I click the rubber heels of my waders, just like a gay Dorothy, but I'm not transported anywhere. I am here. In the middle of nowhere.

It's *The Shining*.

I'm too afraid to go in and write right now, too afraid I'll just type, over and over again, "All work and no play make Wade a very bad boy."

Let's Get Plowed

now blowers are for *fuckin' pussies!*"

This is what the salesman, who looks like an extra from *Fargo,* tells me at a nearby home improvement store after I mistakenly ask about the merits of snow blowers.

And, by the by, I am a fuckin' pussy, but I choose to keep this my little secret.

"Blowers blow the snow around, right?" he informs me. "Plows plow the snow, right? Blowers blow. Plows plow. Got it?"

I want to tell him he's saying the same thing over and over—like "Fuckers fuck"—that one is a noun, and the other is a verb, though they sound the same. But I don't, because I am grateful to be alive.

We have driven nearly an hour in a whiteout to get here, because it has become a matter of life and death to purchase a snow removal system. We shouldn't even be on the roads—birds aren't even dumb enough to be flying in this—but Gary is obsessed, so I white-knuckle the passenger-side seat and air-brake while he slides from ditch to ditch. I so want to ask, "How's it goin', Mr. Magoo?" considering Gary is hunched over the wheel, squinting and going two miles an hour, but I know he would punch me in the balls.

For the first few weeks of winter, Gary and I actually shoveled our driveway *by hand.* It took hours and hours for both of us to shovel the narrow, winding gravel drive meandering back through the woods that we once found so cottage-y cute. Now it's become our personal bobsledding tunnel, our personal hell. We cannot get our SUVs in or out if we get more than six inches of snow. And in Michigan, six inches is just a start.

We would slave for hours, making our way to the end, only to turn around and realize the entire driveway was covered again. After that, we began to shovel when there would be little breaks in the snow, but we'd wake the next morning to find ourselves trapped once again.

Finally, Gary called Snow Plow Man.

We call Snow Plow Man Snow Plow Man because we have never, ever seen his actual face. Snow Plow Man is simply all giant noggin covered with full-face ski mask, ears covered with muffs (though I'm sure he doesn't call them "muffs"), eyes covered with Blublockers, top of head covered with ski hat, which is then covered with parka hood. He does, however, have a cigarette constantly lit and hanging from his ski mask, and though he talks nonstop, the cigarette moves as though it's an extension of his lips.

"Yep. It's a bad storm. You betcha. I'll drop by later this afternoon. Supposed to get a shitload more. Yep. That'll be fifty bucks."

Umm, I'd at least like to see a peek of cheekbone at that price.

He returns six hours later to do the whole thing all over again, because if he doesn't, the National Guard, led by a dog-sledding unit, wouldn't be able to get down our drive.

I continue to be baffled by lake-effect snow. They don't even explain it on the local weather. They just talk about it like it's all well known, like why the sky is blue. All I know is that we are getting roughly a foot of snow every six hours. It doesn't just snow here; the heavens rain snow, the sky vomits snow, big, healthy chunks of snow, over and over and over, like I used to do when I'd drink twenty-six Meister Braus and then eat Nachos Bell Grande.

Which is why we have found ourselves looking at a snowblower-plow thing.

"This'un's like one of those newfangled ridin' mowers," Fargo tells us. "You just stand behind it, and it blasts the shit outta the snow."

"How much?" Gary asks.

"Thousand bucks," Fargo says.

Gary drools. He loves big, expensive things that have the dual power to cause mass destruction while also making others jealous. It's the one straight gene he inherited.

However, the Rouse genes tell me that's a hell of a lot of money to spend, especially since it doesn't involve clothes and shoes, but the Rouse genes also tell me we've spent nearly $300 in the past two weeks and that the snow will not stop any time soon.

At this rate, we'll be either broke or dead by spring.

And I can't decide which is a better option right now.

Suicide Hill

Gary and I have just finished building a snowman, complete with a very impressive thick stick penis. I have peed on his feet to give him yellow boots, but the melting has overpowered the tinting effect, giving the poor fella abnormally underdeveloped calves.

I have to admit that this little outing—which Gary pushed as a way to get me over my fear and loathing of snow—is lovely and child-like and demented, in a John Waters sort of way.

It is late afternoon—nearly dusk—and I am standing at the top of Mount Baldhead, the largest sand dune in town. Mount Baldy is a 282-step climb straight up—a gasp-inducing incline that leaves most folks in need of air-evacuation to a cardiac center—but the views are spectacular: Lake Michigan to the west and our resort town to the east.

I spin around. Saugatuck-Douglas looks like Bavaria. I feel as if I am trapped in a snow globe.

How can pine trees hold so much snow without collapsing? How can the snowflakes be so enormous? The landscape looks like those old paint-by-numbers snow scenes, where you only finish the white on the tree branches and the ground before you grow bored and leave the rest of the portrait uncompleted.

I look back at the towns. Everything is a blur from the snow, but the distant towns glow at dusk, Saugatuck still drenched in white holiday lights, Douglas in colored lights, and everything twinkles and glistens like it's being lit for a movie.

From here, I can see that the "little lake"—Saugatuck's harbor, which collects the Kalamazoo River into a beautiful round holding tank before pouring into Lake Michigan—is finally frozen.

There is a tiny opening in the little lake's frozen basin, a separation in the ice, where geese have flocked—by the hundreds—to eat and drink. It's like nature's version of the town coffee shop, the locals all squawking over the latest gossip.

The yachts—many of which sit in an open shelter—look like ghost ships that are desperately trying to navigate through a blizzard but making no progress.

School has been canceled and kids have flocked to local golf courses or these dunes to sled and tube.

In order to conquer my third lesson, Gary has asked me here to go sledding, on what is the biggest downhill run in town.

Which is why I am looking the world over one final time before I catapult to carnage.

"You need to embrace not only the snow but also your inner child," Gary had said before we left as he was pulling on his long johns.

He can be so Deepak Chopra when he wants to be.

"That sounds very *To Catch a Predator*," I told him. "And, by the way, you look like one of the Waltons. The middle boy, the one no one remembers."

"You are so cynical," he said before dragging me here, to our deaths.

And now here we stand, on top of Old Smokey or whatever, Gary holding a toboggan in front of him, running forward, catapulting himself into the air, and flying down the dune like he's been shot out of a cannon.

I am next.

I stare down the dune, which is like a luge run surrounded on both sides by giant pines. The angle of descent is equivalent to a death drop on a Six Flags roller coaster. The run has been slickened and shined by sleds and toboggans, and the hills call to me, taunt me: *Forget your childhood! Love the snow! Don't be a scaredy-cat!*

I haven't been on a sled much since childhood, since I nearly killed myself, since I was fat and scared and girly and ill prepared for such battles.

But now I'm back in the country, and I have vowed to do better. I told Gary before he barreled down the dune that if I'm disfigured, I will come back and kill him, just like Stockard Channing did in that old Lifetime movie where she exacted revenge on everyone who once thought she was ugly.

I position my body on a rickety old sled we picked up at an estate sale. Gary, of course, took the newer version. I am thankful I am nearly the same body weight as a thirteen-year-old girl, or I'd be Dead Man Sledding. I am pointed face first, staring down my ninety-degree tunnel to hell.

My headband keeps sliding down over my eyes, which is a distraction and comfort. I wanted to wear a headband for the look, not the warmth. This is how I decide most things in my life. Does it look good on me? It doesn't matter if I lose an earlobe due to frostbite as long as I have the Olivia Newton-John "Physical" thing goin' on.

I look around. A small crowd has gathered. People are waiting for their turns. Mount Baldhead is where the big kids sled, the guys who stare death in the face and laugh. I would prefer never to meet death, not even over lattes and scones. All the local tough guys and random idiots are here, wanting their snowy shot at glory. "Go!" someone yells. "Get that girl going!"

Damn my headband!

Suddenly, someone gives me a healthy push, and I scream my final words: "Mother of God, I'm going to die!"

And then I shut my eyes.

When I was in elementary school my family lived for a short while in a rental house close to the town's favorite sledding hill, which was dramatically, but appropriately, named Suicide Hill.

Suicide Hill was actually not a hill at all but a very steep, narrow street a few blocks over that angled dramatically to the left at the very bottom. If sledders didn't judge the hairpin turn correctly, they sailed into a deep ravine that still belched the remains of a few cars and a lot of trash.

I was shamed into going to Suicide Hill on a snowy day by a

group of roughhousing boys who lived close to us, the kind of boys who blew snot rockets and challenged one another to punch each other in the arm until they couldn't take the pain.

Suicide Hill was already packed with such boys when I arrived, me bringing up the rear. I tried to avoid eye contact with anyone, standing toward the back, pantomiming exhaustion like I had just finished and needed a breather. I watched as the boys flew down Suicide Hill, jackknifing their sleds left at the very last minute, everyone screaming and yelling and oohing and aahing.

I delayed for about an hour, standing lock-legged in the frigid air, my joints aching, my eyes tearing, faux-panting over and over and over, until one of the roughhousing boys scanned the crowd and said, "I think everyone's gone except for you."

His finger point might as well have been a spotlight.

The crowd started chanting, "Go! Go! Go! Go!" One of the boys handed me his toboggan, which was scarred, cracked, and dented, although I did notice that it perfectly matched my new silver coat, an exact replica that I'd begged to get after seeing Pam Dawber wear one on *Mork and Mindy*.

I positioned my round body in the round metal, sitting up right on my butt but already feeling a bit tippy in it. My legs were shaking, making the toboggan inch forward on the slick ground. "Lay down in it!" a boy yelled. "It's more fun that way."

The crowd now began to chant, "Lay down! Lay down! Lay down!"

Who are these people? I remember thinking. *Don't any of them have minds of their own?*

I lay down in the toboggan.

I was now on my stomach, face forward, ass in the air, legs jutting out like a captured grasshopper between a thumb and forefinger.

Without warning, two of the snot rocket boys pushed me, hard, and grunted, like they were pushing an elephant on a swing, and suddenly I was flying down the hill, actually hovering above the ground. My eyes were shut, but I decided to open them, thinking it would be a good idea if I wanted to live.

It was a mistake.

I watched houses whir by, my toboggan a blur. It was like riding in one of my grandma's mixing bowls, only a thin piece of metal and a sketchy "steering wheel" standing between death and me.

I was going faster, faster, faster, until, at some point, I could feel the men's ski pants I was wearing come down just a little from the speed and wind shear.

I could feel my snot freezing as it oozed out my nostrils, ice forming in my dewy crack. After twenty seconds, the ride was nearly over, along with my life. I could see the street hook dramatically left and the ravine dead ahead as I neared the bottom of the hill.

Suddenly, I pulled with all my might, my toboggan bulleting forward, until I could feel it start to shimmy ever so slightly to the left. I continued to pull with everything I had, thankfully avoiding the ravine but badly overcompensating, which caused me to shoot my toboggan straight over a ditch, my ride finally coming to a stop when I bounced off an inflatable Rudolph that was luckily still standing from Christmas.

I jumped up, stunned, winded, but gleeful to be alive. I raised my hands to the heavens, to show all of these chanting idiotic villagers my triumph, and, as if on cue, my man-size pants fell down, revealing long johns and more than a hint of ass crack.

Whirring down Mount Baldhead, I have a revelation: This is way worse than Suicide Hill.

I am now traveling the speed of light, my hands gripping the warped wooden steering column, which is like guiding a space shuttle with a kite string. My headband blows off, and I now have the consolation of knowing I will have no bangs when I die.

There is a crowd of what I think are people—though it could be cows or dancing blenders; I can't tell going this fast—and this amorphous group is yelling, "Pull left! Pull left!" or something, and so I pull left and careen down a little side path that quickly slopes up a slight embankment.

I come to a stop. My entire body is quaking, my eyes are watering, my lashes icy.

"I'm alive!" I yell at the group, standing up, lifting my arms triumphantly.

I immediately look down.

"And I'm wearing pants."

Wade's Walden—2. Modern Society—1.

LESSON FOUR
Embrace My Rural Brethren

I sat at a table where were rich food and wine in abundance, and obsequious attendance, but sincerity and truth were not; and I went away hungry from the inhospitable board... There was a man in my neighborhood who lived in a hollow tree. His manners were truly regal.

—Henry David Thoreau, *Walden*

Love Thy Neighbor?

The first neighbor who unofficially comes to Turkey Run brings us—ironically enough—hot, homemade turkey soup. She lives, we learn, through a thicket of woods that makes her house visible from the road only in the dead of winter, when the foliage is gone. This year, however, the never-ending snow has served as a virtual white fence.

"Sorry to drop by, but . . . ," she starts.

I don't like drop-bys, period.

Unless Antonio Sabato Jr. happens to be out of sugar.

Drop-bys don't give me a chance to clean the house or do my hair or put on a façade of perfection. We didn't have drop-bys in the city; everything was preplanned, and then replanned, down to the minute. Urbanites know to call. They have cell phones. And things to do. And places to be.

In fact, the thing I admired most about my city neighbors was their ability to remain strangers, never to intrude into my daily life— nor me into theirs—unless one of us noticed a suspicious odor coming from under the door.

I had lived so long in a city—with so many neighbors constantly coming and going, and so many condos and homes constantly for sale—that I had forgotten country neighbors can be very much like Aunt Bee: annoyingly friendly and always concerned for your welfare. And I have always found genuine kindness in others to be not only baffling but also a bit irritating.

In fact, I moved to the woods—moved outside of our adorable

little resort town—partly due to this reason. I didn't want neighbors for the first time in my adult life. I was tired of living in cramped apartment complexes or houses that were within arm's length of each other. I tired of knowing my neighbors' TV preferences and toilet habits instead of their names.

I grew up without neighbors. I thought I needed that again.

Still, this neighbor sports bright eyes and a wide smile, looks like a very nice woman, and seems amazingly earnest, like a cartoon minister.

"Sorry to drop by, but I made some soup," she says again, this time handing over a Tupperware tub of turkey noodle, "*and* I wanted you to know I've been keeping an eye on your place."

"Thank you. That's very nice," I say.

I, of course, will not eat the soup.

I never eat strangers' food. I do not know if they wash their hands, or pee in their soup, or use cat food as a thickening agent. I do not know if this woman trapped one of my beloved wild turkeys, wrung its neck, plucked it naked, and then threw it in a pot of boiling water, like Glenn Close in *Fatal Attraction*. What I do know is that when I was young and it was Halloween, my mother—the nurse—would inspect every piece of candy, slice open every popcorn ball, after telling us horror stories from the ER that would make Michael Myers cringe and say, "Guurrrl, now that's messed up." And this was in the days before people did too many bad things.

"The soup smells delicious," I lie.

"It is," she says. "Used the dark meat and the turkey scraps. Makes the best soup ever."

That's code for rat poison, I think.

Still, I smile.

"Well, thank you so much for keeping an eye out on our house. Being new . . . and . . . well, you know . . ." (I don't say gay, since it doesn't seem necessary, since two men are standing before her in nearly identical pajama bottoms—one with dancing pine trees and the other with happy canoes.) "Anyway, that's very, very nice of you."

"Oh, it's no problem," she answers happily. "I've got night-vision goggles!"

Now, there's something about that particular string of words—*night* and *vision* and *goggles*—that, when used together, causes my spine to ache, my blood to run cold, much like the phrases "Insert . . . catheter" or "We . . . don't . . . have . . . that . . . in . . . your . . . size."

She walks down our porch, waving good-bye, and disappears into the woods.

"She seems like a very nice woman," Gary says.

And then together we say, "A very nice woman *with night-vision goggles.*"

As she walks away, I envision this woman watching me go about my nightly routine through her infrared binoculars: me, seen through that fuzzy light, giving myself Mary Kay facials, shooting Redi-wip into my mouth, and doing naughty things to Gary.

While she will never do anything to us, except be a great neighbor, our relationship is already tainted, because I believe she's had a front-row view of my insanity.

Thoreau wrote: "I would observe, by the way, that it costs me nothing for curtains, for I have no gazers to shut out but the sun and moon, and I am willing that they should look in. The moon will not sour milk nor taint meat of mine, nor will the sun injure my furniture or fade my carpet; and if he is sometimes too warm a friend, I find it still better economy to retreat behind some curtain which nature has provided, than to add a single item to the details of housekeeping."

But Thoreau didn't have a neighbor with night-vision goggles who could see him clean his pores with a Biore strip from five miles away.

"Call your mother," I tell Gary. "Tell her to make thick burlap liners for every curtain in every window of the house."

Cat Scratch Fever

I meet two more of my neighbors—and by "neighbor," I mean those who live within a few-miles' hike of our home—in one fell swoop, just at the very end of winter when animals and people begin to emerge from hibernation, while I am dog-watching an incredibly stupid beagle named Beavis, owned by a woman from Chicago who brings a shot of the city to the country. She and her family bought a B&B in town, and they go to the opera and symphony and are wonderful chefs and wine aficionados.

We are thrilled to have met people who have hobbies that don't require ammunition.

But they live miles from us and are swamped with their inn. As a friendly gesture, we babysit their beagle when they are busy.

Beavis is one of those dogs who looks at you with a completely blank stare, eyes rotating mindlessly, like a slot machine. He is a dog who only responds to loud commands and hot dogs or stuffed pizza as treats. This is the opposite of Marge, who we intentionally made into a neurotic, codependent bed-wetter in order to prove that she loved and needed us. Marge responds only to quiet talk and baby commands: Going to the bathroom is "potty-pee" or "potty-poo"; eating dinner is "Get'um good'ums"; giving us a good-night smooch is "Gimme a kissy." If we raise our voice to Marge, her tail drops between her hind legs and her ears flop, like we've just caned her.

I am home writing, on a surprisingly pretty and warmish late winter's day, and I am so giddy that the temperature is in the 50s, that I am wearing sleeping shorts. That's it: no shirt, no shoes, no panties. I am pulling a Britney.

Like many beagles, Beavis is a "bolter" who will run after a squirrel or chase a bird right into the middle of traffic, which is why I take Beavis to potty-pee on a leash. But when I take a break to let the dogs out and am almost back in the door—Marge in fact has already gone inside and jumped on the bed—Beavis bolts after a hedgehog in the driveway, ripping the leash out of my hand.

"Beavis!" I yell.

Nothing.

The dog is down the driveway, the leash banging behind like a bad muffler. I run after him. Barefoot and nearly nude.

"Beavis! Come here, boy!"

There is a flash in our woods, and then a rustle, and then he races by my legs, down our driveway, across the street, down our road, and disappears into the woods behind a small house. I sprint into the yard, where a woman in a housecoat—bedazzled with a giant cat playing a guitar and holding a thermometer in its mouth, the moniker CAT SCRATCH FEVER underneath—greets me while an army of cats mew in the background. She is holding something shiny in her pocket: a knife, a handgun, nail clippers, a gum wrapper, I can't tell.

"Excuse me, ma'am. Did you happen to see a beagle run through your yard?"

"Nope. My cats woulda let me know, if it had."

Your cats are climbing your screen door and dangling from the ceiling, I'm thinking. *They wouldn't be doing this unless they're rabid.*

But I say, "I'm Wade. I'm your neighbor. Sorry we haven't met."

"Oh, I know who you are," she says. "I can see a lot of things with my night-vision goggles."

Are you kidding me?

Were these part of the official Welcome Wagon basket that I somehow didn't get?

Either all of our neighbors are undercover police officers, or they firmly believe they are trapped in a Robert Ludlum spy novel.

"Umm, can I take a look in your backyard? I have to find this dog. I'm so sorry."

"Good owners keep an eye on their pets."

"I had him on a leash. He yanked it out of my hand. I'm just watching this dog for a friend."

And then I focus on what she said just before this.

"And I am a *very* good dog owner, ma'am. Marge, that's my own dog's name, is the love of my life."

"The love of your life should be God."

OK, I can't get into semantics or a religious discussion with this woman right now—who, by the way, looks like Harvey Korman in a housecoat—because I'm petrified my friend's dog is going to get crushed by a pickup.

But then I notice in 3-D what I've driven by for months: This woman has opted to go ahead and decorate every inch of her yard with cat tchotchkes. She has a flag of a cat waving an American flag, with the slogan PROUD AMERICAT! She has metal shadows of cats faux-digging in her garden. She has cat wind socks and feline statuary and kitten yard ornaments everywhere.

And this really pisses me off.

How can this woman disrespect nature when nature's inspiration surrounds her? It's like being poorly dressed in the city, when there are windows, magazines, and fellow pedestrians literally telling you what to wear. In the country, you are surrounded by towering sugar maples and majestic pines. You don't really have to do anything to have a million-dollar view. And yet she has opted to fuck it up completely.

So, against my better judgment, I ask this woman about her passion for cats, wondering if perhaps she is a humane shelter volunteer or rescue worker. Maybe her husband had a massive stroke while buying her a kitten.

"Tell me about your cats . . . why you love them so much," I try to ask her, matter-of-factly but in a neighborly sort of way, like I would ask about the weather or her new housedress. "All of this . . . *stuff* . . . is awfully interesting."

"I have a philosophy," she tells me, in the same matter-of-fact tone. "Cat people aren't into themselves like dog people. City people are dog people. They need lots of attention and fuss. Cat people are country people: quiet, keep to themselves, no commotion."

I stare at her, mouth wide open.

This is, in its most basic sense, a nice way of saying, "Fuck you!"

But she isn't done.

"You city folk who move to the country cause all kinds of commotion." She gestures at Beavis, who finally, thankfully, resurfaces before us and stops whipping around like a Cirque du Soleil performer. "You disturb the peace, drive your big cars, tear down the woods for your fancy houses."

What?!

Oh, no she didn't!

They took out about ten trees to plop in our house; she's the one who's desecrated Mother Nature by vomiting cat crap all over the countryside.

Suddenly, Beavis begins licking his balls, like Ron Jeremy.

"Do you know why he does that?" I ask her.

She is staring at me, confused.

"Because he can!"

And then I laugh like a madman.

The woman reaches into the pocket of her housecoat for the shiny thing I saw glinting earlier.

I am going to die.

Cat Woman is going to shoot me in the bridge of my nose and have her cats eat out my brains, like I'm a tin of Fancy Feast.

Instead, she grabs a can opener. Then she reaches into her other pocket and produces a can of cling peaches. It seems I have interrupted her *Judge Judy* snack. She walks back to her house and casually opens her front door, releasing her army of cats.

Beavis bolts.

For some reason, cats petrify me—all that rubbing and clawing and mewing and walking in their own litter boxes—so I, like Beavis, start running, pretty much nude, into her backyard.

I look back. They're not chasing me. They're not lions.

I sprint into the woods, think briefly of yelling "My pussy is faster than your pussies," but then I see Beavis flash through the brambles ahead of me.

Underbrush and thorns are shredding my ankles and bare feet, which are sloshing through mud and snow, aching from the cold.

Jesus Christ, this is like *The Gay Fugitive.*

"Beavis, get your ass over here now!" I am screaming, bellowing, spitting in the woods. "Goddamn it, you stupid little moron. *Stop running!*"

I emerge into a clearing, where I am greeted by a nine-hundred-year-old man and a German shepherd. "You zeem upzet," he says in a thick German accent.

I want very much to scream, "Hoooogaaaaan!"

"I am upzet," I say. "Very upzet."

"I zee your dog." He points with a gnarly old finger to the back of his land, where Beavis is lapping water from his pond. "I'm Ludwig."

But of course.

"What eez your doggy's name?"

"He's not my dog," I say. Ludwig doesn't care. "Beavis."

"Hilda!" he yells at his German shepherd. But of course. *"Holen. Schnell! Schnell!"*

Ludwig, for all I know, could be yelling, "Hilda, kill the naked faggot," but the dog zips by me, barks, shoots forth like a cannon at Beavis, and then chases him back toward us. When I turn, Ludwig has a rope, which he has fashioned into a lasso. When Beavis is within about seven feet of us, Ludwig unfurls the rope, which he ring-tosses right over the beagle's neck. Ludwig jerks the noose tight, gives the rope a tug, and pulls Beavis back to us. He hands me the leash. The beagle, for once, registers a bewildered look, much like the one I am wearing.

"I can't thank you enough, sir," I say. "I'm Wade. We live down the street."

"You love zees land as much as I do," he says. "We are neighborz."

And with that, he and Hilda are off to complete a fence he has started on the back of his property. I look down at Beavis and think seriously about kicking him in the stomach and then tying him down in the middle of the street, but I am bleeding, profusely, from the feet, legs, stomach, and buttocks.

Let's Meet Pablo, Shall We?

Gary meets our nearest neighbor—who lives in the rusting, single-wide trailer with a door trimmed in faded plastic roses the color of rotting meat—for the first time while planting trees on a beautiful late winter/early spring afternoon.

Gary wants to create a tree shield from our unwelcome neighbor and would have opted for a barbed wire fence had it not been so unsightly.

I honestly believed the trailer was temporary, that it would disappear, be hauled off and quickly replaced by a beautiful new home, which is what has begun to happen all around us.

A brand-new rustic contemporary home has just been built on the other side of our lot, a home that was purchased by resorters from the city, a family that looks like it jumped off the cover of a J. Crew catalog. And on the other side of the trailer is a gorgeous yellow Cape Cod, owned by a fabulous gay couple, complete with a pond and artist's studio.

Yet this just shows the complete randomness of our area. Gentrification is happening, but at the pace of a caterpillar, while we prefer that things move at the speed of a cheetah. Zoning seems sketchy in our neck of the woods: There might be a gorgeous new home being built on pine-filled acreage right across from a collapsing mobile home, or a farmhouse being rehabbed next to a yard filled with fallen TV antennas and enraged dogs. If this were the city, we would live in what real estate agents would elegantly term "a transitional neighborhood."

I am filled with guilt, because I believe I forced Gary to live in the country. I still think he would prefer a home in town, directly next to a resorter from Chicago who has a Labradoodle, a Jag, and a puddle of diamonds around her neck.

I grew up with trailers in close proximity. I thought I could handle it. At least temporarily.

In spite of Gary's "love thy neighbor" demeanor, he has purchased roughly twenty small pine trees to plant along our property line to block our view of the trailer. Gary will recount the following story to me, since I have opted to stay in Turkey Run and fake-write in order to avoid manual labor:

The renter, it turns out, is a boyishly handsome Mexican man, whom Gary first sees propped on the hood of his jacked-up Trans Am drinking Busch, listening to the kind of Mexican pop music you hear at all-inclusive resorts in the Mayan Riviera or Dominican Republic.

Gary waves and smiles, like Miss America.

"Hola! Vas a la clase de historia?"

I took four years of Spanish in college, and this—"Hello! Are you going to history class?" along with *"J.Lo es muy bonita!"*—are the only phrases I have taught Gary that seem to have stuck.

If lost in Mexico City, Gary would either get mugged, receive a fabulous education, or become Jennifer Lopez's makeup artist.

The man tilts his Busch in Gary's direction and then scratches his balls.

Gary begins digging a hole with his shovel, the sandy earth collapsing around itself. He plants roughly ten trees before he hears a rustling behind some of the foliage growing on our property line.

"Good luck! Good luck!"

It's our neighbor, and he is standing—barefoot, beer in hand, wearing a dirty wife-beater and pair of low-rider jeans—eerily close.

"Me llamo Pablo," he says. "Good luck!"

"I am Gary!" Gary screams, realizing too late that Pablo is Mexican and not deaf.

Pablo, according to Gary, looks a lot like Pedro from *Napoleon Dynamite,* except with better hair and a better face but slightly worse teeth.

"Good luck!"

"Oh, my God, how sweet!" Gary would later tell me. "I thought he was wishing me good luck."

"Weee'rrreee plaaaannntttinnggg treeeeesss!" Gary tells Pablo, slowly and loudly, like he's talking to a Russian baby. "You know . . . groooowww tallllllyyyy?"

Gary is acting like a tree now, arms outstretched and making wind-blowing-through-limbs noises.

"Good luck!" Pablo says again. Except this time he accompanies his cheery wish with a hand gesture, a backward arm motion that looks like he's either trying to start a lawn mower or lapsing into a seizure.

"Thank you!" Gary exclaims. "Thank-y you-y!"

Pablo laughs and chugs his beer, which he settles against the crotch of his low-rider jeans.

The music is filling the woods, and Gary will tell me it made him want to both dance and flee. Gary can sense nervous energy, tension, and so—as usual—he says something inappropriate.

"Is that Shakira?" he asks. "Love her!"

Pablo giggles and chugs. "Goooodddd luuccccckkk?"

"Good luck to you, too. I have to diggy, diggy." Gary is pointing at the shovel, the ground, and the tree.

Pablo edges closer to him through the foliage. He is smiling loopily. In a self-defense class, the instructor would be telling Gary to blow his rape whistle, knee Pablo in the balls, and run.

"You lucky dog?" Pablo asks before doing the hand gesture again.

Gary is now becoming more than a little panicked.

He tries to remain calm, thinking it must be a cultural gesture, kind of like our thumbs-up. And then it dawns on him: Yes, he thinks he saw Ricky Martin do the same thing once on the MTV Awards after receiving a Moon Man.

Pablo is now, perhaps, three feet away from Gary. He takes another gulp of Busch and then tosses the can behind his head.

Right now, I will later tell Gary, he should have been yelling, "Stranger! Danger!" and running to Mommy.

But then Pablo stretches and rubs his torso slowly, tenderly, like he's giving himself a solo massage. "Do . . . you . . . like . . . deeek?"

This, Gary tells me, he understands clearly.

Pablo's hand gesture, he now realizes, is a masturbation symbol, although backward for some reason, like he's ambidextrous, but with just one arm. He rubs his crotch and groans.

Gary is standing in shock, a shovel in hands, fake-blowing his non-existent bangs out of his eyes, a tic that has remained since the days when he had Wham! hair.

"Vas a la clase de historia!" Gary yells at the top of his lungs. *"Vas a la clase de historia!"*

Pablo retreats, believing, I'm sure, that Gary is either insane or late for history class in the woods.

"He kind of had a good body," Gary will tell me later. "I guess I should have been flattered."

Jesus. *Where have we moved?* I think.

And then a few weeks later, while I'm forced to help Gary plant another screen of trees, a sheet posing as a living room curtain pops open in the trailer, and Pablo is wishing both of us "good luck" in the universal language, his Mexican flag raised in salute, his hand moving quickly backward until his lawn mower overflows.

It seems like Lucy and Ethel have wandered into a rural White Party.

"God, I hope these trees grow fast," Gary says.

"Fucking trailer. Trailer trash!" I scream. "These people are ruining our property values. I hate these rednecks!"

"I guess now is a bad time to tell you I thought that was kinda hot," Gary says.

For the Birds

Gary and I are invited to dinner by our neighbors who own the woods and blueberry fields just behind our property.

They are kind, nice, giving people, devoted to keeping the art of fan carving alive. Fan carving is the process of slicing one piece of wood into thin blades (feathers) and then turning and interlocking them to create a three-dimensional design. The individual blades of wood are not detached and then reattached with glue. Rather, with patience and skill, the blades are turned while the wood is wet, allowing the wood fibers to turn without breaking.

Masters of this art, our neighbors create stunning fans in the shapes of birds, like doves, geese, and hummingbirds.

Over dinner, our neighbors tell us about their work with great passion and share the story of the Russian fan bird legend, the origin of their art.

It seems that in medieval times, families lived in one-room log houses that were covered inside and out with clay. There was just one window covered with a dried animal stomach during the winter and a small smoky stone fireplace. A young boy who was very ill lived in such a house with his family in northern Russia. He lay in his bed covered with furs, and people came from neighboring villages to help him regain his health, but all efforts were in vain. Near the end of winter, the boy's father was sitting by the fireplace making baskets. Tired of lying in a stuffy house, the ill boy asked, "Dad, is summer coming soon?"

"Yes, son, very soon. Just a little more and summer will be here."

Then his father had an idea: "I will make a bird from this piece of wood. I will make it look like a real bird with two wings and a tail. Maybe my son will think summer has come and the birds have returned. That would make him very happy."

The father told the boy, "I will make summer for you."

He made a bird and hung it from the ceiling near the fireplace where his son could see it. The draft from the fire caused the bird to spin. Its wings began to move and suddenly it came to life. The son was filled with joy and his health improved. The people from the neighboring villages returned to ask how the boy was healed. When they heard the story about the bird, they asked the father to make birds for their homes to safeguard and protect their families.

Our neighbors show us their work as Gary and I dine on meatloaf and bean salad and bread.

The meal and the art and the pace are light-years from the food and work and conversations I am used to eating, buying, having.

Everything is so simple, so unpretentious, so, seemingly, not me.

When I left rural America as a kid and made my way in the city as an adult, I began to define people by three main criteria: their looks, their jobs, and their homes.

One of my main priorities became getting invited to what Gary and I termed "A-list gay parties." I considered each party a stepping stone to a bigger, better one, each person a rung on the social ladder, and I would step on whoever was in my way until I reached the top.

What I didn't grasp was that this social ladder was magical. It never ended.

One of the last A-list parties Gary and I attended in the city was a gallery opening for a friend of a friend who was exhibiting charcoal architectural drawings that all looked like giant penises.

Gary went because there was brie, and he likes to pretend at art and theater openings that he is French. He would wear a beret if it didn't make him look like Fievel the mouse, and he often simply yells "Brioche!" when anyone asks his opinion.

The opening was held in a loft that was poorly heated, and my teeth were chattering as I made my way around the room to view the art.

"What a commentary on modern architecture!"

"I see the drawings as concrete stakes through our hearts. Art in architecture is dead."

"It says to me, 'Screw our homogeneous society!' "

Someone was getting screwed, I thought, but it wasn't society.

The drawings were $1,000, and they weren't even framed. There's nothing that irritates me more, unless it's when I have to pay extra for a salad that doesn't automatically come with a $30 entrée.

The after-party was held at a collector's home, a mammoth loft in the city with windows surrounding the entire space.

"Where does he hang his art?" I whispered to Gary.

The place made Mies van der Rohe look like a hoarder. It was filled with a few twigs and funky lamps, and dinner was served at a giant concrete table.

The host was even colder.

Gary and I were separated ("Partners cannot eat together! House rule!"), and I sat in a plastic chair that made me feel as if I was about to get a CAT scan.

"Brioche! Brioche!" I heard Gary say from the end of the table.

I looked around at the guests, many of whom I had wanted to meet for months, and estimated that if I combined all the money that every gay man there had spent on his eyeglasses we could pull our nation out of debt.

A few of these men we considered our friends, but, oddly, we didn't even really know them that well. I mean, I didn't know some of their last names, or what their parents were like, or how some of the couples met.

Perhaps we never asked. Perhaps they never offered.

Everyone at dinner was a bit drunk and yelling over one another, showing their superiority, their knowledge, their refinement. Many were reciting their résumés, hoping, I'm sure, that someone there at some point might either be impressed or be a great contact.

I was slightly intimidated by the group and kept to myself, trying to gag down what looked like an eyeball on a basil leaf.

And then, after three quick glasses of wine, I suddenly found my gumption and began shouting myself, telling everyone I was writing a book.

What followed was a chorus of:

"Oh! I'm a writer!"

"I'm a writer!"

"I'm a writer!"

It was like being trapped in a cage of literary parakeets.

Someone finally yelled to me, "What's your book about?"

"It's a memoir about growing up gay in the Ozarks."

"Oh! I'm writing a memoir about being gay!"

"I'm writing a memoir about being gay!"

"I'm writing a memoir about being gay!"

I quieted back down and concentrated on my eyeball, listening to the roar of the confidently insecure, before peering down the table at Gary, who looked at me, sadly, sweetly, and because he knew I needed to hear it, began yelling, "Brioche! Brioche!"

I carefully study our neighbors' fan carving.

And, ironically, I find myself drawn to it. Drawn to the wood. Drawn to the inordinate amount of time they spend crafting it, perfecting it, honing it, just as I try to perfect every sentence and paragraph, hone the flow, all in a single carving, no glue, no shortcuts.

As Gary and I finish dinner, our neighbors ask us how our transition is going, and say it must be difficult to be so far away from family and friends. Then they pour us a cup of coffee, hand us slices of cake, and wait for a response.

I have tried to forget how hard it is to move from a place you know, have tried to forget that starting over is not as easy as I had imagined.

I do miss my friends, flaws and all.

So Gary and I begin to talk, quietly, slowly, at first, waiting to be interrupted, waiting for them to jump up and air-kiss someone better walking through the door.

But they do not interrupt us. They do not out-shout us. They do not get bored. They listen. They invited us here without any ulterior motives. They invited us here to be neighborly.

We end up hanging one of their doves over our dining room table. When the heat kicks on, or Marge rushes by, or when a window is cracked open, the dove seems to take flight in the current or cross-breeze, and our home comes alive.

The Butcher, the Baker, and the Fudge-Packing Candlestick Maker

Every season, the population in southwest Michigan fluctuates, not only from the influx of summer resorters but also with the influx of Mexican laborers, who return in late winter and early spring to work the fields and fruit farms, to work construction, to prepare for tourist season.

I have wondered why the trailer next to us was often silent at different times, thinking it was the snow, the cold, the wind that kept everyone in hibernation until the final icicle thawed. But I guess it was the seasonal work calendar that slingshots immigrants back and forth, to work in Mexico and then here.

The transition cannot be easy. It is certainly harder than my rural relocation. I have remained in my own country. I do not have to learn a second language. I do not have to labor with my hands. I do not have children who are in Mexican schools part of the year and American schools part of the year. This sacrifice to earn a living—actually, just to live—has to be sacrificing generations of children.

Gary and I make ourselves sick about our investment in Turkey Run, since it is located next to a trailer. We want things to change. Immediately. Beautiful homes are just beginning to dot the landscape, like big hotels on a Monopoly board, and slowly, one by one, the trailers are disappearing. It cannot happen fast enough for me. But this one remains, hangs on, grandfathered into the zoning laws, not rusting out quickly enough.

There are, by my count, at least four to six people who live in this tiny trailer with Pablo, including a very old woman and a very young girl. Many afternoons, the old woman will sit on the front stoop of the trailer—on a plywood platform supported by concrete blocks—and brush the long black hair of the little girl. The old woman rarely smiles, focused solely on brushing the hair of the girl with the same seriousness with which a doctor might examine an X-ray. She uses a giant red brush, which she whips through the girl's hair as though she is brushing a horse's tail. The little girl's hair shimmers in the sunlight. She sits on the old woman's lap, kneading something with her hands—bread, Play-Doh?—I can never tell.

It is a ritual to which I quickly grow accustomed, like being greeted at our door by Marge. I publicly complain about the trailer, what it's doing to our area, but my complaints sound more and more hollow, because I am beginning to realize the trailer is more than a trailer. It is a home.

"Most men appear never to have considered what a house is," Thoreau wrote, "and are actually thought needlessly poor all their lives because they think that they must have such a one as their neighbors have."

What is a home?

According to NPR, the average American house size has more than doubled since the 1950s; it now stands at 2,349 square feet.

I love Turkey Run because it reminds me of my grandparents' log cabin, which, I would estimate, was no more than a thousand square feet: one long, continuous living area that ran the length of the cabin—kitchen, dining, family room—one tiny bath (no tub or shower) in which I could barely turn around, two small bedrooms downstairs, and a sleeping loft upstairs that could sleep eight to ten, depending on how many bunks we wanted to cram into it.

My family was in each other's faces and comfort zones constantly, and I don't know if I would be the person I am today without that. I couldn't hide from my family, and it forced me to get to know them.

I am still proud of that cabin, which seemed like a castle to me as a kid.

Turkey Run is the size of an average home today, but it contains luxuries our old cabin never had, that our neighboring trailer will never have: new appliances, a master suite with a big bathroom and double sinks, a finished basement with custom cabinets and fireplace, a writing studio with wood beams that would make Hemingway jealous. And yet it isn't ostentatious. It is charming, adorable, sweet, unpretentious. Perhaps I need a home that is my alter ego.

A drive down our country lane or onto Lakeshore Drive shows what is happening: Every parcel of land is being developed; larger cottages that loom over the lake are being constructed, each new home seemingly bigger than its neighbor.

And then there are the old lake homes—the tiny cottages and old fishing shacks—that occasionally dot the landscape, virtual doghouses in comparison. And I find these places the most compelling, because you can feel their history.

I am at odds with myself.

Trailers are an eyesore. Architectural pollution. Scars on nature's face.

A trailer doesn't have history. A trailer doesn't qualify as a home.

I mean, didn't everyone see Lucy in *The Long, Long Trailer*?

But then I will walk down our driveway and see the old woman and the young girl, and I can't help but think of my grandmother and me sitting on that old red glider outside our old log cabin.

I can't help but think of my home, of where I grew up.

"I don't want you to come home in a body bag," my mother told me when I was maybe eleven or twelve, right before I headed out in Husky jeans, a pink faux-Polo, a jaunty ascot, and deck shoes to sell candles to my neighbors as part of a school fund-raising project.

Advice like that tends to stick with a man, like "No forks in the electrical socket!" and "Don't let the dog do that to the good pillow!"

I didn't grow up in a subdivision or neighborhood.

I grew up in a beautiful home my parents built outside of our little Ozarks town. Surrounded by a great many trailers and dilapidated homes, our house was a bit like the castle in a really tacky fiefdom.

Still, I believed—as kids do—that people are just people. We're all the same, gingivitis or not.

"Shouldn't I get to know our neighbors?" I asked my mom. "Give them a chance? I'm sure they're nice."

I didn't really believe what I was saying. I just wanted to win the candle contest, win one thing in my life.

My mom got that look that moms get when they don't know if they're making a really brave decision or one they'll regret forever.

"OK, but I'm following you in the car," she said. "I'll be just outside of view."

The first door I knocked on, a number of miles away, was attached to a collapsing trailer whose metal roof sloped and slanted. The trailer was haphazardly set up on concrete blocks, just like the three trucks in the front yard, which, by the way, was constantly smoking because the owners burned their trash in big round metal barrels.

The house belonged to a large, quiet family whose kids I never saw outside of school, or even outside their house, no matter the time of day or how many times we drove by.

"Good morning!" I yelled when the "lady" of the house, accompanied by a throng of children, opened it. "Isn't it a beautiful Saturday morning?"

They all stared at me without saying a word.

"Would you mind if I took a few minutes of your time to show you the best-smelling, longest-burning candles you will ever encounter?"

Nothing.

"May I come in?"

"Why not?" the mother finally said. "We ain't got nothin' to do, I guess."

I walked into their living room, which was filled with doilies, Bibles, and *TV Guides* and smelled like a cereal bowl that had been left out in the sun all day.

I began setting up my wares and launched into my spiel.

"Good morning! I am proud to introduce Karen's Candles, which are guaranteed to smell better and last longer than any candle on today's market. I have set up a few of my bestsellers for you to sample. I encourage you to take your time . . . look, smell, enjoy, buy!"

The kids cautiously approached the candles before one of the girls screamed, "Mama, he set one on a Bible!"

I was already beginning to sweat, that scared sweat that always oozed down my back right before the popular boys picked their teams to play shirts-and-skins basketball in gym class.

I looked down, and at least a dozen cats had me surrounded, and they began to sharpen their claws on my carrying case.

I tried, without being noticed, to shoo the cats away, but I was busted by the littlest girl, who looked as if she'd never had her hair combed. It was big and ratted—unintentionally—and she resembled a hungrier, dirtier, paler Little Orphan Annie.

"Don't you like our cats?" she asked, picking up one that immediately began batting at her locks. "They sure seem to like you."

"Oh, I just love cats!" I lied, like any good salesman, bending over to pick up one that looked like it had mange, big clumps of its hair missing, chunks of white skin flashing through its thin calico coat. It hissed at me. "What're their names?"

"That one you're holdin' is named Muffin," she said. "He's real scrappy. I tried to cut his hair yesterday, but he kept moving."

"And that one over there is Mr. Magoo and the one by Mama is Moondance and that one's Miss Molly and the black one is Nigger."

I dropped Muffin and stumbled backward, mortified. I stared at the cats as they swirled their tails in little circles, now convinced that they were trying to write "Help us!" in the air.

"Have you ever considered naming it Midnight instead?" I suggested happily. "I think it has such a nice ring to it, don't you think?"

"How 'bout mindin' your own fuckin' business?"

I followed the voice into the kitchen, where an old man with no teeth and dried blood on his face was cracking an egg into a dirty skillet.

And then, for good measure, he added, "Fudge packer!"

At that moment, before I asked my mother, who would lie, and before I asked my brother, who wouldn't, I thought *fudge packer* had a quaintness about it, a storybook charm, like "Butcher, baker, candlestick maker."

Fudge packer. Yes, I was a charming chocolatier.

"Fudge packer!" he said again, and this time, the tone of his voice removed the charm and reinvigorated my sweat glands.

"So . . . well, I guess I'll just gather my things . . ."

"Yeah, that's a good idea," the mother said. "Five ninety-nine a candle is highway robbery. What makes you think we have that kinda money layin' around here? And your candles stink anyway."

I looked over and smiled at one of the little girls, who was feeding her boogers to one of the cats, which was eating them hungrily, like kibble.

I threw hot candles into my case—hot wax sloshing everywhere—and hightailed it out of the house and to my mother, who was waiting just down the road.

"How'd it go?" she asked.

And, though I was much too old to do so, I cried.

She drove me down a long dirt road and stopped the car in front of another trailer.

"Not another trailer! I can't do it!"

"Yes, you can," she said. "Go on!"

I knocked on the front door, expecting my previous scenario to repeat itself, but instead was greeted by an attractive, gray-headed woman in a bright green polyester pantsuit. Her home was immaculate, decorated with photos and mementos, and she asked if I wanted a glass of iced tea.

I launched into my presentation, while she sat, listened raptly, and smelled all the candles. When I was done, she said, "Now tell me a little about yourself."

"Excuse me?" I asked. "Ma'am?"

"Tell me about yourself. What do you want to do? Who do you want to be?"

"Erma Bombeck!" I screamed. "Or Thoreau! I love Erma, but my grandma loves Thoreau!"

She laughed, and we talked, and we sipped tea, and she bought ten candles, even Lilac, which I knew—because my brother had said it—would make her smell like "a whore."

"That lady bought ten candles!" I said as I got into the car with my mom. "Ten candles! Can you believe it?"

"Yes, I can. She's a wonderful lady. You were in there quite a while," my mom said. "So, what did you talk about?"

"She wanted to know about me. What I wanted to be when I grew up."

"Well, her son died in the Vietnam War," my mom said. "And her husband died soon after. She's had a tough life, but she's remained a great person."

As my mom drove down the dirt road, she said, "It's not where we live that's important, it's what kind of home we create. It's about who we are, who we strive to be. You know that, right? Not everyone has what we have."

And I nodded, not really listening at the time, wondering if I might actually win the candle contest.

And then one day, as Gary and I are leaving Turkey Run, we spot a FOR SALE sign next door.

Gary and I rejoice when we learn that the land and the trailer are for sale. But my own joy is oddly short-lived, especially when I watch Pablo and his family pack their belongings into the back of an old truck and take off for somewhere, I don't know where, to try to make it through another season.

Though I don't know Pablo—except for a few crucial details that will forever be seared in my brain—I do go over to bid his family good-bye. I feel I must. It's my final attempt to make an effort with a neighbor I've hated from the beginning, to make amends with someone seemingly so different from me.

Pablo approaches me, and I am tentative, fearing that I might see his dick appear, like in a magic trick. But he tells me, in broken English, that it is hard living here, hard liking *"muchachos"* in a Catholic family. Worse, it is hard to never have a home, to move around, to take on work wherever and whenever it comes.

"Ustedes son muy afortunado," he says before leaving.

When everyone is gone and the trailer is empty, I survey the grounds. There are a few things left behind: some beer bottles, a broken lawn chair, a near empty bag of charcoal, that damn wreath the color of rotting meat. And then I find, lying near the trailer, two old red hairbrushes, missing bristles like an old broom, the wood on the handle rubbed shiny from the old woman's hands. I pick up the brush, and I can feel the love reverberate in it.

And then I see, lying a few feet ahead, nearly lost in the underbrush, a little crucifix, dried, faded, and cracking, made of clay, rubbed shiny, like the brush, as only the hands of a little girl could do, a little girl sitting safely outside her home for a few moments in her grandmother's lap, tenderly trying to shape a future over which she has no control.

Wade's Walden—3. Modern Society—1.

Participate in Country Customs

Heaven is under our feet as well as over our heads.

—Henry David Thoreau, *Walden*

All-Points Bulletin

Michigan boasts over 10,000 inland lakes and 3,288 miles of Great Lakes shoreline, making it not only the number one boating state but also a prime area for both commercial and sport fishing.

In the winter, considering the entire state is frozen, one of the prime outdoor sports is ice-fishing, a dangerous way, indeed, for me to kick-start Life Lesson Five.

When you go ahead and factor in my klutziness, fear of things in the wild, and short attention span, me ice-fishing is akin to me standing in a cage of pumas and taunting them with an air horn and T-bone.

Thanks to Gary and Thoreau, I opt to tackle (pardon the pun) this country custom, because it mixes Michigan and the Ozarks and is an offshoot of a hobby I once loved.

My love of fishing was passed on to me by my grandfathers, who spent countless hours with me standing in ice-cold streams teaching me the intricacies of catching minnows, setting the hook, casting. There is a serenity to fishing, as well as an adventure to the process. At a certain point, you leave the world behind and become one with nature: It is you, the sky, a stream, a fish.

I never knew what, if anything, I might catch. And since fish seemed to have little or no personality, unlike deer or rabbits, I could enjoy it. I never saw its face when I snagged one or watched it die in front of me, like when I went hunting once and puked when I shot a rabbit.

I get hooked on ice-fishing by gathering around the bulletin board at the country store, a place you don't want to be with Gary, who studies every poorly Xeroxed flyer and colorful little postcard with blind zealousness, kind of like those religious freaks do potato chips when they want to find one that looks like Jesus.

Bulletin boards are big here in the country: They dispatch the latest area news and happenings on index cards and torn sheets of paper.

Most people update the bulletin boards with new flyers on Fridays, in advance of the weekend and the incoming resort crowd. In the winter, the boards are fairly sparse, info for locals only. Country people gather at bulletin boards, which are typically located in a select few places, like the library, or the grocery store, or the gas station, and stand and stare and point at poorly Xeroxed posters advertising town events, free kittens, and potluck dinners.

"Isn't this nice?" Gary asks. "Everything important that we need to know about our world is on this board."

I nod and rub his back tenderly.

Minutes ago, I was zipping through MySpace, buying a pair of jeans from Banana Republic and reading about Reese and Jake on People.com. Gary, of course, doesn't know this, or he would tack me to the bulletin board with a sign that says RABID STRAY NEEDS TO BE PUT DOWN.

I study the board with fake earnestness. Let's see: I can buy a pit bull mix that looks as though it would like to remove my head; we can purchase a pontoon boat with no engine; we can attend the potluck dinner at the Baptist church and eat Jeannie Lou's "special olive loaf"; there's a garage sale where we can pick up cat bookends and a 1977 Zenith; or we can head on over to a nearby inland lake for a day of ice-fishing—winner of the biggest catch gets $25 and, most likely, a frostbitten nostril removed.

"Anything catch your fancy?" Gary asks.

Jesus, he's become a regular gay Sling Blade in the woods.

I shake my head no.

"How 'bout it? Anything catch your fancy?" Gary asks again.

A plane ticket to Palm Springs and a vintage T-shirt I saw online.

"Not really," I say. "And we are not getting another dog."

"Actually, I was thinking ice-fishing. You said you wanted to try rural traditions. You should give it a shot."

A man in camouflage sporting a crazy *Guinness Book of World Records* beard rips off a tear sheet with a phone number for the rabid dog.

"Ice-fishin' is the sport of kings," he tells us.

"I thought that was polo," I joke.

No one laughs.

My fate is set.

Ice, Ice Baby

A little all-sport lake sits at the end of our road, five or six miles west from our house. It's an *On Golden Pond*-y type lake—serene, filled with reeds and white swans—the perfect complement to monstrous Lake Michigan, which sits just about a mile east of our cottage.

During the summer, the little lake is filled with canoes and pontoon boats and speed boats, the edges lined with fishermen, the center filled with kids water-skiing or tubing.

In the winter, the little lake freezes over solid, the ice as thick as a sumo wrestler's ass. Ice-fisherman shanties pop up like zits on the clean-lined surface.

Despite his initial push, Gary opts not to join me. "Unless it's a skating rink," he tells me, at the last minute, "I won't stand on ice for any length of time. I just don't trust it. It's like ordering clam chowder at a bowling alley. There's just too much risk involved. Didn't you see *Little Women* with Winona Ryder?"

Before I depart, I do a little Internet investigation. It seems that ice-fishing is deemed by its fans to be serious business. It looks more intense than the fishing summers of my youth, when I would often lean against a big, warm rock or lie down in the middle of a canoe—my pole still in the water—and sun, sleep, or just lazily drift away. This looks like it comes down to dropping a line into a hole that's been cut in the ice and praying something hits before you fall into a cold-induced coma.

And yet, to calm myself, I read Thoreau, who wrote, after cutting a hole in frozen Walden Pond, "I look down into the quiet parlor of the fishes, pervaded by a softened light as through a window of ground glass, with its bright sanded floor the same as in summer; there a perennial waveless serenity reigns."

I can do this.

I am ice-fishing with a country couple who have helped do some handiwork around our house. They are the type who feel they will have failed the world if they don't pull something large and scaly from this frigid water.

And I'm pretty sure they really need the food.

This is way too much pressure for me. I didn't even want to come out here on this sunny, breezy 17-degree day. I don't want to sit in a hut, unless it's in the Dominican and Gary and I are being given dual rubdowns by Enrique Iglesias and Ricky Martin.

"Welcome to the Mitten!" my teachers yell from a spot about a third of the way toward the center of the lake.

I wave excitedly, like I'm meeting girlfriends at Starbucks.

"Come on over," the wife yells. "It's safe. The ice won't give."

I am wearing a cashmere turtleneck, a $300 scarf that I bought in Chicago, and a brand-new peacoat that makes me look like I should be having hot tea with Gwyneth and Apple in a London café. I have also opted to wear slick-footed Kenneth Cole Reaction boots with zero traction. There might be a photo op, especially if I win the ice-fishing contest, so I can't wear waders.

I begin to tippy-toe toward the shanty and tumble after three slow steps. The husband hobbles over and picks me up.

"Thanks."

I look up and take stock of my fishing companions. This is what the untrained eye would see right now: Two camouflage-ski-suited puffs of people, smoking cigarettes and drinking Jack Daniel's straight out of the bottle, emerging from a shaky shanty.

I fall again.

As he helps me up, I think of kissing him as a thank-you, but when I look into his face, all I see are two pale blue eyes and a mouth with cracked lips.

It's like *Saw* on ice.

"Thanks again."

"No problem." He smiles. "Gotta watch out for the ice. It's slick."

He laughs at his joke—a deep, hearty smoker's hack. And then he spits a big green loogy right at my feet. It sits shimmering on the ice like jade. I follow him over to the shanty.

"Wanna cigarette?" his wife asks.

"I don't smoke," I say. "Thanks, though."

"Wanna hit then?" she asks, holding up the bottle of Jack.

"No, thanks," I say.

"You better do something up here. It's a long winter," she says. Then they both laugh and drag on their cigarettes.

I tap on the ice with my foot. I can see water underneath, can almost hear it trying to reach the surface. I begin to panic. "Are you sure this is safe?" I ask. "Fishing out here."

"This is solid," the wife answers. "Too cold to break. We wouldn't be out here otherwise."

"What're you catching?"

"A cold," says the husband, and the duo again laughs and hacks.

"We like helping city folk get acclimated to the country. You didn't grow up around here, did you?" the wife asks.

"No," I say. "But I grew up in a small town, and now I'm a proud Michigander."

"Well, welcome to the Mitten! That's what we say up here. The state looks like a mitten; that's the first thing you learn in school up here. See?"

Both of them hold up their gloved hands. Yes, I get it: Michigan *does* look like a mitten. "We're here," she says, pointing toward a lower section of her palm, opposite the state's thumb.

I smile. I haven't seen this much hand action since Gary and I saw *Puppetry of the Penis.*

"The summer folk who decide to live year-round up here can go crazy in the beginning. It's a big switch. Everybody expects it to be like it is all summer. It's not. And it's a long winter. A very long winter."

"Tell me about it," I say. "Can you believe all the snow?"

"Oh, we love it, just love it."

Two friends of the couple suddenly crank up the small heater inside and cram themselves into a corner to get warm. The warmth electrifies their stink of cigarettes and whiskey and BO and fish and outdoors, a lot like the smell Marge gives off when she is wet from the snow and begins to dry in front of the fireplace.

Now that I think about it, I haven't been this close to this many stinky men since I drunkenly wandered into a country-and-western bear bar—as a joke—wearing a *Brokeback Mountain* T-shirt.

"I think there's too much weight on the ice, isn't there?" I ask politely. "Can it hold us?"

"It's fine," one of the men tells me. "I tell you, we wouldn't be out here if it wasn't."

One of the men asks if I need help setting up a pole. I haven't brought anything I need to survive, mind you, except a lot of attitude, which is all I needed in the city.

"Sure," I reply.

He puts a minnow on the end of a rather short, sturdy pole, drops the line into the water through a hole that has already been carved in the ice—kind of like you would core an apple—and hands me the pole.

"Now what do I do?"

"Wait," he laughs. "And stay warm."

And I do. I am handed a folding stool and told to sit. I wait and I wait and I wait, staring into the dark hole. I grow bored and impatient and begin singing "Gone Fishin', Instead of Just A-Wishin'," an old fishing-show theme song my grampa used to sing. And then I have to pee. And then I get cold, despite the fact we're all huddled up and protected from the wind. And then I start to whine.

Usually, city people find my whining cute and adorable. Because they whine, too. We are whining cohorts. Most rural folk don't whine. They are hearty. They can live in the cold and kill animals and remove their fur and cook them over an open fire. I can't do this. But I can whine. I can tell that my shanty friends are getting annoyed, but I don't care. I am not having a good time, and—in my world—that means no one else can have a good time either.

But then one of the men says, in a very clipped tone, "You need to take this seriously. Don't you ever take anything seriously? I mean, things that don't affect only you?"

I shiver. I can't tell if the sting I feel is the brutal cold working its way through my thin layers of wool and cotton or the truthfulness of his words.

I stare at him meanly.

He is wearing a stocking cap that has pressed his eyes into tiny slits.

Fuck you, Miss Saigon, I think to myself.

I think this is very, very funny. So I start laughing.

Everyone stands and takes their folding stools and turns away from me like I'm five and throwing a tantrum.

I am alone.

And that's fine by me.

Bye, country couple.

Bye, stinky rednecks.

The wind whistles across the tent, making that canvassy flap-flap-flap sound of complete and utter isolation.

Why didn't I bring my iPod? Oh, I'm supposed to be Thoreau, and Thoreau didn't have an iPod. Something makes me think, however, that he would have listened to the Scissor Sisters if he'd had the opportunity.

I can hear the ice creak, the lake moan. I can hear my heart thumping. I begin to drift off, into a cold-induced, sleepy-land place.

And then I see a fish slink by the hole in front of my feet.

I get a hit.

The tip of my pole bobs and then grows taut. I have fished before but only in wide open space. This is a mystery, pulling something I can barely see from a hole in frozen water. I stand, and the fish pulls me. I slide in my Kenneth Cole boots, slowly, but most decidedly, toward the hole. I have no traction. I so want to catch dinner for my man. I want to impress all of these people I don't know. I want to undo all the wrongs from my country childhood, make everything right with a single fish. I want to be a man of the wild, a caveman.

In a jaunty scarf.

Then I can feel my line go slack, the tip of my pole go lax. My fish has gagged up my hook and minnow.

"Nice try," one of the men says.

"You almost had him," another says. "You gave it a good fight. Maybe next time."

I hand my pole to him and start to take off my gloves, to rub my fingers, which are achy and cold. As I remove my right glove, the mood ring I am wearing—yes, I adore mood rings—flies off my finger, a combination of my Mary Kay hand lotion and sweat making my hands slick and overly lubed.

My mood ring goes up, and then down, and then *plunk!*, deep into the hole, down into the icy water. A fish darts by, thinking it's a minnow.

Everyone awaits my reaction.

But I do not get mad or pissy this time.

Instead, I grab my pole, sit back down on my folding stool, and try again.

Bewitched, Bothered, and Bewildered

As we pull into the gravel parking lot of a ramshackle country bar featuring a giant sign that says HUNTERS ALWAYS WELCOME!, I rub my brand-new mood ring for good luck. For once in its history, a mood ring is accurately reflecting my emotional truth: My stone is black, even though I am hot and sweating profusely.

"Ready for your debut, Shania?" one of our friends asks.

A group of friends Gary and I have met recently very much want to be involved with Life Lesson Five. They want to watch me karaoke for the first time in my life. And one of the few places that karaokes is a bar renowned for its rowdy rednecks.

I know karaoke started in Japan and later became a fun, hip thing to do in the city, but I knew karaoke—before Chris Tucker did it or *High School Musical*—when it was performed in seedy country bars by lonely, drunken rednecks pretending to be Hank Williams Jr. Many of our new friends—both gay and straight—are younger and loved to karaoke at bars in the city. But I—and they—have never done it in a bar that looks exactly like the one where Jodie Foster got raped in *The Accused*.

"It's either this or bowling," Gary says. "And you like the bowling shoes too much for that to be a challenge."

A friend shuts off his SUV headlights, which had been illuminating a parking lot filled with Harleys sitting alongside a half-wooden, half-aluminum pole barn–esque structure covered in NASCAR flags and stickers. I can hear George Strait or George Jones or some other country George pumping from the jukebox, the tin roof of the bar shimmying.

I take stock of the outfit I have worn in which to make my singing debut: Banana Republic hip-huggers, a retro long-sleeve waffle T-shirt that says BEWITCHED on the front, and leather shoes featuring stripes of electroshock blue.

I open the door, and the smell of old beer, whiskey, cigarette smoke, vomit, Old Spice, and Jovan Musk hits me. Followed by a man who looks like Billy Ray Cyrus.

"Ouch," I say, rubbing my shoulder.

"Gotcher ID?"

"Umm, yeah, sure. Wow. I haven't been carded in years."

I smile broadly. Billy Ray doesn't.

"You're a model?"

Oh, my God, I think. *Is everyone around here gay?* I smile and blush, looking apologetically at Gary.

"Me? Oh, God, no. But how very flattering and kind of you."

Gary and the man are staring at me. And then I remember my friend who had the same thing happen to her when she was getting her car fixed in a rural repair shop. She had mistakenly thought—just like I did—that the man had asked "You're a model?" instead of "Year and model?"

"You're an idiot," Gary says. "He wants to know the year and model of the SUV. He likes it. It's not our car, sir. It's our friends' car."

"And I'm forty-one and, yes, I have modeled. I was a Sears Winnie the Pooh children's clothing model, thank you very much," I mumble.

This is going to be a long night. Especially after I see that karaoke night will feature a gaggle of drunk, gangly women in cowboy boots and feathered bangs and drunk, gangly men in Wranglers and cowboy boots and mullets screaming a bunch of angst-ridden songs about cows and trucks and moonlight and whiskey into a plastic mic.

Gary and I squeeze into a booth near the back, while our friends head to the bathrooms, a challenge I am not yet up to.

A waitress who looks like Kellie Pickler comes to our table. I scream my order—a bottle of Mich Ultra—and end up with warm Budweiser in a plastic cup. A throng of folks are already boot-scootin' and line-dancing in an area off to the side of the shed.

"We'll be dead by midnight, you know," Gary yells, nonplussed, kind of like he'd say "We're out of milk" or "It's supposed to rain to-morrow."

He's right. I put our odds at around 40–60 we'll make it out without an incident.

Then our odds worsen.

Two little country gals totter over drunkenly and invite themselves to sit down, scooting Gary and me over in the booth seats with their asses.

"Hi, I'm GeriLynn!"

"Hi, I'm Donna Lou!"

GeriLynn is a size 16 who has squeezed herself into size 8 jeans and a sequined black country-and-western shirt whose buttons are a single jalapeño popper away from busting free and exposing overly tanned breasts the size of honeydews. Her hair is supposed to be dark brown, I think, but it's been colored a blackish red, and, under the barlight, she looks a bit like a rural Elvira who just got back from spring break. Donna Lou is obviously a whore. She is sloppy drunk, a sprayed mass of teased, permed bleach-blond hair and shellacked makeup, wearing a cropped T-shirt that says HARLEY GIRL and a short denim mini paired with shiny new cowboy boots. She smells like liquor and '80s hair-band rock.

"Whachoo cute young cowpokes doin' here without any ladies?" Donna Lou slurs.

GeriLynn giggles nervously and eats the stale popcorn that's been sitting on our table since, probably, the late '70s. Her nails are the color of fresh blood.

I want to lie. To stay alive. Gary knows I want to lie. He's shaking his head at me.

"Fresh out of a nasty double breakup," I say. "We were dating twins, if you can believe it. Found out they were cheating on us. With the same guy."

I can tell Gary wants to be pissed but is actually quite impressed.

"Oh, my God!" Donna Lou says. "Why, that is the saddest thing I ever did hear."

GeriLynn is staring, her mouth open and still filled with popcorn. She looks just like the chipmunks that sit off our screen porch.

"Well, you fellas could use some cheerin' up," Donna Lou says. "And we're just the gals to do it."

Donna Lou scoots over next to me and throws her arm around me. "Ooo-wheee, you're a tiny thing, ain'tcha? I need to get some meat on those bones. Unless your bone already has some meat."

Donna Lou is a fast worker.

She orders boilermakers for the table, and, when Gary announces he doesn't drink ("Safe driver," he says), Donna Lou replies, "More for us!"

I do a boilermaker and suddenly feel a bit more flirty. Gary knows this; my eyes always get narrower when I am buzzed.

"Looks like you have a tattoo on your big ol' booby, GeriLynn. Am I right? Am I right?"

GeriLynn giggles, eats popcorn, and says, "It's my baby's name. Travis. After Travis Tritt. He's my angel."

"I think I'll call your tattoo 'Travis Tit.' "

Donna Lou laughs heartily and rubs my thigh.

I stiffen. But not in the way Donna Lou expects.

"Are you OK? You seem nervous."

"We're gay," Gary says. "Queer. In the Liza Fan Club. OK? We don't mean to lead you girls on. Some friends we know dragged us here. We don't want any trouble."

"Oh, my God! I knew it!" GeriLynn screams. "I told Donna Lou you were gay. She thought you looked too manly."

"In this outfit?" I say.

"Donna Lou thought *Bewitched* was the name of your softball team. God, everyone in this area is either gay or straight. Oh, God, that doesn't even make sense."

With that, GeriLynn bursts out laughing and spews popcorn like a firehose. "At least we have good karaoke partners."

"I can't sing," Gary says. "Not a lick. Tone deaf. I'm out."

"I know you can sing," GeriLynn says to me. "I betcher reeeaaal sexy when you sing."

And before I can twitch my nose and vanish like Samantha, the Dixie Chicks have me standing in line to sing. They hand me the playlist and I scan the options, becoming more and more panicked.

OK, I think, *I know Gretchen Wilson's "Redneck Woman," or I could sing "Man! I Feel Like a Woman!" by Shania Twain. Oooh, and there's "D-I-V-O-R-C-E." Love that.*

Then I look out on the crowd.

Remember *The Blues Brothers,* when Jake and Elwood sing behind the fence? That's how this crowd looks. Drunk, angry, and wound up after working on the line all week making refrigerator parts. A man singing a woman's song about being a woman might not be right; I learned my lesson singing "Delta Dawn" when I was young.

But then I see it. There, shining on the list, mistakenly, unbelievably, is Kelly Clarkson's "Since U Been Gone." Not only do I know this song, I can sing this song. Both in my own voice and falsetto. I know every word. *I might be killed,* I think, *but at least I won't vocally embarrass myself the last three minutes of my life.*

"Number twenty-seven," I say to the karaoke guy.

"Ummm . . . ," he begins to say.

"Yeah, I know, OK?"

My heart is pounding in my head; my legs are shaking. I listen, panicked, wanting to flee, to run, but the girls have me locked in their arms. I stand between them, silently, as they sing some duet by the Judds. And then they're done. And I can't do anything but stand there and sing. Kelly Clarkson. I look out at Gary, and he gives me a smart-ass thumbs-up. I look over at our friends. They collectively make a slicing motion across their throats.

I am noticeably flinching, like I have MS, waiting for a bottle of Bud to be thrown at my head. But then our waitress yells, "You go, guy! Kelly's the real American Idol."

People are clapping, rocking their heads. They may be confused, but at least they know when someone's in tune.

I sing as though my life depends on it. And it very well may.

As I approach the chorus, I feel my oats and improvise a bit to test the crowd.

"Jump!"

"Since U been gone, I can breathe for the first time."

And they do as told . . . they jump.

Kind of, anyway, as high as you can in boots and skintight jeans while line dancing.

I finish to a standing ovation—with people staring at me, kind of like they might if they saw a unicorn cross the highway—and walk back to our booth feeling not only glad to be alive but also feeling very much alive.

It's the first time I've been myself in a rural setting. And I realize, in my semi-euphoric, semi-drunken stupor, just what my mom had tried to teach me long ago: It's not *where* you choose to live. It's *how* you choose to live.

Eat My Dust, Tractor!

There are also smaller daily customs in the country to which I must acclimate myself, just as there were those I adapted to in the city.

I now dodge deer and raccoons in the road instead of bicyclists and buses. I now pop in for rock salt and whole-kernel corn instead of a latte or new table runner.

These bizarre rituals are slowly becoming routine, like living on Mars and still heading to Walgreens.

Thoreau eventually found comfort in his routine of bathing in Walden Pond or making a daily fire to cook his meals.

And I, too, am learning to be at peace with my rural customs, like:

Driving: The Angry Commuter vs. the Ambling Country Driver

People drive differently in the country.

For one, there seem to be few turn signals. We have this thing called "the Michigan U-Turn," where instead of pulling to a stoplight and getting an arrow to turn left or right onto another street, like in the city, here you must propel your vehicle 180 degrees into oncoming traffic in order to go a different direction. It's comically chaotic, almost as if Gilbert Gottfried and Chelsea Handler had been tapped to design our highway system.

Far worse, there is no driver urgency to get somewhere, no I-have-to-cross-six-lanes-of-interstate-traffic-right-now-to-make-my-exit-or-

I'll-be-late, no cell-phone-talking, makeup-applying, fast-food-eating, coffee-drinking, change-the-radio-station, pull-a-gun drivers to enrage you.

Gary and I miss those drivers.

Locals amble, giving a polite country wave even to drivers who steam by on narrow roads. Everyone here gives "the country wave"— the two-fingered don't-lift-your-left-wrist-off-the-steering-wheel wave.

Where are our black girls with bedazzled Tip Top nails yelling, "Hey, baby!"

Gary and I have purposely tried to enrage a country driver, and it's nearly impossible. They simply pull to the side of the road, roll down their window, and wave us on by. The last time we visited the city Gary cut off a woman who was eating a Mrs. Fields cookie the size of a Frisbee. She sped up to 90 to catch us, at which point she swerved within inches of Gary's car door and screamed, "Fuck you! Fuck you! Fuck you!" with cookie crumbs spewing from her mouth like a dessert geyser.

"We love you!" Gary yelled.

The closest we have actually come to pissing off a country driver was the time I rolled down my window at a stop sign and told a rather demented-looking hunter that it probably wasn't the best idea to have his two dogs riding loose in the bed of his pickup.

"It's, you know, dangerous," I said nervously, fidgeting with my choker.

He flashed me a Skoal-infused smile and then pointed at the well-stocked shotgun rack he had displayed on the window behind him.

"Thanks for your time, sir," I replied.

Small-Town Friendliness

The notion that getting things done in a small town is somehow faster or easier than in a city is completely false. While there is little or no car traffic in a tiny town, there is foot and mouth traffic.

You cannot pass someone you know with a simple "Hello" or "Howdy hey." Each local must be greeted with a lengthy recounting of your day, and/or week, and/or month to date. And you, in turn, must ask, and nod, and smile. Which is why running to the hardware store or to pick up toilet paper takes a minimum of, oh, two hours.

I make the mistake of ignoring everyone in town one day as I rush through the drugstore, only to discover later the next day that I:

1) had broken up with Gary (not true)
2) was an asshole (true)
3) was hard of hearing (not true)
4) had spastic diarrhea (ummm, true, which is why I was rushing in the first place)

I chose not to poop on myself by staying quiet and paid a much bigger and dirtier price.

You cannot afford to be unfriendly in a small town.

DOING YOUR OWN YARD WORK

The first thing that gay men must do when they move to the country is rearrange the woods.

We must mulch paths and groom trails and build bermed, lentil-shaped gardens and plant thousands of dollars' worth of native plants and pick up every leaf and stick that might happen to fall on our acreage.

Which, unfortunately, happens every time there is the slightest wisp of wind.

That's why they are called "woods."

But Gary is obsessed.

In St. Louis, we had two parallel squares of grass in the front yard the size of saltines. Our fenced-in backyard was perhaps the size of a giant waffle, and Gary kept it spotless, no leaf, twig, or piece of pollen to be found. It was rimmed with flowers and filled with overflowing pots. It was stunning. It was stunningly small.

Here, we don't have a yard. We have a shitload of land. Though we have only a little over three acres, our land seems to go on forever. There are no visual dividers in the country. There are no fences, there are very few houses, and those are hidden back in the woods, tucked away. From the screen porch, I look around and see only our yard and our woods.

It is nerve jangling to have this much acreage with Gary, a man who borders on having yard-care OCD. At first, we worked together on projects, like picking up sticks and twigs and tree limbs, using them to build a "natural fence" by stacking them on top of one another. The effect, believe it or not, is visually stunning, a patchwork of intricately shaped boughs and branches interconnecting to make borders, paths, and fences throughout our acreage.

However, it was pointed out, during my impromptu performance review, that I wasn't—and I quote—"stacking the sticks right."

"What exactly does that mean?" I ask Gary.

"Well, based on the size, design, and type of stick it is, you have to find the perfect place for it and then work it into the structure. You, umm, are just kind of tossing one on top of another."

"Yeah?"

"It's not a brush pile."

"You've lost your mind."

"Why don't you try mowing? It's a wide open space. You can buzz through it without, you know, thinking."

Mowing our yard with a push mower takes hours. I have to wind my way up and down hillsides, and weave around mini-gardens and—up front, near the road—the nearly fifty pine trees Gary has planted.

Just when I think I am done, I see another property stake shimmering a little farther in the distance, and I have to crank the mower back up.

Problem is, I crank 'er back up over a ground nest of hornets, which—considering I'm not Bill Nye the Science Guy—I wasn't aware lived in the ground. Ten seconds later, I am covered in hornets, which are swarming my body. I have, I now realize, mistakenly worn an adorable Gap T-shirt with literary quotes on it, J. Crew patchwork plaid shorts, and flip-flops. I stare in horror at my arms swelling from the stings.

I look like Will Smith in *Hitch*.

So I run screaming down our driveway, smacking at the hornets with my retro mesh ballcap from the Gap. Gary is waiting . . . with a hose. He turns it on me full blast, soaking me head to toe, in seemingly slow motion, like I'm Tawny Kitaen in a Whitesnake video.

"Why don't you just wheelbarrow the garden clippings to the trash can?" Gary says sweetly.

"I don't ride the short bus!" I yell.

"Right . . . ," he says.

I pick up the yard waste until I begin to break out all over my arms.

"Are you really allergic to poison ivy?" Gary asks.

Obviously, I am.

Gary doesn't let me stop helping him in the yard. Instead, he dresses me, covering every inch of skin, from head to toe, outfitting me in jeans, tube socks, a long-sleeve T-shirt, sweatshirt, gloves, and waders. I look like one of those people who test attack dogs.

So I come up with my own plan.

I call a local lawn service company, which sweeps in, little nymphs riding mowers and wielding magical weed eaters, and thirty minutes later, they are done. Thoreau would not have used his hard-earned

money to pay an army of shirtless O-Town boys to come in and manicure his yard. That would have polluted his nirvana.

But, I realize as I rub ointment on my stings and gladly say sayonara
to Life Lesson Five, Thoreau was not a gay man from the city, either.

Wade's Walden—3. Modern Society—2.

LESSON SIX
Live off the Land

My beans, the length of whose rows, added together, was seven miles already planted, were impatient to be hoed, for the earliest had grown considerably before the latest were in the ground; indeed they were not easily to be put off. What was the meaning of this so steady and self-respecting, this small Herculean labor, I knew not ... What shall I learn of beans or beans of me? I cherish them, I hoe them, early and late I have an eye to them; and this is my day's work.

—Henry David Thoreau, *Walden*

Is That Cucumber for the Salad?

T here comes a point in every man's life," a city friend once told me, "when he feels an overwhelming desire to live off the land."

Of course, he told me this as we were waiting for our fish to be grilled at Whole Foods.

"Are you kidding me?" I asked him. "I'll never be like that."

"It's primal," he continued. "It's like cavemen making fire. That's why reality shows like *Survivor* are so popular. Just wait."

And I'll be darned if he wasn't right.

Part of the reason Gary and I moved to rural Michigan from the city was to test ourselves—emotionally, spiritually, physically. We wanted to live more independently. We wanted to respect our planet. We wanted to grow our own food, sustain ourselves.

So we vowed that we would cultivate our own vegetable garden, just like Thoreau. Thus, Life Lesson Six.

I mean, we watched *An Inconvenient Truth* and were outraged, which is why we replaced every standard $3 Walgreens lightbulb in Turkey Run with energy-efficient LED bulbs, at a cost of roughly $500. I could have had Zoom! whitening and highlights for that price, but, damn it, I felt good about the choices we were making, despite the tiny little fact we purchased an SUV the size of Costa Rica simply because I thought I looked like Adrian Grenier riding that high in the air.

Anyway, the good choices cancel out the bad ones, right? Like when you eat 150 mini-Snickers on Halloween. They never really add up to one normal-size bar.

The point is: We always had the best of intentions.

And I honestly believed—out of all the Wade's Walden Life Lessons that I had deliriously developed back in the city—that this one would be a slam-dunk.

For one, Gary is a gifted flower gardener.

And secondly, I love to eat vegetables.

Moreover, my parents had nurtured a wonderful Ozarks vegetable garden when I was a child. I remember turning the hard clay soil with my parents, digging, digging, turning, turning, through tree roots and stone, until an arrowhead or two would appear, which I would scrub off and save and make into a choker. I remember walking behind our house, to the edge of our woods, and plucking hot Big Boy tomatoes off the vine and eating them like apples. I remember having a bounty of veggies and herbs, from spring through fall, that tasted so fresh—and fresh is not even the right word—that they could never be re-created. They made all grocery vegetables taste frozen, mushy, altered.

Which is why, when we moved, Gary had said to me, "We have three point five acres of land—we should be able to use our God-given wits to grow something besides flowers. Just imagine how cool it would be to walk outside in the evening and pick our own home-grown salad."

I spent endless days imagining the future he had dreamed: me, carrying a cute basket, wearing little gloves, looking innocently sexy as I make my own balsamic vinaigrette with fresh herbs to top our very own hand-picked produce, which I will showcase in Pottery Barn salad bowls. I will be June Cleaver and Martha Stewart and Ron Jeremy all rolled into one: a lady in the streets and a freak in the sheets. We will use our giant cucumbers for salads and . . . well, other things.

But not the same one for both.

Definitely not the same one for both.

I mean, the Amish live off the land, and they do it wearing big hats and long beards. I can, at least, wear tank tops and use Off! Gary isn't asking that we raise cattle. He's simply asking that we cultivate a cucumber, pamper some peppers, sustain some strawberries.

We're simply asking ourselves to grow some of our own food, to provide for ourselves for a little while, to give back to the planet for once instead of only taking from it.

We can do this.

Spring Has Sprung

Spring arrives one day in Michigan like a forgotten castaway who manages to row his way onto the beach using two coconuts.

I sport exactly the same expression as an old Jewish woman in Naples who sashays out to the beach in her gold sandals before the breakfast buffet at the Ritz-Carlton to claim a beach chair by covering it with a towel and a Janet Evanovich paperback and instead discovers Robinson Crusoe gasping in front of her.

I step outside my front door in early April, wrapped in my winter layers—sweats, robe, and a thick plaid blanket—expecting to be bitch-slapped by the cold, but instead the snow is melting, sliding off our cottage roof in chunks. It is actually warm, the wind from a direction other than Ungodly. Birds are chirping and circling, diving into puddles created by the snow. I shrug off my blanket, and then my robe, and finally the sweatshirt, until I am standing in short sleeves.

I inhale deeply, and, for once, my lungs don't burn.

I can smell wet pine.

I can already hear the sounds of "the peepers," which is what the baby bullfrogs and crickets are called in the country, as they noisily come to life.

"One attraction in coming to the woods to live was that I should have leisure and opportunity to see the Spring come in," Thoreau writes.

I pull on my waders and circle Gary's gardens. I can see the heads of crocus and daffodils just starting to penetrate the once frozen earth, a tiny paintbrush of wet green against a sludgy white canvas.

It is time.

Our Bean Field

We start simply enough.

Gary and I choose a tiny plot of land—perhaps twenty feet by twenty feet—that sits just beyond our driveway, on a cusp of forest overgrown with Michigan bamboo, a sort of invasive but pretty rubber tree–ish plant. It seems a manageable space—much more manageable than Thoreau's seven miles of bean rows, which helped sustain him during his stay at Walden—until we begin to whack and thwack at the native bamboo; it seems to have a *Friday the 13th* unwillingness to die.

I stand by, mostly watching, occasionally bending the tree back as far as it will go and then—*whoosh!*—letting it fly back into its upright position.

"It's like a giant, leafy penis," I tell Gary.

He stops and stares at me. With a lot of hatred.

"Are you going to help me, Thoreau?"

"I *am* helping."

"Well, first you need to change. I'm sure Thoreau didn't hoe his bean garden in leather slides featuring, at the very least, a one-inch man heel," Gary says.

"What if people drop by to see us?" I ask.

"Well, unless you're expecting Joan and Melissa, I think most locals would commit you if they saw you planting a vegetable garden in three-hundred-dollar slides."

I go inside and begrudgingly change into my waders.

"Good choice," Gary says. "Nice look."

"I *am* very serious about this," I tell him.

We spend weeks clearing the space for the garden, pulling roots that seem embedded into the earth's core, clearing brush, hoeing, amending the sandy soil with compost and humus. I am covered with so many mosquito bites I am convinced I have contracted malaria. My face is cut, my fingers ache, and we haven't even planted anything.

Still, Gary forges on with the warlike determination of a Norseman.

I lean on my shovel and watch the man I love.

Gary is a dreamer. He does have a grand desire to live off the land, to be natural and woodsman-y. He even grows a beard for inspiration, to fit the part. The beard is hot. Extremely hot. It's like I'm dating someone else. Like a hot woodsman with a beard. I ask Gary to chainsaw something and cuss. He nearly cuts off his arm and says, "Shit!"

"This takes two," Gary says. "Just remember, Thoreau went it alone. I was looking through *Walden*. There's a chapter on his bean garden. He loved being outside, he loved the earth. Shame on you for giving up already."

I want to tell Gary that I'm getting worked up watching him dig with a beard. But Gary knows me too well. He knows he needs to shame me and motivate me, a tactic that never fails to excite me. I always need motivation. I need a young guy to try to beat me in a marathon or someone who says I can't do something. Defeating someone always makes me feel better about myself.

So I decide to defeat Thoreau, by growing so many beans that Del Monte will beg us for them.

We Blow Our IRAs on a Vegetable Garden

Finally, the day arrives—a bright, windy, warmish day where the clouds bounce quickly along the sky like tumbleweeds—when we can venture out to the local nursery and pick our veggies along with other gardeners' brains.

The nursery is a virtual Woodstock of horticulturists, a hidden oasis near the lakeshore where avid gardeners flock to buy and talk and exchange secrets, like creepy Harry Potter fans.

I obviously look like a newbie, because people start approaching me, talking to me, advising me, and I don't like to be approached by people. My instinct is to run and hide in the car or make fun of them. I guess I probably shouldn't have dressed like I'm going to a Britney concert.

An old man who looks like Moses instructs me on the virtues of Big Boy tomatoes, while a woman who resembles Charlize Theron in *Monster* implores me not to "fuck with the jumbo green peppers" because they make her throat break out. I'm thinking it might be the testosterone injections, but I keep that to myself. Another couple in matching overalls and buttons that say GARDENERS KNOW THE BEST DIRT inform me, as though their lives depend on it, on which is the best humus to purchase. They stick their hands into the dark, steaming poop-soil and inhale it deeply, like it's a $300 bottle of Merlot, and then hold their fingers out for me to sniff.

"I take your word for it," I say, backing away.

I suck on an organic Tootsie Pop and nod continuously with faux enthusiasm as we spend the day with people who should first be bathed and then euthanized. But Gary, already a gifted flower gardener, is fully enthused.

I had printed out the following from *Walden* and brought it with me, so Thoreau could help guide our efforts and our spending:

My outgoes were,—

For a hoe, ...$0.54
Plowing, harrowing, and furrowing, ... 7.50 Too much.
Beans for seed, ...3.12 ½
Potatoes, ...1.33
Peas, ...0.40
Turnip seed, ...0.06
White line for crow fence, ... 0.02
Horse cultivator and boy three hours, ... 1.00
Horse and cart to get crop, ... 0.75
In all, ...$14.72 ½

My income was from

Nine bushels & twelve quarts of beans sold, .. $16.94
Five large potatoes, ... 2.50
Nine small, ... 2.25
Grass, ...1.00
Stalks, ... 0.75
In all, ... $23.44

Leaving a pecuniary profit, as I have elsewhere said, of $8.71½.

"OK," I tell Gary. "I've never read a ledger before, but I believe that Thoreau spent fourteen seventy-two and a half and ended up making twenty-three forty-four, meaning he came out ahead in this gig. So, let's just keep this in mind, all right? We can probably grow enough to sustain us all summer and then sell our overage at a makeshift road-side stand to stupid Chicagoans who will pay eight dollars for a tomato because our sign is so fucking cute."

Gary laughs.

I say this, really, as a preemptive strike, because Gary would go ahead and debit a Lexus SUV if he felt like it. His excitement too often occludes his judgment.

But he is good today. Or so I think.

I lose track, because everything seems so small and manageable: packets of seeds and cute little plants and six-packs of herbs and veggie accessories. It's not like buying a Stickley dining room table.

However, when I walk to the register, I learn that—after spending six hours shopping—we have spent a total of nearly $500 on seeds, plants, soil, and adorable garden stakes of smiling tomatoes and happy cucumbers and ornery onions.

"We could have flown in P. Allen Smith for less," I tell Gary. "We will not buy a single vegetable the rest of the year, got it?"

He nods and blows his nonexistent bangs out of his eyes.

On the way home, I make our own bean field list, like Thoreau.

Our Garden of Eden will overflow with the following fruits and vegetables:

- Tomatoes
- Onions (green and white)
- Green peppers
- Red-leaf lettuce
- Spinach
- Cucumbers
- Zucchini
- Yellow squash
- Radishes
- Strawberries
- And, of course, green beans

The time has come for the earth to give us our bounty. The time has come for me to channel Thoreau.

This Land Is Your Land, This Land Is My Land

Our land.

We have a lot of it now.

This is the first sizable piece of land—not just a postage-stamp-size yard or a common courtyard in an apartment complex—that Gary and I have ever owned.

We have nearly four acres. We are the Donald Trumps of the country, for Christ's sake. We *should* be able to use our God-given wits to grow something, anything, besides flowers.

Thoreau lived off the land, and he went it alone. He hoed his bean garden, tended his beans, watered them, nurtured them, picked them, ate them, and sold them. He even made a small profit. And he was a writer. I'm not asking that we wring the necks of our own chickens or hunt down squirrel for supper. I'm simply asking that we grow a tomato to dice in our salads, that we grow a green pepper to stuff, that we can walk out and pick a bowl full of fresh strawberries that we have planted.

It would seem an easy thing to ask. Gary is a talented gardener. He can grow anything, anywhere. He can grow trees and shrubs and flowers and ground cover from seeds, starts, and transplants. He can grow flowers in sand, soil, or clay.

He is Martha.

With body hair.

And a penis.

Thus, the logical transition is: If he can grow any flower, surely he can grow any fruit or vegetable. And I can be his apprentice, his gardening sous chef, if you will, helping him dig and prep. I will follow his direction. Together, we will grow a garden that will make Al Gore weep.

But I quickly learn there is a cavernous difference between flowers and vegetables, plants that are pretty versus plants that are edible. For one, you cannot stare out your dining room window and look admiringly at lettuce. You cannot sniff a radish with the same fervor with which you inhale the drooping bloom on a peony. You cannot put an arrangement of green onions in a cute little McCoy vase.

They stink.

Gary is a baker, too. My theory is that bakers tend to be flower gardeners and that cooks tend to be vegetable gardeners, and the two are very different breeds, like dachshunds and Great Danes. Flower gardeners/bakers tend to be: a dash of this, a dash of that (be it ferns and phlox or cinnamon and nutmeg), sugar and spice and everything nice, they arrange the chocolate chip cookies on a pretty cake plate or a cottage bouquet in a McCoy vase, and then watch everyone ooh and aah and enjoy. Vegetable gardeners/cooks tend to be: by-the-recipe types, follow-the-rules types, who can spend all day cooking a six-course meal using fresh ingredients from their gardens and time everything down to the last minute before whipping it on the table and watching everyone devour it.

This is why Gary prefers to bake rather than cook. He is not good at timing things so the parts of the meal all come out together. He'd prefer to spend forty minutes on the potato casserole and three minutes checking the turkey. He'd prefer to gossip or change a holiday CD than baste.

This is also why he loves flowers.

His gardens are a dash of this and that, many plants started from hundreds of different flowers and plants given to him by family and friends. Gary's garden blooms continuously and in unexpected ways. If something works, it works; if it doesn't, he'll try again.

Still, despite his outward appearance, Gary—unlike me—really is a man of the earth. When he dies, he wants—honest to God—to be buried in a burlap bag under his favorite pine tree in our woods, so his body can more quickly decompose and be given back to the earth.

I would prefer a more elaborate affair, perhaps with a horse-drawn carriage, celebrities, and Bette Midler singing "Wind Beneath My Wings." Fireworks would be perfect, if I pass in the summer. Releasing doves would be appropriate in the spring. Jauntily dressed carolers would be a nice touch in the winter.

Still, I honestly believe that a little bit of Gary will rub off on me and that, together, we can have a big, beautiful garden.

I remember, when I was little, my father carefully tending to his own garden every night after work and every weekend morning. My mom and I would carry a giant red-speckled enamelware bowl out into the garden on early summer evenings and pick what we wanted in our salads that night, or we would pull onions to slice, batter, and dump in the fryer alongside chicken livers.

But time has smoothed the rough edges off my memory.

I have forgotten that the few minutes I spent in my father's garden translated into endless hours of work for him.

And my father was an engineer who loved to cook.

You do the math.

Gary and Wade Grow a Single Bean

There should be some thrill about sticking your hands deep in the ground, planting seeds, nurturing new life, being responsible for growing your own food, food you know has not been chemically altered in any way.

I should be able to do this. I should take pride in this. I should enjoy it.

But I plant awkwardly, stiffly, like a frightened robot. I hover above the earth, my knees over the ground, too scared to get them dirty. My back aches. I dig my hands in the soil—uncovering earthworms and slugs and creepy-crawlers—and gag audibly. But I make myself persevere, like when I tried out for the freshman football team in high school—to prove I could be normal and fit in—and ended up breaking my little finger in three places, the bone actually protruding through my skin.

I try to wear cloth gloves, but they eventually become wet and muddy, so I switch to rubber gloves, which are cold and very prostate-exam, and they rub blisters on my fingers and forearms.

I just don't like dirt. I never liked to make mud pies. I never liked to get my new white Keds dirty by walking anywhere there might be dust. I don't consider this work beneath me—though, quite literally, it *is*—it's just dirty work. I don't like gunk under my fingernails. I don't like to look like one of the Little Rascals.

A local even gives me a hat with netting, to thwart the mosquitoes, but I wear it only once, after I catch a glimpse of myself looking like Katharine Hepburn in *The African Queen.*

All of this just doesn't come naturally to me.

I can't tell Gary. He loves working in the earth, planting, getting muddy. It's kind of a turn-on. He is the anti-me. And I know he is doing this largely for me.

So, I make a good go of it, pretending to be happy, putting on a good front, coating my body in deet, itching my mosquito bites until I bleed, and then silently crying in the shower while scrubbing my hands until my fingerprints disappear.

For the first few weeks, I diligently help Gary water and nurture the garden with much care and tenderness, like we've found the baby Moses floating in a bassinet. We prune trees so additional light can reach the garden, we add iron to the soil, we sprinkle manure and toss Marge's poop around the plants. We weed, and whack, and watch, and wait. And wait. And wait.

Another month in, by the time other gardeners are bragging about their hand-grown produce, we have only tomatoes the size of pimples; lettuce so gritty that running it through the dishwasher can't remove the dirt; onions that look like pearls; a single green pepper the size of a booger; and three—count 'em, three—green beans, which are already shriveled. Our strawberries blossom with the cutest white flowers but never produce a single berry.

We don't have enough produce to make a salad for the Keebler Elves. Experienced vegetable gardeners offer their friendly assessments: "Not enough light."

"A vegetable garden needs full sun."

"Soil is too sandy. Didn't amend it enough. Won't hold the water."

Personally, I attribute our problems to a wormy beetle-y larva thing that I find on a leaf. It looks exactly like an insect I saw on the Discovery Channel that got into a man's body in the jungle and grew to be about twenty-five feet long. They showed an X-ray of it curled from head to toe in the man, crushing his organs, suffocating his brain—although it looked very relaxed, lounging really, like it was enjoying a mojito and cigar.

I was convinced this thing was eating our garden.

And probably my kidneys.

No matter the reasons, though, we had nada.

What would Lucy do?

Lucy, I know, like every good gay man, would take a different tactic with her garden.

So Gary and I perform an extreme makeover. Rather than try to figure out what's going on inside our garden, we focus on its exterior, knowing if it looks good, it will surely feel better about itself.

We make a front gate out of sticks and willow and adorn it with a handmade birch-bark sign that says TURKEY RUN PRODUCE. We buy additional, adorable garden stakes of smiling peppers and jaunty onions, we buy little signs that say GARDEN OF WEEDIN'. We begin placing tiki torches around the edges of the garden to give it "grandeur" and "presence."

Our garden looks like "da bomb," but the only thing it produces is a bout of diarrhea after we eat a cucumber that resembles a moldy dildo.

When I walk with Gary to check our garden one more time—him secretly believing, I know, that perhaps a beanstalk has miraculously grown into the clouds—I immediately see the look of complete devastation on his face. Gary cannot fail at this. Why? He is, truly, a gifted gardener. While I have a vendetta against dirt, Gary has a pact with the earth: He will nurture it. That's why his flower gardens look as if they should be featured in *Better Homes and Gardens* or *Midwest Living.* They are, truly, breathtaking. People hear about his gardens and now stop by our cottage just to see them.

But today, Gary retreats into our cottage, dejected.

So I pick a few of his flowers, which I take inside and make into a pretty arrangement. I stand back and look at it. *This is how Gary says "thank you" to the earth,* I think. *This is how he gives back.*

When Gary walks in, he smiles.

"You can't shove a tomato and a cucumber in a vase, can you?" I say.

One Particular Fella

OK, let's be honest here.

Our country garden isn't going to feed us for a day, much less a week, unless we can live off twenty dirty, worm-infested lettuce leaves, a cucumber the size of a sweet midget pickle, and an onion smaller than a cubic zirconium.

So I head to a rural grocery about forty-five minutes away, since I don't want anyone to see me shopping in town. They'll know I'm a fraud. And yet the store I go to is the kind that makes the old IGAs from my Ozarks youth look like the Four Seasons.

I enter and begin to make my rounds.

There is no ground turkey breast.

There is no soy butter.

There are no Morningstar black bean burgers.

In short, the store carries none of the foods on which I used to survive.

I forget that rural country grocery stores don't even carry crunchy peanut butter, much less organic bread and deli honey turkey.

I have no garden. I have no grocery. I have no food.

I cannot continue to eat sleeves of cookie dough and drink bottles of wine as my staples. I don't think those items comprise the base of the FDA's food pyramid. I mean, there's nothing sexy about a chubby diabetic with a colostomy bag, and I am well on my way.

Thoreau once contemplated eating a rat. I cannot do that. My family tried to cook turtle soup at our cabin on Sugar Creek when I was young. Simply watching my kin slaughter a turtle and then try to rip its shell off was worse than anything *Hostel* has to offer. I swore off wild game after that.

However, I do consider Kashi Go Lean cereal to be very country, very natural, very organic, since I think it's made of tree bark and gravel. It just happens to come in a convenient box, which is easier than going outside every morning, putting crushed stone into a bowl, and milking a cow.

But this store doesn't carry Kashi.

"Can you special order it?"

I am more yelling this at the clerk than asking politely.

"Us's cereals issh over there."

The clerk is probably fifty—all ashy gray skin and yellow finger-nails and auburny-silver hair that's been pulled into a bun the size of Sputnik—she looks at least eighty. She has to give her "gums a break," I hear her tell a morbidly obese young woman in produce, so she's chosen not to wear her dentures today. This bad fashion and hygiene decision has given her the look of a confused, rotting jack-o'-lantern whose mouth is simply caving into its head. And then the clerk looks at the fat woman and says, "Oh, hon, you's pregnant! Congratula-tions!"

The fat woman looks at her happily, not offended in the least—unlike every woman I know, who would have bitch-slapped the clerk into the soda aisle—and fondles her apron stomach, turning it over and kneading it like bread dough before saying, "Nope! Just looks that way!"

I have to get out of this store, so I tell the clerk, "Listen, I've seen your cereals. You only carry Corn Flakes, Cocoa Puffs, and Lucky Charms. You don't even have Shredded Wheat."

"Corn Flakes is good for you."

I stop and think about if, conjugation-wise, she is right: Corn Flakes *is* good or Corn Flakes *are* good. Actually, astonishingly, I think she's right, considering Corn Flakes is probably considered sin-gular.

She is running her index finger over her gums, moaning in delight.

"Actually, corn cereals . . . is . . . are not that great for you. They're . . . corn. They don't have enough fiber or protein. They inflate my blood sugar."

She is staring at me through dirty, perfectly round Alvin the Chipmunk glasses.

"You don't have sugar in your blood, sweetheart. You have blood in your blood."

She is laughing at herself, her sore, red gums open and mocking me. She is not as dumb as I have made her out to be. Anyone with that much sarcasm can't be that stupid.

"Listen, can you do me a big favor, since it looks like you're the one who knows how to get things done around here?"

I am fake-smiling, like a jackass, winking.

She grunts. She isn't falling for flattery. I guess three decades of drinking Stroh's for breakfast tends to suck all the charm out of life.

The clerk is crazy skinny, the malnourished, TV-dinner-and-Winston-diet skinny, not the Kate Moss–on-crack-but-still-able-to-look-OK-with-makeup skinny.

"What do you want?" she asks.

"I have a little list of suggested items I'd like the store to carry. Can I jot them down for you?"

She rips the edge off a paper grocery bag and hands me a bowling pencil. I feel like I'm asking her out for a date after League Night.

I write a list of some twenty items I'd like the store to carry . . . *for me,* although I try to convince her that I am completely certain resorters would also buy these items and that the store's purchases wouldn't be in vain, or strictly *for me.*

My list includes:

- Kashi Go Lean cereal (must be Go Lean, *not* the puffs)
- Silver Palate rough-cut oatmeal (must be the slow-cook kind, *not* the instant)
- Detour protein bars (must be the old Detour bars, *not* the "new flavor")

- Ground turkey *breast* (*not* just ground turkey; it still has too much fat)
- *Fresh* Brussels sprouts
- *Fresh* spinach
- *Fresh* carrots (not the baby carrots)
- *Fresh* broccoli (not just the bagged or frozen)
- Jicama
- Lentils
- Edamame (a *must* item)
- Hodgson Mill whole-grain pastas (must have at least nine grams protein, five grams fiber per serving)
- Starbucks espresso roast coffee (must be the espresso whole bean, *not* the ground morning blend)
- Ghirardelli white chocolate syrup (must be the syrup, *not* the powder—mixes better in lattes)
- Morningstar Farms spicy black bean burgers (the soy veggie burgers will also work; the pizza burgers will *not*)
- Turkey pepperoni (preferably low-fat Hormel)
- Healthy Choice honey turkey in the deli (*only* Healthy Choice is acceptable)
- Boneless, skinless chicken breasts stuffed with feta, roasted red peppers, and sun-dried tomatoes (the Cajun turkey sausages will work, in a pinch)
- Garden of Eatin' blue corn tortilla chips
- Zone drinks ("My partner, Gary, watches his sugar intake; he does the One Touch, like Patti LaBelle," I tell her.)
- Splenda for baking ("You should try it; fabulous!")

I hand her my list.

Proudly, mind you.

"Zowie zooks!" she says. "You is one particular little fella. Is you kiddin' me with all this?"

"I isn't," I reply. "I'll pay extra."

"I have a suggestion: Why don't you just grow your own veggie garden and raise a coupla turkeys?" she says.

I think briefly about pushing the bowling pencil into her jugular and am convinced that if I explained all of this to a jury of my peers, I would be acquitted.

But I know I have no "peers."

Instead, I purchase a sleeve of cookie dough and a bottle of wine, and drive home, thinking about the least-noticeable place on my leg to wrap my new colostomy bag.

Tomato, Toe-mah-toe, Let's Call the Whole Thing Off

It matters little comparatively whether the fields fill the farmer's barns. The true husbandman will cease from anxiety, as the squirrels manifest no concern whether the woods will bear chestnuts this year or not, and finish his labor with every day, relinquishing all claim to the produce of his fields, and sacrificing in his mind not only his first but his last fruits also.

I read this excerpt from *Walden* to Gary in bed the night of my grocery debacle.

It is a few weeks later, and summer is about to begin.

"It's more about our relationship with the earth than it is about growing anything," I say. "And we are trying to respect our earth. Hello? Hello? Anyone there? Bueller? Bueller?"

But Gary is not listening. I know because he asks me, first, what a "husbandman" is; second, if the Mary Kay line reducer is working on that trough on his forehead; and, third, if a movie is ever made from one of my books, if I would sign a legal contract stating that only Shia LaBeouf be allowed to play him.

I quickly answer "yes" to number three, because I want to move on already, but then stop and ask, "Why?"

"Because someone said I looked like Garry Shandling today. And I don't want some movie producer to get a bad, pre–weight loss photo of me and hire somebody like William Shatner to play me."

"Good night, Ricky!" I say.

"Good night, Lucy," Gary says.

I roll over and go to sleep.

The next morning, Gary wakes me early. "Sorry I wasn't listening last night. Let's go for a drive around the countryside today. We'll get scarves and open the sunroof, and be all Thelma and Louise, OK?"

We drive along the lake, taking the scenic route, and pop into little galleries and coffee shops. The drive reminds me of why I—and so many tourists and resorters—love our little rustic, artsy coast.

On the drive, we stop at the cutest little roadside vegetable stand you have ever seen. The kind with the bright flags that whip in the wind, the little wooden carts holding the season's latest produce, and a hand-painted sign that says GWYN'S GARDEN GOODIES. A woman who looks exactly like Tanya Tucker—you know, in her "Delta Dawn" heyday, same hair, same eyes, same teeth, same overalls with pretty little flowers sewn onto the straps—is manning the tomato cart.

"Are you Gwyn?" I ask.

"Yep," she says.

She doesn't sound like Tanya Tucker. Everyone in Michigan sounds like they were in the movie *Fargo*. Everyone. They all say "Yep" or "You betcha" when they answer and then insert a "Well, you know" when there should be silence instead. And when they're done speaking with you, they say "All righty then," which is a polite northern country way of saying "Wouldja shut the fuck up already?"

"You have some mighty fine tomatoes, Gwyn," I say.

Gwyn blushes. I realize too late that I sound like a pervert. Gary walks up and puts his arm around me. Gwyn looks slightly upset to discover I play for the other team.

Gwyn's perfectly round, perfectly red, perfectly plump vine-ripened tomatoes are sitting in cute little straw baskets, like Gary's mom uses for her Easter displays, which she fills with jelly beans and plastic grass.

I pluck a tomato out of the basket and hold it up for Gwyn. "How much for one?" I ask.

"Yep . . . well, you know, we don't really just sell a single tomato, you know. They're four for a dollar . . . that's why there's four per basket. Yep. You betcha. Well, you know."

I want just one tomato. We will never eat four tomatoes in two days. They will rot and turn to mush sitting on our kitchen windowsill. It happens every time.

I tell all of this to Gwyn.

"Well, you know, it's just how we do it," she says.

Country people do not do well with change, I have come to realize. Everything must follow a code or rule; everything must be done exactly the same, no surprises. The farmer's market in St. Louis was like bartering for pottery in Mexico: no holds barred, yelling, screaming, making a deal. Not in the country. Everything is quiet and polite; everything has a passive-aggressive edge. I'm not in the mood for this today. I'm jonesing for some city cynicism, some urban rage, some good old-fashioned deal making.

"Well, you know, it's not how normal people do it, Gwyn. It's not how grocery stores do it, Gwyn. It's not how you do it in the city. You can buy a single tomato in a grocery store. But since there's not a grocery store around that I like, I'm forced to buy everything alongside the road, like a Gypsy. We're two people here, Gwyn. Not a family of wolverines who can devour a basket of tomatoes in a single day. Cut us some slack."

"All righty then," Gwyn says. She is done with this conversation.

"Oh, no. Oh, no you don't. You don't *all righty then* me, sweetie. I want to buy one tomato. So we can split it on our salad tonight. You can sell a basket of three tomatoes to someone else for seventy-five cents. Don't you see how this works? It can be done. This is a democracy. No one has declared that all garden tomatoes must be sold four to a basket for a buck. You can change it up. Why can't anyone change it up around here?"

Gary sidles up to me and whispers, "What the fuck is wrong with you? Just buy four tomatoes. It's only a buck. We can make spaghetti sauce or put them on burritos. We've got tomato options."

"I just want Tanya Tucker to sell me one fuckin' tomato," I whisper.

"Jesus, just take a look at yourself. You are insane."

I leave my body and float somewhere above, where I see myself holding a single tomato straight out in front of my body, like I've caught a grenade that was tossed my way. I see Gwyn still saying "All righty then, all righty then" over and over.

We are failures.

We can't grow our own tomatoes.

I can't even find food that I can eat.

I'm trying to be uncomplicated, but I'm actually a walking Rubik's Cube.

And now I'm being forced to buy a zillion tomatoes from some woman who probably has an army plucking tomatoes at her farm right now. She looks sweet, but I'm sure she's the Martha Stewart of produce and lives in a mansion with an infinity pool overlooking Lake Michigan.

And then I see her husband, who looks like Billy Jack—you know, from the Billy Jack movies—coming from behind the cute little red-and-white-striped tent with a baseball bat.

What would Lucy do?

My soul reenters my body and I say, very politely, "All righty then. Four tomatoes it will be."

I hand Gwyn a dollar, and Gary ushers me to the car.

"You need to pull it together," he says. "You're the one who wanted to move. You wanted to live in the country, Thoreau. We don't have any Whole Foods or Trader Joe's. You got Gwyn. And, just to remind you, a tomato in the city costs like six dollars."

I am hugging my basket of tomatoes. I miss Trader Joe's. I miss paying six dollars for lettuce I've never heard of.

I miss . . . me.

An Apple a Day

Gary doesn't lecture me. In fact, he doesn't talk the entire way home. He doesn't even go home. Rather, he pulls into a U-Pick not far from Turkey Run.

Though there is nothing to pick this early in the season, he wants to set the scene.

"Do you remember the first time we picked apples here?" he asks.

"I do," I say. "But I have chosen not to remember."

"Well, remember," he says. And then he turns off the car, and we sit in silence, staring at the expanse of orchards.

Orchards and vineyards dot the west Michigan landscape, endless, rolling hillsides filled with fruit trees. In my short time in rural America, these orchards have come to define the time of year, tell me what season we are enjoying: blueberries and sweet cherries in July, peaches in August, apples summer through fall, as well as plums, nectarines, pumpkins, squash, Indian corn. These seasonal crops have replaced my office calendar.

The U-Pick Gary has pulled into—down a long, dusty gravel drive—is a local icon. Tourists and locals alike flock to it, like locusts. I used to pick strawberries at U-Picks growing up as a kid. Usually, I would simply walk out of our house or cabin and into the surrounding woods and fields to pick wild blackberries or raspberries. The cuts and scrapes seemed worth the pain, especially when I would present a big bowl full of fruit to my parents, who would turn it into a pie or cobbler. But that magic faded over the years. I didn't like to get cut. I didn't like to get dirty. I didn't want to eat pie. I didn't want stains on my clothes.

Gary gets out of the car and disappears behind a row of flowering trees.

I remember last fall.

There was a crowd that day, but the orchard could hold a throng, thanks to its hundreds of acres. People seem dwarfed by the sheer size.

"Why are we here?" I had asked Gary.

"Because you need a dose of this," he had said, dramatically gesturing out the car window like a *Price Is Right* girl.

"You need a dose of this," I said, grabbing my crotch like Kanye West.

It was a beautiful day, the kind where city people raised their faces to the sun and looked around in awe, remembering what it was like to see open, green space and not to be crowded, bumped, rushed.

Instead I had said, "I'm wearing flip-flops. My feet will get filthy."

We departed the car, and a woman in a sky-colored bonnet pointed us in two directions, one for picking apples, another for picking peaches.

"Everything's better . . . with Blue Bonnet on it," I sang quietly to Gary as we walked away with four large sacks.

He glared at me.

I remembered bitching, as we walked that day, about the dust, my feet, the fact that it was easier to walk into a grocery and pick out five shiny Fuji apples than meander around a fucking farm to do labor that should already have been done for us.

Still, we had meandered to one of the few rows not clotted with weekenders, and I watched Gary stretch to pick perfect red, cartoon-looking apples clinging to branches. Through a row, I remember seeing a stunning woman—think young Jane Seymour—watch a group of commercial-ready children pick apples as she conducted business on her cell phone.

"Not that, Cooper!" she had yelled at a boy. "It's not red enough! . . . Sophia, no, no, no! That one was on the ground! . . . Cooper! Don't eat one! They're not clean!"

She'd walked between the rows, closer to me and Gary, and she had whispered, "I don't know. We're at some bumfuck orchard with a bunch of rednecks. The children wanted apples. Everything is so dusty here. I didn't even know fruit had seasons. I mean, we can always find what we want at Whole Foods, right?" She had laughed. "We'll be back in the city late this afternoon. I can't wait. I've had enough of the country."

Then the woman had busted me listening to her. I hadn't even picked an apple. I was just standing there watching her. So I smiled at her. She turned away.

The car door slammed, shaking me from this memory.

"Remember now? That's still you," Gary says. "It's not pretty, is it? You can check off as many of your little Life Lessons as you want, but you really haven't learned or embraced a thing yet."

I am so angry and pissed and embarrassed that I subconsciously pick up and squeeze one of Gwyn's tomatoes until it explodes in my hand.

It looks like I've committed murder, which is what I was thinking of doing.

Instead, I am thankful we were forced to buy four tomatoes, because now I only have three to spare.

Frond Memories

Our woods, too—like the lake and the U-Picks—reflect a different personality based on the season. In the winter, the woods are paint-by-numbers white, the tree trunks blasted with snow on the north side, the limbs facing south still dark and unfinished looking, as though a child had gotten bored with his work and wandered away to watch cartoons.

In the fall, the woods bask in an otherworldly yellow-gold glow, the leaves of the sugar maples reflecting the fading intensity of the sun, like stage lights covered in color gels.

In the summer, the woods stand strong and proud, at full height, chest out, a teen boy full of life.

And yet the spring, I think, may be the most beautiful time of all for our woods, as it pulls out all the stops, mesmerizing you—like a Meryl Streep performance—with subtle nuance after subtle nuance.

The emerging leaves aren't just green, they are Day-Glo green, a bright, limey, iridescent green, before they stretch into their deeper adulthood green. The earth begins to consume the remaining wet leaves, and emerging in their place is a treasure trove of plant life: delicate white trillium; thick beds of mayapples; an army of lilies of the valley; purple phlox; and an array of ferns, all shapes and sizes, each one a forest snowflake, stretching their way, slowly, slowly, into the warm air, awakened after a long winter's sleep.

This is the view from my office window now. No cars, no buildings, no noise.

I used to notice spring in our city parks or our botanical gardens, but really only in a half-assed way: looking but not seeing, walking but not stopping.

When I was little, we lived on five acres of woods in the country and spent our summers at a log cabin along a crystal-clear creek. When my older brother, Todd, wasn't hunting, or fishing, or getting dirty, he would often drag me out of the house—away from *Gilligan's Island* or *The Brady Bunch* or *I Love Lucy*—to walk through our woods, me whining, my brother holding branches back for me so I could pass without getting cut. As we walked, he would quiz me about a certain tree, if its bark might make a solid canoe, or he would point out a particular fern or mushroom and ask me if it was OK to eat, or explain the difference between an oak and a sassafras leaf. When I would begin to whine—like I always did—he would pointedly ask me if I even cared about where I lived, where I grew up, what surrounded me.

"You're so worried about getting out of here, you don't even pay attention to what you have," he once told me.

My brother's dream, before he was killed the summer after graduating high school, was to be a conservation agent. My dream was simply to run like hell.

Many years ago—and many years after my brother passed—I went to a fancy dinner at a fancy restaurant in Chicago, a place you waited six months to get into, where people were raving about the chef and his latest creations. I was engrossed in conversation when someone passed me an appetizer that tasted so familiar yet so foreign. I was certain I'd never ordered it before, but the taste whirled me somewhere else.

"What is this?" I asked. "It's fabulous."

"Fiddlehead fern," someone said. "Can you believe it? Ferns! They can only get them for a few weeks a year. We're very lucky to be here tonight."

And then I remembered: My brother had made these for me at our cabin one spring; fiddlehead ferns, or some sort of edible fern, that he had picked and cooked himself on our cabin's old gas stove, tossing them in butter, garlic, onion, a little salt and pepper, and maybe some crisp bacon he dropped in at the last minute.

This day, I leave my office and walk into our woods, foraging for ferns—one hour, two hours; I am on a mission. I see nests of young fern fronds that have not yet unfurled. Some look just like the scroll at the top of a fiddle.

I remember my brother's voice: "You can eat these, Wade. Did you know that? Remember that, OK?"

But I am too scared that I will make a mistake and end up poisoning Gary, and find myself in prison being the boyfriend of a murderer nicknamed "Anvil" after trying to explain to a jury that I was only trying to channel Thoreau.

I stand in the woods and cry because I'm a big fuckin' crybaby, but mostly because I do care about where I live, about where I grew up. It just took me a while. And it's not too late, which is why I hit a local market to buy fiddlehead ferns. It's not too late, even if Gary asks at dinner, "What are these? Are you trying to kill me?" And then he says, "These are incredible."

We don't need a garden, I want to say. *We already have a garden. I just need to open my eyes.*

But if I say this I will sound insane. Because it sounds insane, even in my own head.

"Are you OK?" Gary asks.

"I'm just . . . happy, I guess."

And I am, despite the fact I realize I have tanked Lesson Six and knotted my scorecard in a tie. I mean, if Joan Rivers and I were each left to our wits alone, she would have done a better job living off the land.

Wade's Walden—3. Modern Society—3.

LESSON SEVEN
Nurture Our Country Critters

Fishermen, hunters, woodchoppers, and others, spending their lives in the fields and woods, in a peculiar sense a part of Nature themselves, are often in a more favorable mood for observing her, in the intervals of their pursuits, than philosophers or poets even, who approach her with expectation. She is not afraid to exhibit herself to them . . .

—Henry David Thoreau, *Walden*

Talkin' Turkey

There's a big crowd—a throng actually—at the country store today. It's like a half-off sale at Macy's, except I'm not being clawed by a woman with a French manicure or a gay man swaddled in scarves.

No, this is all straight men: hunters in jeans and camouflage and boots and hats that promote cattle feed or farm equipment.

All the men are lined up in the back of the store. I grab a copy of a hunting newspaper and fake-read it behind the fellas. I try to fix my hair—to "wear it down"—so I fit in more with the guys.

Which is kind of like sending Charles Nelson Reilly on a spy mission.

"Ready, Bob?" one guy with a beard and John Deere cap says.

"I'm always ready. Gonna fill my freezer with turkey!" says another guy with a beard and a John Deere cap. I realize they all look the same. I half expect them to start shooting their rifles up into the air and then chug from a bottle of moonshine.

And then my heart drops like a roller coaster.

I forgot.

I heard on the radio that it's opening day for turkey hunting season tomorrow, and hunters are getting their licenses, ammo, turkey calls.

You learn these things in the country, like you know when a new musical opens in the city. Many kids out here take off, or get off, the first day of a particular hunting season, be it deer, or turkey, or salmon. It turns wives into hunting widows and men into killers. It turns our surrounding countryside into a live-action Game Boy.

It was similar for me growing up. Our house was surrounded by gunfire during hunting season, and deer served as hood ornaments for a few long months.

Turkey hunting season seems even harder on me as an adult.

I remember one of the first mornings after we moved, when we were awoken by the deafening sound of thunder. We looked out our bedroom window and saw a shadow of clouds flying past, like a hundred wicked witches on their brooms. It was early, the sun barely brightening the horizon, and we heard thunder, followed a few seconds later by rumbles of more thunder, followed by even more thunder, the echo continuing, like screaming "Hello!" into a canyon.

It was not the familiar echo of a storm over the lake, but something different.

And then we saw them, a horde of wild turkeys, taking flight from the surrounding pines to our yard. You could hardly call it flying, really, because it was more half-assed, drunken, can't-fly-a-straight-line flapping. Though nervous at first around our presence, they slowly warmed to our companionship as well as the corn that we bought at the feed store and tossed around our yard. Since I had no coworkers or latte friends anymore, these turkeys became my "companions." They became the very first to hear what I wrote, as I would stand on our screen porch and read aloud my work while they strutted and pecked at the ground, occasionally looking up at me and clucking, as if to say, "You can do waaaay better, Thoreau!"

"You can't kill them! They're our friends!"

I actually say this.

Out loud.

To this group of hunters.

Who want to kill them.

My words shift them into an ultra-alert stance. They look poised to shoot me.

I know I sound like a whack-job, one of those PETA devotees, the model who protests the fur industry while encased in leather. But I am a lover of the wild turkey, the toms with their hideous red beards that nearly drag the ground, fluffing their proud feathers and strutting, the tactics they use to impress their ladies.

They are ugly-cute. Like Marge.

I analyze the crowd of hunters glaring at me.

OK, this is one of my strengths, I think: I have an innate ability to quickly sum up any competitor, or nemesis, and decide how best to wage battle.

But I quickly realize, as one of the hunters begins to talk about his favorite shotgun, that my superpower was probably only good back in the day when I did battle with wealthy women or gay men, people who used words as weapons instead of live ammunition.

Right now, I am the only one *not* wearing camouflage, the only one who does not look like a moving bush, the only man wearing a pink vintage-fit American Eagle polo and beaded choker. I mean, I would be visible from Mars. I knew I should have worn that cute pair of camouflage pants I just bought at Old Navy.

"What's the bag limit around here?"

The reporter on the local radio had used the term "bag limit," which I figure makes it safe to bandy about in a desperate situation like this. In fact, the reporter had estimated that nearly a hundred thousand hunters would kill over thirty thousand turkeys this season in Michigan. Which basically means that every single person in Michigan hunts turkeys. Except me.

"You know," one of the men says to me, "we got too damn many turkey. They're overpopulated, like the deer. Did *you* know that?"

Remember the movie *Boys Don't Cry?* This is what I picture happening to me.

And then I hear:

"Since U been gone . . . I can breathe for the first time . . ."

It's Gary.

He's calling my cell, a flamingo-pink Razr, which has triggered my Kelly Clarkson ringtone.

I might as well gobble, put the end of a rifle up my ass, and pull the trigger. It would be a less agonizing way to die.

"Get some Hamburger Helper. Cheeseburger Macaroni. That's my favorite. We're having a trailer park supper tonight. Nothing but the best for my baby."

"I'm about to be killed by a group of hunters."

I try to whisper this, of course, but it comes out, "Emmabootshe-keellimagoobahuns."

"Snap! Crackle! Pop!" he says, and hangs up.

I smile broadly at the hunters.

"No, sir. I didn't know that," I say, trying to suppress my panic.

"I didn't think so," the man says. "We use every part of every turkey we kill. We use every part of every deer we kill. We need to feed our families. You folks move from the city . . . you've never had to worry about things like that."

"I live here year-round, sir," I say. "What makes you think I'm from the city?"

The men laugh. And whisper. I realize I'm gesturing with my pink Razr in my pink shirt and pink choker. I am gay Barbie.

This cultural divide is one of the hardest parts of moving back to the country: There is an incredible dichotomy between how I view animals and how many of the locals view animals.

In rural America, animals tend to be animals. Dogs are not adorned in sailor outfits, cats are not declawed, and the only times birds are in a house are when they're mounted to a wall or in an oven. Marge would be living in a doghouse outside during the winter and used for hunting, not bedecked in a Cinco de Mayo bandana, snuggled in our comforter, and taken to the groomer.

I don't eat much red meat anymore. I do eat chicken, turkey breast (though even that pains me more and more), and fish. But what if I couldn't be so picky? What if I didn't have options? What if, quite simply, I had no other option for food than hunting?

"Since U been gone . . . I can breathe for the first time . . ."

Jesus Christ! Mother Mary! And the apostles!

It's Gary again.

"Oooh, and pick up some Rotel, Velveeta, and those frozen Jeno's pizza rolls I used to have as a kid."

The Waffle House

As I walk to my car one morning, two chipmunks confront me—like little furry robbers—as I attempt to open the garage door. They seem pissed that I have encroached upon *their* territory.

"This is my house, kids!" I yell.

They scamper into a little hole at the base of one of our walls—a storage space in the middle of the garage for the lawn mower and garden tools.

"Hey, you little bastards! Come out of there!"

I am poking at them through the hole with the handle of a shovel, but they are too far back, somewhere in the bowels of our house, eating our wires, I'm sure.

"You can poison them, trap them, or just seal them up in their own grave, although the stink is awful bad," a local tells us. "But you have to get rid of them. They're cute, but they're pains in the ass."

But we don't just have chipmunks, I quickly discover. We also have baby rabbits, nestled in little nests along the gardens that border our cottage, two here, three there, five in the hydrangeas, which we watch and nurture, feeding them lettuce and carrots, until they are big enough to stand and then hop over to Gary's flower gardens and whittle them to the ground.

Soon, Gary has only stalks, as if a nuclear bomb that targets only leaves, flowers, and foliage has detonated in the yard. Within weeks, the baby rabbits are as big as VW Bugs.

Locals return with advice. "Cute as hell, aren't they? But they'll ravage your gardens. You can shoot them, poison them, or hit them with a shovel when they're asleep."

This last option intrigues me, in a sick sort of way, like the time Gary and I attended a Leather Night pageant. Gary stuck one of those leather torture gag balls in my mouth, and I squealed like a Christmas pig and posed like Paris while he took pictures with a digital camera. A rather serious leather man—dressed as a cop—was not amused and said I was "mocking the beauty of leather." I pointed at my Banana Republic jacket, belt, and shoes, and angrily mumbled—through the torture ball still crammed in my mouth—"Thith ith the real gay man'th leather, thweety!"

But I can't kill an animal, no matter what they do. I battled a raccoon with lip balm and breath spray. It scared me—like I scared it—but I still didn't want to kill it.

I have an odd connection with animals, probably more so than with people. I will delve into a deep, dark funk once Marge dies. If it were possible for me to have birthed Marge through my mangina, I would have. I worship Marge. I love the way she starts to stink when she hasn't had a bath. I love to nuzzle her ears. She actually kicks Gary out of the way with her paws so she can spoon me. It's creepy but sweet, and I would have it no other way. When I look in her eyes, I see only innocence and love and loyalty. There is no game, no hidden agenda. I cannot say this about many people in my life.

However, since premeditated animal murder is not an option for either the rabbits or the chipmunks, Gary and I instead decide to "displace" them.

We adopt a woodland immigration policy of sorts. Our goal is to relocate them back to their home turf instead of burying them alive in a wall or striking them with anvils. We begin to capture them—in traps and Tupperware containers, using veggies and corn and peanut butter—and then drive them a few miles away (in my car, of course, which is used for all the dirty work), where we dump their furry little asses in the middle of nowhere, which we deem is far enough away from our middle of nowhere.

The first time we attempt to relocate a horde of woodland creatures, I feel, as I drive, like I'm in the middle of a scene from *Enchanted*.

We dump an entire batch of rabbits and chipmunks into an empty field, waving good-bye, but as we begin to pull away, we hear a distinct thump and then what sounds like a tennis shoe in the spin cycle of a washer.

"What the hell was that?" Gary asks.

I get out of the car and look underneath it, and then glance back up at Gary as though I just found Jimmy Hoffa.

"Oh, my God! No!" he cries. "Do you think it's OK?"

Considering it now looks like a bloody waffle, I'm guessing no.

Gary is, quite literally, crying and screaming, "Bugs! We killed Bugs Bunny!"

"Stop it," I beg. "You're making me feel like shit."

"You should. You could've swerved."

"I didn't even see it. It was Stealth Rabbit."

"Well, you could have swerved. That's all I'm saying. Let me drive."

And then, as God is my witness, we hear a similar ka-thunk-a-thunk, and when I look under the car once again, Gary has crushed a chipmunk.

"It's not a rabbit, at least," I say.

"They were attached to us!" he cries. "We fed them. They knew our voices. Oh, my God. Look again. Is it alive?"

Considering the tire is still resting on it, I'm guessing no.

This time, Gary makes me stand outside the car and watch for any other suicidal animals as he pulls back onto the side of the road.

Un-Stable Boy

We live roughly a mile from a horse stable, and when the winds are calm, or when it is silent after a winter's snowstorm, you can hear the ponies laugh and the jackasses whinny.

When the winds are blowing, you can also smell their shit.

Sometimes, Gary and I like to walk Marge up our little road to watch the horses, which she—by her intimidated reaction—thinks are big dogs.

Sometimes, the horses wear adorably trendy little outfits, and we like to imagine that they're headed to dinner somewhere very nice, like Spago.

Someplace with candles. And sugar cubes. And hay.

Like all gay city boys, Gary and I humanize animals, making every pig Babe, every skunk Pepe LePew, every deer Bambi, and every field mouse Fievel Goes West. So it is with our horse neighbors down the street.

One spring day, when the wind is whipping the new leaves off the trees, we take a drive through the country and notice a horse farm in an inland town that we have yet to visit. We stop in order to critique the horses' outfits and are so amused by our repartee that we say to the horses' owners, "Is there a wedding? Or a horse fund-raiser?"

The owners cock their heads, just like the horses. They do not see the incredible adorableness of their own animals, which irks me. I mean, Marge is wearing a spring bandana, resplendent in bright tulips.

She looks as though she should be holding a Gucci bag and an iced mocha.

I am lost in this thought when the owners ask, "Wanna go for a ride?"

Gary yells "Yes!" while I shake my head no.

We view horses very differently.

Gary loves being around horses.

I love being around horses, too. Preferably from a private suite at the finish line with a daiquiri in my hand and a pane of Plexiglas to separate us.

Gary loves riding a horse.

I prefer getting mounted.

And still I find myself, mere moments later, attempting to top a rather bony but boyishly handsome horse named Zeus, which I believe looks a lot like an equine Justin Timberlake.

Mind you, I am not, nor will I ever be, "dressed to ride." I am wearing jeans so tight that the oversize buttons on the pockets have ground into my ass cheeks, making it possible to plant a large-size birch tree; long, long, pointy, pointy shoes, which look like leather canoes; a tight, stretchy Lycra-blend Banana Republic long-sleeve shirt that looks like a wetsuit; and knockoff Chanel sunglasses. I am wearing multiple chokers, a leather bracelet, and a silver ring. I should be in a photo shoot for *Metropolitan Home,* not trying to climb onto the bony ass of a horse in a windstorm.

I mean, I cannot even mount my horse. None of my clothes has enough give to allow me to actually bend a limb, which is the reason I had previously been leaning rigidly against the leather seat in Gary's SUV like a bolt of fabric.

I look up, and Gary is already prancing around the perimeter of the stable like Elizabeth Taylor in *National Velvet.*

I try repeatedly to jump and mount my horse, like I've been instructed, but to no avail. Finally, from out of nowhere, two hands grip my ass and lift me onto the horse, like I'm a ballerina.

"Grab the reins," a voice says.

I look down and a stable boy with dusty blond locks and a sexy cowboy hat is holding my horse still. I swivel my head in a circle.

Gary is still riding Secretariat, making weird horse command noises with his tongue.

The stable boy smiles at me.

"Grab what?" I ask.

"Here." He hands me the reins and provides a rundown of instructions.

I lick my already dry lips and smile coyly.

I feel like I am about to be in a bad direct-to-DVD porn movie.

I kick Zeus with my pointy shoes, which are obviously too pointy, because he takes off across the stable like a missile.

"Pull back on the reins," the stable boy yells.

I pull back. The horse stops.

With a touch more instruction, I get it down and ride Zeus for about ten minutes, until my legs go numb and my nipples are chafed.

I motion to Gary that I'm stopping, and the stable boy helps me off the horse. I briefly want him to spoon me for a while, to make me pancakes and cowboy coffee over an open fire, to *Brokeback Mountain* me, but Gary is yelling, "Get the digital camera!" so I end up taking pictures of my man, who is a very good horse rider, and spend the rest of the day feeling very much like I just got banged.

He's Baa-aack!

Something, it seems, is crawling up our trees, deck, and porch, and literally ripping the bird feeders open, shredding the little cages, destroying the cute perches. Our adorable deco feeders look as if they've been struck by lightning.

All our birds—the iridescent blue indigo buntings, like the ones that carried the train of Cinderella's dress; the ruby-red-throated woodpeckers; the fragile hummingbirds; the cardinals; the yield-sign-yellow-finches—flap around the screen porch, looking in at us, wings on hips, as if to say, "Hello? What's going on around here?"

"Raccoons," neighbors tell us. "They'll destroy anything."

We already knew, considering our trash was still being ransacked every week.

I remember as a kid at our log cabin at Sugar Creek how raccoons could open anything. They could pop open our minnow buckets, which we left sitting in the spring, even when we wired them shut. They would rip fish right off the stringer, leaving just the lips attached. Raccoons are cunning little thieves who can quietly rob the shirt off your back without you even knowing.

I should know. My original raccoon nemesis even stole my super-shimmery lip balm, which means war in my world.

Gary and I hung a bird feeder on the side of our house—on the deck just beyond our screen porch—sticking it to a window overlooking the woods. Finches flock to this feeder, extracting sunflower seeds from it. All day long, I hear alternating sounds of singing and knocking as birds land, eat, and take flight, banging the feeder against the window. This morning, I discovered that the feeder had been ripped off the window, and the majority of the paint had been clawed off of it as well. The plastic cylinder holding the seed had been torn open, and it sat empty, like the carcass of an antelope in the desert.

I had walked outside to inspect; bending down, I noticed a pile of poop on our deck near the feeder. Upon further inspection, I saw something bright and plastic-y. I knelt and studied the hunk of crap. Scraps of a lip balm tube were layered in the poop, like an edgy Andy Warhol pop art project, like Andy decided to create cutting-edge collages from excrement and newspaper headlines.

The poop art said, more or less, BURT'S BEES.

My raccoon!

Was this his work?

I believed it was, because the rabid bastard certainly had impeccable taste.

You Will Pay for This

I wait with a flashlight on the screen porch, like I'm Judith Light waiting to exact revenge on my rapist in a Lifetime movie.

Gary and I have strewn a line of trash—chicken bones, corn, potato skins, and lettuce leaves—leading to a suet-filled bird feeder. It's a trap for my raccoon. Literally. We cannot kill our tormentor, so we will relocate him, just like we tried to do with our bunnies and chipmunks.

It's not cute anymore, all the destruction and mayhem. The bottom line is this: We are spending a minimum of $100 a month to feed the birds and purchase new feeders to replace the damaged ones. We spend another $20 on corn for the wild turkeys and $20 on salt licks for the deer. This does not include flowers. If I had a child, he would not be going to college. I would be sitting him on the edge of his bed, explaining, "Listen, we love you, but your daddies have spent your tuition money on sunflower seeds and wayward animals."

There is a soft breeze tonight, and between the rustling of the leaves, we can hear things rustling in the woods. We wait, occasionally turning on the flashlight and shining it into the vast darkness. After an hour, we have no guest. After two, we have fallen asleep on the porch. Gary begins snoring loudly, which wakes me.

Out of boredom, I shine the flashlight into his open mouth. His cheeks turn red. He looks like a human jack-o'-lantern.

I lean in and point the flashlight down his throat. I didn't know he had that many gold fillings. I could buy a Viper with his dental work.

And then I hear a noise and zip my flashlight toward it, taking part of Gary's jawbone along with it.

There is my masked boyfriend, sitting on his hind legs, eating my food, oblivious to my emotions, just like all my past lovers.

Damn you, Burt! I think.

I nudge Gary awake. A string of drool dangles from his arm to his mouth, like a spit jump rope. He sees the spotlighted raccoon and goes, "Wha'?"

"It's Burt!" I say.

"Who?" Gary asks. "The raccoon has a name?"

"Yes. Burt. I've named him after my lip shimmer."

Gary claps twice to try to scare the raccoon, but Burt isn't afraid. He likes the attention. He's like an animal Nathan Lane.

He picks up a hunk of bread, fake washes it, holds it out for us to see, analyzes it, and then devours it before grabbing a chunk of chicken.

He looks kind of cute, not like the rabid beast that rode my head.

My God, he *is* just like my old boyfriends.

"How do you know that's him?" Gary asks. "There are probably a zillion raccoons out here."

"I know," I say. "I know. It sounds crazy. But look at him. No other raccoon has that much moxie. And he had seven rings on his tail. I counted when it was flipped over my shoulder. Burt has seven rings. Count 'em. Oh, and he had a notched ear, like someone had three-hole-punched it."

Our neighbors have told us that coons like one of my personal favorite snack foods, marshmallows (all sugar, no fat!), so we have loaded those in the trap, along with chicken, corn, and dog food. Our trap is a wire mesh cage with a spring-loaded door. When the raccoon enters, the door will shut, just like the Bat Cave, and we can then relocate Burt, preferably to Saskatchewan.

But this is not what happens. For the next half hour, Burt is a virtual Criss Angel, picking and plucking food from the trap, squeezing its furry ass around the trip without slamming the door shut. No wonder raccoons can uncork wine bottles and pick pocket lint from your navel. Burt has all the grace and dexterity I lack.

Thinking that Burt simply needs a big surprise to trigger the door, Gary screams something along the lines of "Whoozawoozamoozit!"

Burt turns, staring into our flashlight, and then seems to point at me and cackle, scaring the shit out of me, like Robert De Niro did in *Cape Fear* when he went to the movie theater and sat behind Nick Nolte and Jessica Lange.

Then Burt calmly exits the cage, picking out the last few crumbs of food without setting off the trapdoor, and proceeds to climb the cute little gate we have on the back porch and terrorize our latest bird feeder.

"That's enough! This isn't Denny's!" I scream. "Get out of here, you stinky little bastard!"

The raccoon, finally scared, remembering those exact words and, I'm sure, my voice from its previous attack, scrambles down the porch and into the woods, stuffed from the free buffet.

"What are we gonna do?" I ask Gary. "We can't kill him. We can't catch him. We can't destroy him. He's like Michael Myers."

Rest in Peace

I take Marge for a walk in our woods a few days later. She is finally getting acclimated to a life with no sidewalks, although Gary's mulched and carefully manicured trails are a nice substitute.

We walk along a trail that meanders along our neighbor's vast property. Our neighbors have trenched a creek that runs through their land, near the outer edges of their blueberry fields, and it flows steadily in the spring, after the snow has melted and the rains have come. When it begins to dry in the summer, a carpet of ferns—of every shape, size, and variety—blankets the creek bed.

This day, as Marge charges through the woods, the scent of something new directing her right and then left and then right again, I stop to stare at a fern that is *Jurassic Park* big. It stands, from the bottom of the creek bed, which is roughly three feet deep, nearly to my waist. Its base is as thick as the trunk of a baby birch, and yet its leaves are tender and fringed.

And then I hear the buzzing. The thick, sick sound of buzzing flies swarming something dead. I look into the creek bed, through the forest of ferns, and see the tail of a raccoon. There are seven thick rings. My heart jumps.

I reangle my body, and it is then I see the head, split wide open, flies dining on the open eye and brain. I start to turn away, sick from the view, and my movement dispels the flies for an instant, just long enough for me to see an ear: It is notched.

Burt!

I scoot down the hill and into the creek bed, moving back the ferns, and find Burt, dead and bloated, his head open, his body severely scarred, as though he has been attacked by another animal, perhaps a coyote. Marge tries to get closer, but I hold her at bay.

It seems silly, but I kneel beside Burt and stare into his face. The defiance is gone, his body just a shell now being eaten by flies. I have an overwhelming urge to cry, to mourn his passing. He was, in many ways, my first country frenemy.

I cannot leave Burt like this.

I trudge back along the trail and retrieve a shovel and trash bag from home. When Gary gets home, I tell him the news, on the verge of tears.

"This is just silly, right?" I ask, my lip quivering.

Gary digs a little grave on the edge of our woods, and we bury Burt. For a cross, I lash together two tubes of lip shimmer with string.

It just seems fitting.

Later in the evening, as we have dinner on the screen porch, we look out to discover that Marge has been trying to unearth Burt. In doing so, it seems, she had become intrigued by the smell of the lip-balm cross and somehow managed to open and eat the contents, which has coated her lips, mouth, chin, and snout in shiny, shimmering jelly.

"You're beautiful!" I yell, half laughing, half crying.

Doe, a Deer, a Female Deer

A few weeks later, Gary and I go for a walk through the woods. I am inexplicably sad over the death of Burt and feel bizarrely responsible for it. I encroached onto his home. He was fine before we came. He would still be here if it weren't for me.

As we walk, Marge bays loudly and then stiffens, pointing at a grove of trees just beyond the running creek. We squint into the woods, and there, lying in a pile of leaves and sticks, is a baby deer. Marge jumps the creek and begins pawing at the leaves surrounding the baby, sniffing her find.

"Leave it, girl," Gary yells.

The deer is shaking, and it sounds as though it is choking.

"She's dying!" I cry.

But Gary, Mr. Nature, calmly explains she is simply clearing her lungs, like any newborn, and that the mother is most likely standing nearby, frightened away by our arrival.

We walk on, hiding behind a thicket of overgrown underbrush, and eventually the mother returns. She begins licking her baby, standing over it, protective and on guard. We stand this way for what seems like an eternity, and, finally, the baby stands, wobbly, shaking, like a child taking its first steps. It makes its way through the forest, slowly at first, and then it is off, a kid showing its energy.

We have our hands clamped over Marge's jaw so she won't bark, and when Gary and I finally look at each other, we are crying.

Wade's Walden—4. Modern Society—3.

LESSON EIGHT
Rediscover Religion

God himself culminates in the present moment, and will never be more divine in the
lapse of all the ages. And we are enabled
to apprehend at all what is sublime and
noble only by the perpetual instilling and
drenching of the reality that surrounds us.

—Henry David Thoreau, *Walden*

Why Is There Never Pot at a Potluck?

Gary and I have been asked to attend a potluck at a local church in order to "meet some nice folks."

Gary decides to go because he doesn't want to seem impolite, doesn't want to alienate anyone in a small town lest he be ostracized forever, and, most notably, doesn't want anyone to miss out on his "famed" cheesy hash brown casserole.

If any event, no matter how pathetic—be it a Tupperware party, a fund-raiser for Rick Santorum, or an orgy of octogenarians—involves bringing a casserole, Gary is there.

I go only because I feel deep down that if you say no to something involving a church it's bad karma, like the time I snatched an old woman's parking place before a wedding and then proceeded to shut the car door on my toe.

The church to which we have been invited is small, white, and old, like Helen Hayes, and it sits alone on the edge of a field in one of those barren spots that always seems to get decimated by a tornado, and people are surprised when it happens, although five men with average lung capacity could probably blow this church off its foundation.

In my lifelong search for religion, which constitutes Life Lesson Eight, I have attended enough church potlucks to last a lifetime, been handed hundreds of bowls of chili along with innumerable paths to salvation. It almost worked once, when I nearly became a Seventh-Day Adventist because the recruiter looked like Orlando Bloom.

I thought I needed saving at one time in my life—from myself, my sins—but I ended up finding myself, saving myself, and then finding God as an adult. I believe that I discovered religion without outside interference, and, as a result, received my own personal cell phone—with no lost calls—to God.

I believe it is painful but necessary to fall, fail, and be shunned before true faith can be found in this world.

And though I am happy with my relationship with God, I still question myself.

Do I need organized religion?

Do I need to attend church?

Though I have faith, do I need to be surrounded by the "faithful"?

I knew religion would be a struggle once again in rural America, where many folks wear their beliefs on their sleeves.

And perhaps my cantankerous relationship with organized religion is why I have chosen not to wear sleeves tonight at all, but rather a flaming red Abercrombie tank top that looks like body paint.

If the congregation doesn't like it, they can kiss my devil's tail.

This is a fitting analogy, by the way, considering it's about 480 degrees in the church basement.

"It's hotter than hell down here," Gary whispers.

"That's because we're in hell," I say, rolling my eyes toward a woman the size of a Viking who is sitting alone at a table, protecting with her meaty forearms at least five bowls of stew and ten plates filled with dips and chips and cakes, as if an army of her peers were going to rush in to pillage the Crock Pots and loot her Chinet.

The Viking is wearing a caftan featuring an embroidered Holly Hobby–ish cat. She is plucking a ham hock or bone or hoof or something from her bowl and is gnawing the marrow out of it.

"My pussy is hungry." This is what I whisper to Gary. "That's what her enormous shift should really say. And why are cat clothes so popular in the country?"

Gary aspirates his breath mint and tells me politely to "shut the hell up."

Our hushed merriment inspires an immediate visit from one of the church fellows, who instantly starts talking to us about the church, the importance of community, the way of the Lord.

"We're glad you're here. We're glad you've come home," he says.

I smile.

"Do you *believe*?" he asks me.

"Oh, yes. In many things," I say.

Like fashion, for instance.

The man is wearing a bolo. *If you had truly talked to the Lord today,* I'm thinking, *He would have told you to wear a real tie.*

The elder escorts us to the kitchen, which looks kind of like the one Ma used in *The Texas Chain Saw Massacre*.

"Hash brown casserole!" Gary screams excitedly to a group of women who obviously have never heard of this amazing little invention called the tweezer.

This is more painful and intrusive than my hernia surgery, I think. *And why is there never pot at a potluck? It's when you need it the most.*

The last time I participated in what I would call organized religion was when I was an early teen and my mother sent me to a rural church camp.

Like most teenagers, I went through that phase of surly indignation where every word my parents uttered was met with a scowl, a smirk, a put-down. Much to the chagrin of my mother, a woman of great faith, my favorite term to convey parental annoyance was "God!"

With each shout-out to our Lord and Savior, my mother recoiled, her eyes darting around nervously as though she expected God Himself to appear before us and smite me down.

"James Wade! I will not tolerate that language in this house, do you understand me? It's disrespectful. Do you think the Lord stands around and says, 'Oh, my Wade!' or 'For Wade's sake'?"

"God, Mom, whatever."

And then my mother came home from work one day just before school was to end for the summer—ensconced in her bloodstained nurse's scrubs—and found me lying in my usual place: on a beanbag in front of the TV upstairs, surrounded by Funyons and French onion dip, watching reruns of *I Love Lucy*.

She stood between me and the TV.

"God, Mom! Move!" I remember saying. "Lucy and Ethel are going to charm school!"

She held in front of my face a poorly Xeroxed pamphlet featuring ink-smeared crooked crosses and paper so thin you could see through it.

"Jesus! Was that professionally designed?" I said, pushing it out of my face.

"Church camp," she said to me, tossing the brochure onto our heavy, dark wood living room coffee table, which was covered with water rings that looked like crop circles. "You need an attitude adjustment."

So just a few weeks later, on a blistering June morning, I was dropped off—quite literally—in the middle of a hay field, holding two trash bags filled with clothes.

My mother did a smart-ass wave good-bye and tore down the dirt road in our Rambler, leaving me alone in a cloud of dust, surrounded by nothing but hay, a prefabricated church, and a U of trailers behind it.

Before she disappeared, however, I saw her face in the mirror, and I could swear that she was crying. It was then I knew: My mom just wanted me to make friends. She just wanted me to be respectful. More than anything, she just wanted me to be OK the first summer after my brother died, and she wasn't quite sure if I—or any of us—ever would be again.

It was then I noticed that the church's weather-warped, hand-lettered sign read GOD HATES SINERS! instead of GOD HATES SINNERS!, a statement that summed up the area and era in which I was raised. It was a time and culture long before church signs carried cute, clever religious ad slogans like "Got God?" or "Hot outside? Come on in, we have prayer conditioning."

Ozarks church slogans were simple and direct, always slightly threatening.

I stared at the sign, irritated by the typo, a precursor to my brief career as a copy editor and a curse with which I would always live; to this day I proof restaurant menus and alert waiters and waitresses to the horrifying fact that they are serving a Wafle Breakfast or Hamburfer Basket.

I was wearing my favorite school outfit the day I was handed over to the Lord—a knockoff pink Polo, Husky jeans, a gold chain that held a dangling lightning bolt, an armful of multicolored rubber bracelets, and white Keds whose laces were covered in "friendship pins"—when I was suddenly greeted by a swarm of pasty teens: makeup-free girls who wore their waist-length hair pulled back with bobby pins and ankle-length denim skirts, and boys in overalls and long-sleeve flannel shirts.

Dark rings of sweat had pooled under my arms and boy-breasts, turning my pink polo a bloody red. Suddenly, there were shouts of "Amen!" and "Praise the Lord!"

My magical appearance in this dust bowl, it seemed, was a sign of either the Apocalypse or the Resurrection.

My first thought? *Jesus, what a bunch of freaks.*

I spent a week with "the God Squad," as I instantly termed them, and a large part of our "redemption" involved child labor.

Every day, we performed chores. We baled hay, we cleaned floors, we patched roads. And then, every night, after a dinner of chicken nuggets and mushy fries, we thanked God for our hideous food and back-breaking day.

For two hours every evening, the camp held a church service and testimony, the highlight of which was when a woman I'll call Millie Jo channeled the Lord by speaking in tongues.

I, of course, could never discern the Lord's voice in Millie Jo's. I only heard Millie Jo screeching in a heavy Ozarks twang, "Hebbedy, humma, modderuhzizo!" before being lifted off the floor, presumably by God, and tossed rather unceremoniously around; she continued writhing for nearly a half hour, breaking only toward the end to re-trieve a cup of stale coffee.

The second night or so, when it came time for lights-out in the boys' bunkhouse trailer, I asked aloud if Millie Jo could really speak in tongues.

And a boy, whom I had not yet seen during my time with the God Squad, walked into our sleeping quarters wearing only a pair of white briefs and said, "She can speak in tongues. And so can I."

His name, I believe, was Carl, and I remember him saying that he traveled around to different youth camps giving testimony.

He said, basically, "The Lord speaks through me; I am His instru-ment. You have to let yourself go, feel the words of God, feel the power of God, feel His presence wherever you may be, let him into your body, and he will fill your soul. When I speak, my words become His words, my actions His. I cannot contain His glory, and so it must come out."

His voice, so deep, so confident, gave me a boner.

I knew I shouldn't harbor bad thoughts about a prophet, but I couldn't help it. I desperately wanted to play Carl's instrument, just like God.

But then I wondered why God would come to a series of trailers in the middle of nowhere and speak through Carl and Millie Jo. Wasn't that a lot of the Lord's focus on just a hay field in the Ozarks?

To impress Carl, I began studying his and Millie Jo's techniques, the way they fell to the floor, their vocal inflections and word patterns.

Every night, I followed Carl around like a groupie. "You were amazing tonight," I'd say. "That was your best tongue thing yet."

Carl tended to talk to me like I was a puppy. "Thank you," he would say softly, the dim lights in the bunk room illuminating his body. "Did you have a good talk with the Lord tonight?"

"Uh-huh," I would say, waiting for him to strip and get into bed in his underwear.

Carl's body was perfect. He was tan, toned, and had that damn little trail of hair disappearing into his tighty whities.

Toward the end of my week at church camp, I could tell that Carl was getting impatient that I hadn't been as committed to the program as he and others had been. "Why haven't you given testimony yet?" he asked. "Everyone else has. Don't you have something to say to the Lord?"

And I did.

I wanted to ask Him how He could be cruel enough to take my brother and leave me alone in rural America. I wanted to ask Him why I liked boys, no matter how many Farrah Fawcett or Raquel Welch posters I hung in my room. I wanted to ask him when it would be OK to stop hating myself. I wanted to ask God how many blows I was going to take and if my faith was supposed to be shaken and rocked at such an early age in order for me to fully grasp what faith is all about.

So, that night, when the pastor announced that it was time for testimony, I walked to the front of the prayer trailer and said aloud, "I feel closer to God than I have in a long time. I can feel His spirit in me.

"My brother died last summer . . ." I hesitated, taking a deep breath, and the crowd immediately stopped fanning themselves with their hands, almost as if I had pushed Pause on a remote. "I still can't believe he's gone. It's not fair. I . . . miss . . . him.

"I'm just thankful that God has taken such good care of me and my family," I said, not believing a word of it. "I can feel Him in my life."

People began to softly say, "Amen!"

"I can feel Him!" I started to scream. "I can feel Him!"

People were standing now, screaming, "Amen, brother! Amen!"

I felt emboldened.

"Amen, brother! Feel His presence!"

"Hebbedy, humma, mettahuzzo!" I screamed. "Hebbedy, humma, mettahuzzo!"

And with that, I was on the floor, rolling partway down the aisle, desperately trying to aim my body toward Carl, who was seated a few rows back. But my chubby body was not meant for rolling, unless it was into a very shallow grave by a very strong murderer, and I found myself lodged under an empty folding chair, my lightning bolt chain somehow managing to hook itself under one of the legs. I popped an eye open to see if he was still watching me. Carl was yelling, "Praise the Lord!" so I kicked over the chair that my necklace was caught on and continued rolling until I ran into his leg.

"Hebbedy, humma, mettahuzzo," I chanted. "Hebbedy, humma, mettahuzzo!"

Suddenly, I fell silent and lay there stiffly, letting a little drool fall out one side of my mouth. I felt someone's hands on my chest. I was being touched by Carl, which was way better than being touched by God.

"You understand now."

He was looking at me with his dark brown doe eyes, his polyester dress shirt clinging to his perfect body. I had already forgiven him for his clothes; I could change that.

He helped me off the ground and put his arm around me. I leaned in, for just a second, and put my head on his strong shoulder.

I popped testimony wood.

And then camp kids and parishioners began to flock to me, offering their blessings, and Carl slipped away.

After the service, I searched the grounds, nabbing a dreamsicle out of the cafeteria freezer to cool my body and soul on this hot and steamy night. But Carl was nowhere to be found. I walked outside, feeling terribly guilty about my Oscar-worthy performance. I still couldn't believe my brother was gone, and I honestly didn't feel like God had taken such good care of my family.

He, I honestly believed, had turned his back on us.

I walked toward the hay barn, and suddenly I had my first vision: I saw God spit in my face.

In the distance, I could see Carl making out with a girl who looked like Marie Osmond.

"Hebbedy, humma, mettahuzzo!" I screamed, spewing orange juice everywhere. "I hate you!"

Carl and Marie looked over at me, confused, and started kissing again.

And it was then I realized that Carl was lying, too, doing exactly what people expected of him and then, when no one was looking, doing what he wanted.

There was really only one tongue he was interested in, and it wasn't mine or God's.

By week's end at church camp, I actually looked forward to the time we had set aside for silent reflection.

It was my time to look God in the eye.

I had already spent much of life trying to avoid direct eye contact with God—like I did country dogs that people kept chained to a post all winter—worried that He would see into my soul, see my darkest secrets, know what I was thinking, and want to rip me apart.

But, sitting alone there, in that tiny church that fronted a makeshift prayer compound of trailers, was the first time I actually realized that God already knew me, inside and out. It was the first time I had inklings that perhaps, just perhaps, I had been born gay and that this was simply a part of who I was. And whether others saw that as good or bad, it was—like getting brown eyes instead of blue, freckles instead of perfect skin, red hair and not blond—the way it was supposed to be.

It was God's will.

I addressed God personally in these moments of reflection and sought His guidance. For a few hours this one week, I did not beg for him to change who I was, nor did I wish to be dead, like my brother; I only wanted to talk and listen.

It was a short period of time in my youth when I allowed myself to release all my anger, my tears, and my frustration, when I allowed myself to scream at my brother for leaving me, at God for taking him, at myself for never telling him I loved him.

And when I began to go hoarse, I listened to God speak in the humid silence of that church. And, for the first time, I found just a sliver of peace, a sliver of hope that brought tears to my eyes, tears of red and green and gold and violet, which reflected the colors of the lone stained glass window, falling down my cheeks, the colors rolling away, like the morning sun on the ripples of Sugar Creek as they danced downstream.

God *was* speaking to me, and I realized I didn't have to speak in tongues to be heard.

I "graduated" from church camp during a huge outdoor revival on a Saturday evening.

Throngs of men, women, and children—every inch of skin covered, even in the sweltering heat—spilled out of dusty pickups and rusty Gremlins carrying dog-eared Bibles and Snickers bars and giant Big Gulps.

Often, those "matriculating" from neighboring church camps would be invited, along with their families, to one of these revivals, the hidden goal, I believe, to recruit members before they were tossed back out into the unwashed masses.

I remember my parents showing up to my coming-out party, my mother vaporizing from our Rambler dressed like she was heading on over to Studio 54. She was bedazzled in black gaucho pants that flared like parachutes at the bottom, a sleeveless black top with overlapping pieces of fabric that billowed when she walked, a flowy black linen jacket, a gold cross around her neck big enough to make the Pope jealous, and strappy gold heels, my father trailing behind her chugging a can of Coors.

My parents looked like Elizabeth Taylor and Richard Burton.

Worshippers crammed into a single tent, the overflow hanging outside, the flaps of the brightly lit tent pulled back and pinned like the too-long bangs of the Mennonite girls.

Without warning, without hymnals, the crowd began to sing, everyone knowing every word to every song, it seemed, except us. I looked at my mother, panic stricken, and she mouthed, "Banana," which was our way of covering in church when people sang hymns with which we weren't familiar. *Banana* had a lot of syllables and it worked the entire mouth—lips and tongue—so that it looked like you were in sync with the group when you were actually clueless. For ten minutes, my mother and I fake-sang *banana* over and over, my father standing like a mute, nervously fingering the can of once-cold Coors he had shoved into his pants pocket.

The pastor, on cue, sprinted into the tent from outside and asked that all church campers and their families stand to be recognized.

"Amen!" the crowd said to us as we rose from our seats. "The Lord loves you!"

My mother looked around in shock, really looked around at those surrounding us, finally realizing where she had sent me and what she had subjected me to for a week.

"Oh, my God, I'm so sorry!" she said to me.

"Don't say *God,* Mother!" I mouthed.

She smiled appreciatively.

And then the preacher began to whip the crowd into his typical frenzy, screaming, "Do you love the Lord? How much do you love the Lord? Show me how much you love the Lord!"

The crowd broke into song, and my mother, feeling the power, began to sway, slowly at first, then with her hips, and then she was off, dancing, boogying, clapping, snapping her fingers, lifting her feet, and twisting back and forth. A large swath around us suddenly stopped— like when a certain section of the crowd at a football game decides it no longer wants to do the wave—and stared aghast at my mother, who was boogying and singing, "Banana! Banana! Banana!"

A man with muttonchops and one of those mustaches that's not really a mustache anymore but a criminal offense looked at my mother like he wanted to burn her at the stake, like he actually had experience in human sacrifices, and yelled, "There is no dancin' here, lady! *No dancin'!*"

My mom stopped, startled, and stared at the man.

"Dancin' is an abomination to the Lord," a heavy, sweaty woman in a denim jumper added somewhat apologetically to my mom, nodding her head.

"I don't understand," my mother said.

"No dancin'!" the man's mustache bellowed.

And like a perfectly timed movie moment, the crowd quieted and my mother yelled, "Have you all even read the Bible?"

People gasped, and my father stepped forward and raised his fists like there was going to be a brawl of biblical proportion.

"Dancing to honor God is a big part of the Bible," my mother shouted. "There's more dancing in the Bible than *West Side Story.*"

And in the silence of that tent, my father simply popped the top of his stowaway beer and said, "The Rouses are outta here!"

When we got home, my dad said, "No more church camp, boy," and headed to bed.

I stayed up with my mother, who had apologized to me nonstop since we got in the car.

I said, "You're all dressed up and didn't even get to dance," so I played my Kool and the Gang album, and we danced to "Ladies' Night."

The next morning, a Sunday, I woke early—used to my morning camp routine for at least another day—and asked my mother if she would like to go to church. She was standing in the kitchen, making coffee, in her short pink, fluffy bathrobe that my dad said made her look like a Playboy Bunny. Tears welled in her eyes.

"No, but I'm glad you asked. Someone finally asked," she said softly, her voice cracking. "My faith has been so tested, Wade. My relationship with God so rocked. Would you mind sitting with me in the family room while I read the Bible?"

And slowly, this became our Sunday routine; our church became the family room in the woods or the bluff beside our cabin or the patio outside under the giant elm—the best churches I've ever attended— my mother reading, me listening and asking questions, finally understanding what true faith means, that in the face of unimaginable tragedy there is hope, there is always hope.

"Who wants more casserole?"

Gary is sashaying around the church basement, now wearing an apron and oven mitt.

"It's hot and cheesy!"

He *is* Bree from *Desperate Housewives*. Except with a pronounced Adam's apple.

I can't take it anymore, so I play one of our favorite "bored games." When bored out of our minds at certain events, Gary and I will look around a setting—be it a restaurant, an amusement park line, a fundraiser, a movie theater, a gas station—and ask, "If you were single again and were forced at gunpoint to choose only one person here to sleep with, who would it be and why?"

I look over at Gary.

"Lots of melty cheese, right?" he asks as the women tear into the casserole with plastic spoons.

I am free to analyze.

But my options are sadly limited.

Most of the men in the church basement are wearing overalls, or suspenders, like country Larry Kings.

Now, there's a lot to be said for a "fixer-upper," especially once you get him naked, but there's no one here I'd like to see unclothed. Lots of "dunlaps"—the stomach has "done lapped over their privates"—and a lot of apron bellies, the kind they cut off and hold up to the camera on those extreme makeover shows.

Then a woman eating an entire lemon meringue pie straight out of the tin and a man with one of those creepy Amish beards that doesn't have a mustache suddenly part ways to expose a virtual Brad Pitt.

OK, so he's not Brad Pitt, but in this crowd, he looks very close, despite the severe part in his hair and the fact he has way too much gumline in proportion to his teeth. But a good dentist can stretch those gums, and a stylist can revamp his hair. The important things are that he's naturally blond, in very good I've-just-jumped-off-a-tractor kind of shape, and wearing jeans that make it look as though he's smuggling a cantaloupe in his crotch.

Brothers and sisters, we have a winner. Amen!

I stare.

Too long.

At his crotch.

In a church.

He busts me.

Usually, I'm a good starer. I can glance and turn away. Gary and my mother are the worst starers in the world. They stare like they're watching *Dancing with the Stars.*

"It's not TV," I tell them when we're out in public. "You're not home alone. You cannot just stare with a glazed-over expression. These are real people."

Doesn't matter. They stare, especially at restaurants, and then talk about the people while they continue to stare, and then point at them. And now, this annoying habit is beginning to rub off on me.

And then this guy scratches his cantaloupe.

While staring back at me.

I try to grab Gary while still staring but graze the church elder in the process.

"Question, young man?" he asks.

"Who's that guy over there?" This just comes out, because I have nothing else to say.

"Oh, that's Elder Diggleworth's son. He works the family farm."

"Married man?" I ask.

Now Gary glares at me.

"No. A bachelor. Still on the search for a God-fearing woman."

"Mmm-hmmm," I say, twisting the words to fit what I want to hear.

"Excuse us," Gary finally says, extricating himself from the group and dragging me into a corner by the refrigerator, which smells like bleach and onions. "What are you doing? This is a church."

"I'm just playing our game. I'm bored. Who would you pick?"

"We can't do this right now. What's wrong with you?"

But, because Gary is Gary, he still searches the room before eye-pointing at a very tall man who looks like Larry Bird. "You're full of crap," I whisper. "There is no way."

"Look how tall he is. I'm sure his thingy is gigantic."

I look at Gary and laugh. We are officially going to hell.

But then I think, *Why?*

We are good people. And we try hard to be good people. We believe in God. Our faith is important to us. But we hold it close to our souls, like family. We do not brandish it around violently like a firearm. We believe deeply, but we have been disenfranchised by religion. So why should we choose to participate in something that fights so hard to keep us out?

I am well aware of the scriptures that seem to condemn me. I have read the Bible. I have studied the Bible. But we all fall short, every day, in one way or another. Our goal is to try to make the right decisions, to be good people. When all is said and done, I believe our final spiritual test will be akin to *Who Wants to Be a Millionaire?*: Each of us, one-on-one, with God, trying to answer some hard-ass questions. And all without a phone-a-friend or fifty-fifty.

I study the church crowd again. Kids are talking about summer camp. People are talking about holding a fund-raiser for a family whose mother has cancer. I am a cynical son of a bitch. These people have invited us here as a *couple,* knowing we are together, that we are one. This is a first in my life. They aren't judging me. I am judging them.

I take Gary by the arm, grab a bowl of ham and beans, and make an attempt to talk to the man in the bolo, who is now chatting with the Viking.

He tells us that we are all God's creations and that we are perfect. We all sin, but we must strive to be good human beings. Part of me wants very much to cry, to run upstairs and fall on the little wooden altar and tell God that I'm sorry and happy and trying to do what's right in life, and that I sometimes fail, and, occasionally, succeed. I can even feel my lip quiver and a palsy in my cheek.

But then, suddenly, the man and the Viking start giving me and Gary the full-court biblical press to attend their church, telling us "it is the only way to get to know your Lord and Savior" and that "our way is the *true* way."

Which is why another part of me—the bigger part, actually—wants to rip off the man's bolo and throw it in the nearby punch bowl. While I'm at it, I'd also like to slam-dunk the Viking's earrings, which look exactly like gallstones.

She sees me staring at her earrings and asks if I like them. I want to ask if she passed them recently, but I reply, "Oh, they're such a wonderful shade of . . . *ash*." It's all I can muster, unless I'd like to ask how in the world she ever managed to turn her adenoids into jewelry.

Moments like this are where I succeed and fail all at the same time. God has his work cut out. With me. With all of us.

I smile at the man and woman. They are probably very nice people. But being here, in this church, makes me feel claustrophobic, nauseous, angry, kind of like how the two of them might feel if they ever got a mirror in their houses and happened to catch a glimpse of the way they were dressed.

I Find a Path

I am watering plants at the front of our property, where our land butts up against a two-lane country road, when Marge—whose leash I have momentarily tied to our split-rail fence, like a horse to a hitching post—begins baying.

I jump out of my skin, especially when I see a group of robed men walking my way.

The men, many older, are walking with their heads down, silently chanting.

It's all very *Being John Malkovich,* as if they have mistakenly walked through a crack in the universe and been spit out here, in the middle of nowhere.

"Hello?" I sing. "Good morning!"

They do not respond.

"Hello!" I call, a bit more loudly.

Nothing.

OK, which one is Ashton Kutcher in makeup? I'm being Punk'd.

"Hello!!!"

Anyone? Bueller? Bueller?

One of the men looks up at me and whispers—in a snaky hiss—not pleased in the least, "We're *meditating.* We must remain *silent.* We are not supposed to communicate with the outside world."

I smile.

My bad.

"I am sooo sorry," I say. "It's just so weird to see—"

And then he shushes me.

Well, I never! I think. And then I realize I'm watering Marge's back; she is trying to lap the liquid falling from the can.

But then, oddly, the first mental domino in my brain is pushed over, and everything seems to fall into place in my head.

A rather large Hindu-based monastery and an interfaith retreat sit just down our country road, a couple of miles from our home.

Moreover, Gary and I live in a township called Ganges. Just now, after months of being here, have I put two and two together, after finally hearing the locals pronounce our township name out loud. Only then do I realize it is not pronounced "Gang-us," like Genghis Khan, but rather "Gan-geez," like the river in India that is held sacred by Hindus.

On a few occasions, I have seen men in robes or women with their heads down walking along our little country lane, praying, meditating, chanting, but I have been too self-absorbed in my country world to do much of anything besides avoid hitting them with my car.

I think back to my comparative religion class in college and remember that many Hindus believe that the water from the Ganges can cleanse a person's soul of all past sins, and that people travel from great distances to bathe in the river at least once in their lifetime.

And then the final domino falls—I can actually hear it in my head—and I have to confess to myself that the water here, Lake Michigan, and the area's magnetic energy pulled me to this spot and would not let me go until I moved. There was something unspoken, almost magical, that drew me, and that energy seems to manifest a creativity in me, a force that drives me to write, a force that makes me want to change the world. Some locals say that crystals exist on the floor of the lake. I don't know if that's true—although I'm still convinced there are freshwater sharks—it's just all so odd, and I don't easily embrace the odd, but there is something I can feel, a vibe, a hippie tension, a feeling as though a balloon is being dragged all over my naked body, and the static electric energy has me on edge.

I look at the robed men, heads bowed, walking down our road, meditating.

"The lake?" I yell. I have to ask. I'm so Lucy.

The men turn. I swear they even roll their eyes.

"Lake Michigan? . . . Is it . . . *sacred*?"

One of the men smiles broadly, hands clasped, and bows his head in my direction.

When I was young, my family attended a grand church, and as soon as the service finished and we walked outside, I would look beyond the great steeple that seemed to touch the clouds, worried that fire and brimstone were going to rain down on my head at any given moment.

The minister at our church would often rant at his lectern at a world gone mad, a world going to hell, a world that was most certainly in its final days. He would discuss the sins of the world with his parishioners—more as a politician than a preacher—sharing lessons I had never heard when my mother read me the Bible.

"Jesus is mad!" he would say. "There is only one true way to the Lord!"

And then he would conclude each of his sermons with the same question: "Are you going to hell?"

And even at age seven, I felt I already knew the answer: "Yes, I am."

All of which is why I relished my summers at our log cabin on Sugar Creek. It was there that even my grandma—one of God's true foot soldiers—took a break from her Sunday church routine, waking early to appreciate God's simple handiwork in nature before anyone could awake to disrupt it.

Most summer evenings at dusk, my grandma and I would walk down to Sugar Creek and out to a point on our rocky beach where the water slowed, pooled, and became deep. Here, the creek ran still and gave off a coolness and scent that was instantly calming.

"Water always draws us back to God," my grandma told me. "It's where we wash our sins away."

We would hold hands and lean over the water, staring at our reflection. On occasion, we would toss a shattered piece of black shale into the water, and our image would break.

I would stare into the water, giggling at our distorted picture, waiting for the ripples finally to slow, in order to see my grandmother and me holding hands once again.

"We all lose ourselves in this world," my grandma told me more than once, "but the secret is to slow and wait for the ripples to stop, and then you will be reconnected and able to see yourself clearly."

Some mornings I would wake at dawn and join her on our barn-red glider, which sat on a bluff overlooking Sugar Creek. My grandma would pat the damp cushioned seat of the glider, and I would slide over to her, my butt shooshing air, before settling into her arms, onto her bosom, while she drank a steaming mug of coffee, copies of the Bible and *Walden* in the lap of the paisley housedress she loved to wear.

"Look at what's in front of us, Wade," she would say, sighing, watching fish jump, hawks dive, the fog that settled deep into the banks of the river bluffs like a bad cough every night slowly begin to dissipate. "We ignore what's around us, the fact that God is present in everything. Too many people try to reinterpret God's word in order to make themselves more powerful, more right, more blessed. But in God's eyes, each of us is no bigger or better than the mosquitoes buzzing around our heads right now. If you think we have a magnificent perspective on the world from here, imagine what God sees."

I would begin to drift off in my grandma's arms on many Sunday mornings, just as the sun began to rise above the bluffs.

"We all have a special purpose here," my grandma would whisper to me, the breeze rising up and over the lip of the bluff to jangle one of her Avon earrings like a wind chime. "The mosquitoes feed the birds; the fog provides moisture to all those trees you see jutting out of the bluff and into nothingness. We all have a special purpose during our time on earth. The hard part is understanding what our purpose in life is and then setting out to accomplish it. If we don't, our precious time here is wasted."

And then I would fall asleep, a child in my grandmother's arms, a baby in an angel's wings, both of us high above the earth, seemingly floating heavenward.

I don't know if I ever felt closer to God.

Later on in the week, on a lovely early summer's morning, Gary and I go for a walk. We hike through our woods until we find ourselves at the monastery down our rural road. It is a rambling, whitewashed building hidden away in the woods and not detectable from the road. It is quiet and still. There is no sign of life. We open the giant front doors of the monastery and are greeted with a rush of warm, woody air. A sign instructs us to take off our shoes.

I refuse.

An open chapel stands in front of us, light pouring in from all angles. I close my eyes and breathe deeply. It smells like a spiritual open-air library.

And then a voice surprises us. "Welcome."

"Are you . . . a swami?" I ask the man.

"No," he says. "But I am here to help."

There is a calmness and genuineness to his voice that puts me at ease, offsetting my panic at the fact that he is barefoot.

He tells us the monastery is a minisanctuary in the countryside that provides a place for spiritual seekers to engage in prayer, meditation, and study away from the distractions and cares of daily life. This little rural retreat provides an atmosphere conducive to solitude and meditation in a nonsectarian context of reverence for all faiths.

The man invites us into the chapel and asks us to sit, cross-legged, on the floor. I want to ask when we get to fingerpaint, but he inhales deeply and closes his eyes.

Freak show! I think to myself.

I look over at Gary. His eyes are closed. He *loves* shit like this.

Freak show, part deux! I think. If this man asked Gary to strip nude and sing "Amazing Grace," I know Gary would. Because a "higher power" told him to.

If Jim Jones had looked like David Beckham, Gary would be dead.

After an eternally uncomfortable silence, the man opens his eyes and tells us that a carload of Hindu swamis, seeking a meditation retreat away from the stress of the city, happened to drive through Ganges and stopped, intrigued by the name and also spiritually tugged by something more. They ended up purchasing a large orchard and turning it into a retreat.

Vedanta, we learn, is one of the six major philosophies of Hinduism. Vedanta teaches that man's real nature is divine and that the aim of human life is to realize that divinity through selfless work, devotion to God, control of the inner forces, and discrimination between the real and the unreal. It accepts all religions, properly understood, as valid means of realizing the truth. Religion is a way of life rather than a set of dogmas, and Vedanta places great importance on actually experiencing the truth for ourselves.

Shockingly, I find myself listening closely to the man, almost as intently as if I were trying to learn the lyrics on the new Kelly Clarkson CD. I even ask a question: "So you accept people of all religions?"

The man answers: "We accept all religions as valid paths to God. Where Vedanta differs from some other faiths is that we believe God has incarnated many times: as Jesus, as Buddha, as Sri Ramakrishna, and many others, which is why we embrace them all. We don't convert; we accept all religions as valid paths to God. There is only one God, although people may use different names, such as Jesus, Allah, Brahman."

The man looks at me and says, "I can sense that you need time to reflect. I suggest that you go across the street to the interfaith retreat and walk along their paths. It may help you contemplate where it is you are headed."

Gary and I cross our little rural road and head into the pretty interfaith retreat that we see filled on many Sunday mornings and afternoons.

We enter and a nice woman offers to give us a tour.

She asks that we remove our shoes.

I refuse.

She tells us that this interfaith retreat is dedicated to education and dialogue, as a way to promote understanding and peaceful relationships among people of differing beliefs in the community and in the world.

"Differences need not separate," she says, "but enrich our lives and deepen our capacity to love."

"The man at the monastery suggested we walk your trails?" I ask hesitantly.

"Oh, yes, please," she says. "Our meditation trails are marked with signs that have sayings from different faiths and religions. The trails are used for reflection."

We are directed to a tree-lined route behind the retreat that winds through the woods.

I think of what the man at the monastery said just before disappearing like a ghostly spirit behind the big front doors.

"Whenever you have leisure, go into solitude for a day or two. At that time, don't hold any conversation on worldly affairs. Live either in solitude or in the company of the Holy."

The meditation path leads into the woods, forking in many directions. Gary and I never knew this existed. We begin meandering and find, marking the trail every ten feet or so, hanging in or on the trees, handmade signs—painted, stenciled, written, weathered—that carry quotes from different religions or spiritual leaders.

Gary and I walk along, quietly reading passages, occasionally sharing one that resonates with us deeply.

"Live either in solitude or in the company of the Holy."

What I have been doing is a sham. I have been living in solitude without being at peace. I have been yelling at those seeking peace. I have been lost out here, in more ways than one.

I motion for Gary to come over, and we take a seat on adjoining stumps and grab hands.

We pray.

For a moment, I mentally stop running.

Insert (Nasty) Foot in Mouth

n order to continue on our spiritual path, Gary and I attend a Buddhist seminar on chanting and meditation at the interfaith retreat.

Which means I have to remove my shoes.

Which is like asking Tom Cruise and Brooke Shields to hang out for a while.

Taking risks in life is very important to Gary. He will eat a hotdog from a street vendor or do doughnuts in a snowstorm. I prefer routine. I like my things. I like Kashi and Purell and Dolce & Gabbana. I don't like to remove my shoes and walk barefoot on floors where other people walk barefoot. I have a foot fetish, albeit a different kind of fetish: I don't like feet. I don't like to look at them, or see them, or think about them.

Feet are pedestrian. They should be covered. When Gary asks me to rub his feet, I gag and tell him he should just get reshoed, like a horse.

Ironically, I have cute feet, and Gary does not.

His second toe—the one closest to his big toe, which, by the way, is the size of a Buick LeSabre—is mangled and rough-hewn. The end looks like it was simply hacked off and grew back in the shape of Gumby's head. It catches on everything when he's barefoot, seemingly the smallest flecks of dust, and the toe seems boneless, allowing it to bend completely under his foot without breaking. If it were lumber on the back of a pickup, it would be marked with a pink flag as a hazard to passersby.

On the tips of his little toes, Gary has just a speck of nail, like a grain of sand on the beach. A friend's eleven-year-old daughter recently challenged him to see if she could even get paint on the nail, and she tried valiantly, utilizing every weapon in her pink Hello Kitty toolbelt, slowly minimizing her chosen weapons from brush to Q-tip and finally to toothpick.

She failed. "You have weird feet," she said, directly, honestly, as only a child can.

Gary can pick things up with his feet ambidextrously. He can hand me a fork, or a full package of Doritos, or even a smaller magazine (think *People* or *Consumer Reports,* not *InStyle*).

He begs me to rub his feet, to pay attention to them, to love the simple fact that they are a part of him.

I cannot.

While he thinks feet can be fun and sexy, I think feet are simply, well, pedestrian. They should be covered at all times in expensive shoes.

Which is why asking me to meditate barefoot is like severing a baker's arms and then asking him to ice a cake.

We enter the retreat center, where I am immediately surrounded by a lot of earthy people, the kind who wear Desmond Tutu hats even though they're not black and drive Subarus and wear Crocs.

I tend to hang with people who look like they spend way too much time getting ready.

The Buddhist teacher is an older bald man with a giant smile—think Gandhi meets Julia Roberts. He is swathed in robes the color of blood oranges. He begins to speak:

"Butta alf fuzzy wuzzy contact senses zippeedoodah."

I can't understand a word this guy is saying. Who voluntarily lectures if he can't enunciate a syllable? I would be booed off the stage if I did this.

After he babbles, he laughs.

And then all these barefoot earth freaks laugh, too. *What did he just say?* I want to yell. I'll give you a bar of Ivory and a gift certificate to Nine West if you tell me one single word he just uttered.

And then it happens. A woman sitting next to me stretches her legs and her foot grazes mine. But then she refuses to move it. When

I inch mine away, hers follows, like our soles are Velcroed together. I have an overwhelming desire to vomit. I tap Gary, and even though we have been instructed not to talk, I whisper, "Her feet are touching mine."

He mouths, "Snap! Crackle! Pop!" and then shushes me. The woman's toes graze my sole, and I gag; then, out of sheer desperation and revulsion, I kick her foot away, like it's a rat in a sewer.

"Ow!" she says. "What are you doing?"

"Sorry. You were touching my foot."

"You didn't have to kick me."

"You didn't have to keep touching my foot."

"I didn't know I was touching your foot."

"How could you not know you were touching my foot? It's like we were conjoined twins for a few minutes."

And then this woman shushes me—*me!*—so I give her the snakebite, like Bette Midler did in *Big Business*.

The Buddhist teacher continues mumbling. "Butta alf fuzzy wuzzy contact senses zippeedoodah." He laughs. The barefoot lemmings laugh.

I decide to sit cross-legged in my folding chair, which instantly deadens my spinal column, but I feel better knowing I can't get ringworm.

I shut my eyes and listen very closely.

He is saying that Buddhism is separating function from desire. The function of my tongue is to taste. When I taste something good, I desire it. But the goal is to remove the desire, the wanting, the yearning, from your life. Then, and only then, can you move to a new plane, move to a new level of spiritual understanding with yourself and the world around you.

I'm all about desire. All about tongue and taste and wanting more. That's kind of like my personal business card. In fact, I can taste a white chocolate latte right now.

And suddenly a group of robed Buddhists begin to chant, in unison, and it is beautiful and unsettling, sincere, centered, and resonant. It gives me goose bumps. It makes me feel very shallow and silly.

I think of my childhood, of church camp, of all the things that came spewing out of people's mouths that didn't mean a damn thing.

Perhaps, I realize, it's about listening to myself, listening to God, and not to everyone else who is talking in tongues, talking in circles around my head. Perhaps it's about planting my feet on the ground and finding my own path.

So I unfurl my legs and place my feet firmly on the ground. I can do this. Separate function from feeling. My feet are for walking. Finding my path. They are pedestrian. I can do this.

Another teacher begins to teach us to meditate, to breathe at 60 percent of our capacity and follow the breath's trail throughout our body until we release it. She instructs us to keep our focus, not to fall asleep or drift in our thinking but to meditate, to ground ourselves.

I concentrate.

Feet.

I concentrate.

Dirt.

I concentrate.

Ringworm.

And then people are clapping, and I am running for my shoes and a shower and a bucket of Purell.

My Church

Sometimes the fog rolls off the lake, heavy and thick, like a moving curtain, and the morning simply becomes stalled, the sunlight choked in darkness. Our house disappears—like the castles you see in English paintings or in the photos of lighthouses on Cape Cod—the fog hungry to eat anything in its path.

There are many spring and summer days when the weather will stay this way until noon, until the warmth and the height of the sun have a chance to do their magic, to burn away the overcast, and the world can reappear, cloaked in golden light.

These foggy-starting days give me a different perspective on the world, a different perspective on my life. These days give me pause, allow time to reflect on my connection to this world, to ask the questions, *Why am I here? What is God's plan for me?*

I think of my grandma and me sitting high on a bluff—seemingly an arm's length from heaven—exhaling deeply into the morning fog, our breaths freeze-framed for just a brief second before they become one with the fog. And then, like today, we would watch the fog slowly dissipate, the world below coming into crystal-clear focus.

I look around me as the fog lifts and realize the lakeshore has become my sanctuary, the stump my pew, the woods my church.

I have found God simply by popping my eyes open in the middle of a fog—as I am doing right now—to see what is directly in front of me: an old pine, a red-breasted woodpecker, two rabbits, and rhododendrons the size of small cars lifting their purple and white blooms to the emerging sun.

Here is God.

Though he was deeply spiritual, Henry David Thoreau was not considered a religious man during his life. In fact, he removed his name from the rolls of his Unitarian congregation in his twenties, according to Cindy McGroarty, who writes that Thoreau "stopped attending organized services because he was convinced that church was the last place one might find God." Thoreau even wrote, "The church is a sort of hospital for men's souls and as full of quackery as the hospital for their bodies."

So today I follow what my grandmother, mother, and Thoreau—*my* spiritual leaders—have taught me.

Later in the day, I head to Lake Michigan, which is as flat as glass.

The sunsets are pure drama, a kaleidoscope of color and light that stretches as far and wide as the eye can see.

I return to this—these sunsets of swirling color—because I can see God in all his glory.

I catch my reflection in the flat water, a pink, blue, and purple mirror. I am aging. My face is more lined. I reach down to touch my face, and my image shatters and then reconnects.

It is me.

It is not me.

"Nevertheless, of all the characters I have known," Thoreau wrote, "perhaps Walden wears best, and best preserves its purity. Many men have been likened to it, but few deserve that honor. Though the woodchoppers have laid bare first this shore and then that, and the Irish have built their sties by it, and the railroad has infringed on its border, and the ice-men have skimmed it once, it is itself unchanged, the same water which my youthful eyes fell on; all the change is in me. It has not acquired one permanent wrinkle after all its ripples. It is perennially young."

I then go home and wander into my true place of worship—the woods—pull up a stump, and simply stare at our lilac trees, the fragrance so intense it's like being in the perfume aisle at Neiman Marcus during the holidays. These lilac trees simply grow wild in our woods, and in late spring and early summer, the trees' arms grow heavy, and their purple, scented hands wave for the butterflies to come.

And they do, hundreds of them, from tiny white fluttering specks to giant monarchs, flitting, flying, their collective wings actually fanning the lilacs. The fading sunlight through the trees illuminates the butterflies' wings for a split second, a kaleidoscope of color, blue, then yellow, then green, then white. I watch the simple beauty of this scene: lilacs and butterflies on a beautiful evening in the woods.

A yellow butterfly lands on my forearm. I hold very still, and it stops fluttering for a little while, resting, catching its breath. I sigh heavily, and the butterfly tilts its head toward me and then softly opens its wings and catches a ride on my contentment, flying up toward the sun, flying up toward heaven.

Wade's Walden—5. Modern Society—3.

LESSON NINE
Let Go of My City Cynicism

What sort of space is that which separates a man from his fellows and makes him solitary? I have found that no exertion of the legs can bring two minds much nearer to one another.

—Henry David Thoreau, *Walden*

A Berry Good Time

With a renewed sense of spirituality, I set out to conquer what may be my most challenging Life Lesson, number nine: release my city cynicism.

One cannot be both spiritual and cynical, right? I mean, Jesus never said, "Your sandals are *so* B.C.," did He?

I have used my cynicism like a body condom to protect myself all these years—first in the country and then in the city—and I cannot remember what it is like to insert myself into life without protection, to view the world as a child might, without mocking others.

And what better time to embrace innocence than summer?

Summer!

A Michigan summer in a lakeshore resort town is sheer perfection. It is Paris in the spring, Concord in the fall, Aspen in the winter.

The temperatures are ideal: low 80s in the day, 50s at night, zero humidity. Most days are bright and blue, the sun shimmering off the water, gulls exercising their wings and then resting on the waves, sailboats spreading their canvas and then zipping across the water, each and every wave seemingly offering a glimmering and flickering reminder of what it is like to be happy, hopeful, innocent, and young.

Most of all, summer means the return of civilization, of sanity. This is what I have been waiting for.

One of our first summer visitors is a whirlwind of a woman named Elise, who is one of our best friends.

Elise is a former cabaret performer whose second "calling" in life was to be an architect. She is wildly successful. She is wildly flamboyant. She is wildly lovable.

Elise prides herself on being Zen, feng shui, at one with nature, but she is conditioned to be all tornadic city energy, a woman who has found it much easier to reach her state of peace by simply paying a reflexologist $300 to work out those kinks, a psychic $100 to chart her future, and an herbologist $60 for an ounce of green tea. Still, Elise is a woman of great intention and great courage, a woman who has worked only for herself her whole life, a woman who helped me see my own light, who helped us take a leap of faith, who taught us to believe in ourselves.

Elise arrives from New York to stay for a week. In the back of my head, I hear my mother saying, "Guests are like fish. After three days, they turn bad."

But I adore Elise and her funnel cloud of a personality. I need a dose of the city.

Elise is all choppy black hair and funky jewelry and enormous sunglasses and big boobies and three-inch heels. While she is generous, kind, thoughtful, and very funny, she also makes the girls from *Sex and the City* look like the Steel Curtain, especially when you take her out of her natural environment and plop her here, in the woods. It's like taking Queen Elizabeth and putting her in a trailer park. You're going to notice something's just not right.

When Elise arrives, she is wearing a black cape with a shocking-pink liner. She is wearing Chanel sunglasses the size of her rental Hummer and a white linen minitunic she says she picked up in Chinatown. She is wearing chunky white heels with thick straps and at least a three-inch lift. She has a cell phone pressed to an ear, and she emerges onto our gravel drive to scream, "My darlings! Dolls? . . . No concrete? No sidewalks? Oh, my! Oh, my! This is very Adirondacks!"

She immediately trips on a flagstone. And then, seemingly, on a leaf.

I could not be happier to see someone.

She stumbles along, gesturing wildly at a tree, a flower, the air, holding three conversations—one with the caller, one with me, and one with a bee that seems entranced by her perfume—but holding only her giant pink clutch.

"I'm exhausted, doll," she whispers to me, gesturing back to her car with her head as though I'm a valet. "Could you be a lamb and get the rest? Oh, and can I have an Evian?"

She continues this routine for three days—going from the bedroom, to the kitchen, to the beach, to the shops, to the restaurants. An entire pot of Starbucks each morning does not help quell her animation.

On the fourth day, I am alone with Elise, trying to write, which is an impossibility, like trying to meditate in the middle of a 50 Cent video shoot.

I fake-write for an hour as Elise relays the dilemmas of her life: rude clients, rich people with no taste, trendy shoes that don't hold up, the power of edamame.

"Doll, I don't know what I'd do if I weren't so centered in my life."

I look at her. She chugs a cup of coffee and then says, "Oooh, gotta go. Weak bladder."

"Let's go for a walk," I say suddenly when she reappears from the bathroom.

But a walk for Elise entails a wardrobe change, à la Celine. She has brought four Jimmy Hoffa–size suitcases for her stay and shipped ahead two packages, and she will ship four boxes home upon leaving. Elise slips into a Sporty Spice melange complete with sunglasses and "walking heels" that she feels will be more harmonious with nature.

I take her to our neighbor's blueberry field, where we have been granted exclusive picking rights—as many and as often as we choose. Our neighbors have rows and rows of blueberry bushes, and they are sectioned by variety: Some are sweet and oh-so-tiny for eating; some are bigger and bluer—a bit more tart—for baking.

Elise is abuzz as she walks, one conversation running into another—about buying shoes in Manhattan, having a crush on a manager at Nordstrom who she worries "might be gay." She does not notice, as she talks and gestures and giggles and laughs, that birds take flight, squirrels run for cover, and turkeys strut in the other direction.

"These are perfect," I tell Elise, standing beside a row of bushes whose limbs are literally falling from the weight of ripe blueberries. I pluck them off the bush and eat them. They are warm and sweet.

"Shouldn't you wash them first? What about pesticides? Do we need to ask before we pick? Will we get shot? I think blueberries might give me the runs. What if I get some on my new shirt? Do I look bloated in this outfit?"

I realize, watching her swat at bees, fluff her hair, and rub lotion onto her legs, that she is me. Or the version of me I used to be: the suitcases, the sunglasses, the clothes, the hair, the lotion.

I look at myself: I am wearing cargo shorts, a coffee-stained T-shirt, tube socks, and my green waders, along with the free pig ball cap Gary gave me from the feed store.

Who have I become?

But that's not the question I should be asking now, I know.

Who was I?

Elise tells me—standing nervously in front of a bush—that she doesn't want to stain her fingers blue. "Doll, I just got a manicure from the top salon in Manhattan. I want to show my hands at dinner tonight, not have to wear white gloves to cover them up!"

Just be quiet and pick some fucking blueberries! Just be still for a minute! OK?

I say this out loud. I don't mean to, but I do. Elise looks stunned and hurt, like I've just taken a razor to her new clutch.

I should apologize. I have hurt her feelings. She looks like a little girl who wants to cry because she didn't get a Snickers in the checkout aisle at Target.

But then a cardinal lands in the bush beside her and chirps happily, plucking a few berries straight off the bush. It flies off, low to the ground, over a field of unmowed Indian paintbrush, a flash of bright red against a sea of waving orange. The sun is out, and Elise lifts her face to receive its warmth. A heron dips into our neighbor's pond, which sits at the end of the field, emerging with breakfast.

Elise looks at me and smiles.

For the next half hour, she picks blueberries, and she eats blueberries, in total silence.

She will later tell me it was one of the loudest and most profound conversations she has ever had with herself.

Swing Time

They're here!"

I sprint out of my cottage, the screen door banging my exit, to greet some of our next visitors, best friends who have come to stay with us in Michigan for the very first time. When their kids step out of the SUV, I begin pelting them with the following dorky, precalculated greetings. I want them to *feel* the excitement of summer at the lake. I want these city kids to embrace the country. I will drown them in a flood of folksy charm.

"Welcome to the Mitten!"

Nothing.

"This is Wade's Walden!"

Nada.

My greetings fall on deaf ears. More accurately, they fall silently onto ears that are already filled with Fergie from attached iPods.

The sun is shining, the sky a brilliant blue, the smell of pine in the air, the sugar maples so heavy with leaves they look as if they might just reach down and give you a hug. And yet these kids don't see this. Their ears are still filled with words and not birds; their eyes are still riveted to their cell phones, their fingers flying, delivering text messages to friends in the city.

"Do you, like, have wireless and cable way out here?"

This is the little girl's first question.

I point at the two dishes sitting on the edge of the woods.

Her brother thumps his hand on his thigh to the beat of the music and gives me a thumbs-up.

"But no indoor plumbing," I say.

They look at me as though Fergie has just begun singing Rosemary Clooney tunes.

"Just joking," I answer.

Fears calmed, they sprint inside the cottage, take a seat on the couch, and continue their routine before I can even say, "Who wants to go to the beach?"

I have planned their visit with as much precision as a Cirque du Soleil show, down to my scripted introductory remarks. I want these cynical city kids to experience the wonderment of summer like I did when I was a child at my grandparents' log cabin. I want this modern-day, ultra-urban Hannah Montana and pocket-size Justin Timberlake to have a Mayberry-esque experience.

But I go to bed defeated. Without even making s'mores, which I had planned for 9:00 P.M.

The next day brings a summer morning that is a pure Michigan stunner: a cloudless, cool start that quickly morphs into sunny, humidity-free warmth, T-shirts replacing sweatshirts. Gary makes blueberry pancakes for the crew. I say, sleepily, innocently, before caffeine has even taken hold of my synapses, that the blueberries in the pancakes were picked fresh from our neighbors' farm, just beyond our woods.

Two pairs of blue-stained lips purse with a question. "Can we, like, go see that?"

Ten minutes later, we are all out the door, veering along the trails Gary has made in our woods. Each bend in the path—past a mushroom patch, along a grove of still-upright mayapples, through a grove of baby pines, across a field of ferns—elicits *ooohhhs* and *aaahhs,* a closer inspection.

Even from me.

When we emerge from the woods into our neighbors' blueberry field, the kids sprint to the bushes, immediately drop their buckets, and begin cramming the sweet, warm berries into their mouths. They gobble until full, until they look like Oompa-Loompas, and then they begin to fill their pails, until they, too, are full.

"Can we walk the long way through the woods?" the kids then ask me.

Along with their blueberry fields, our neighbors own a mini–national park of acreage, land that is also marked by beautifully meandering trails.

We walk alongside their creek, the kids launching leaves and pine needles as their boats. They giggle as they watch wild turkeys run in the woods. They watch in complete fascination as a family of deer forage for food.

When we return, it is well past lunchtime, and the kids excitedly relay their stories to their parents and then to their friends via text message.

As I hand the little boy a sandwich, he suddenly holds up a list he has found on the kitchen counter. "What's this?"

"Oh, it's nothing," I say.

But it's too late. My calendar and itemized list of activities for them to do—actually broken down into hour and half-hour intervals—has been discovered.

He begins to recite from the list: "Things to do at the beach . . . find driftwood that looks like a seal; a dog; a snake; . . . collect lake rocks; build a sand fort . . ."

"OK, OK, that's enough," I reply.

And then, as the little girl texts another friend about her morning, she says to me without looking up—in this somewhat distracted and yet completely focused way—"You know, it's cool to, like, chill once in a while."

I stare into her freckled face as she continues to text, and I realize she's, like, right.

It isn't they who need a heavy-handed reminder about letting go and having fun this summer; it's me, the Neurotic, Manic Bionic Man.

I toss my list, and the three of us spend the afternoon rocking in a single hammock, looking up at a sky so perfectly blue it makes your heart ache, and then falling asleep.

I haven't really accomplished anything on my list today, except to have one of the best summer days of my life.

I have turned the corner.

How Much Ice in Your Iced Latte?

have turned the corner and run smack-dab into a wall of people, it seems.

While I'm hightailing out of the woods every summer day to enjoy the Currier and Ives perfection of the resort towns of Saugatuck-Douglas, the rest of the world is hightailing out of the city to get a whopping dose of quaint and charm as well.

Summer is high season in any resort town, obviously, but I didn't expect this. I didn't expect resorters to arrive in droves, like the swarm of Japanese beetles that recently descended upon Gary's flower gardens.

Where were you when it was 10 degrees? I think. *And, in order to control your spread, can I go ahead and spray herbicide directly on anything wearing a mint-green shift or baggy Nautica swimsuit that looks like an American flag?*

And yet, I know they're here for largely the same reasons I'm here. It's why Gary and I—like all our friends do now—used to escape the city to come here on vacation.

Each and every summer day in Saugatuck-Douglas is filled with anticipation and excitement, a touch of giddiness.

Every summer day is like the opening day of school.

Except for fags and rich people.

I head into town nearly every summer morning to grab a triple-shot Caramel Silk at Uncommon Grounds. It's my midmorning break from writing. I love to sip my latte as I walk along the pier watching the yachts and sailboats, which have emerged from hibernation to dominate the waterfront. I love to breathe the warm wind of summer, inhale the smell of flowers and freshly mowed grass and gas from the boats drifting off the water as they motor down the channel.

There's only one small problem: My morning meeting with summer innocence is becoming more and more delayed in July. I now wait in long lines that snake beyond the screen door of the coffeehouse, down the stairs, and onto the sidewalk. The artsy baristas I have become friends with are now too busy to chat, too busy fending off demands from visitors who sound, well, a lot like the rich, self-absorbed clientele with whom I used to work.

"I said, 'No-foam latte.' I can't drink a wet latte."

"Is your coffee fair-trade?"

"Are your scones low-fat or no-fat?"

I hear the following exchange this morning between a young barista sporting a bright blue bandana and a young husband and wife in freshly pressed linen who check their closely matching Invicta diving watches every few seconds, as if a bomb is about to detonate in their pants unless they ingest an iced mocha immediately.

Husband: We'd like two nonfat iced mocha lattes.

Barista (writing order on cups): Yes, sir. Anything else?

Wife: Yes. May I ask you a question? Do you still use that nasty
    chocolate powder you did last year, or did you switch to
    syrup, as I'd asked?

Barista: Excuse me, ma'am?

Wife: Don't you remember *us* from last year? Don't you remem-
    ber our request?

Barista: No, ma'am. I didn't work here last summer.

Wife: It's just so hard to tell, because you all wear those . . . *ban-
    danas.*

Husband: Did I say nonfat?

Barista: Yes, sir.

Husband: Did I say whipped cream?

Barista (checking cup): No, sir. Would you like whipped cream?

Husband: Did I *say* whipped cream?

Barista: No, sir. I was just making sure, so there was no confusion.

Wife: Just how many ice cubes do you use in an iced latte?

Barista: Excuse me, ma'am?

Wife: How . . . many . . . ice cubes do you use in your iced latte?

Barista: Umm, I've never counted.

Wife: Could you give me an estimate?

Barista (looking at the cup): We fill it, I guess, about three quarters full, especially since it's so warm out today.

Husband: Do you use cubes or pellets?

Barista: Excuse me, sir?

Husband: Ice cubes or ice pellets?

Barista: Cubes.

Wife: So, using cubes, how many would you estimate that you put in a cup?

Barista: I'm not sure, ma'am.

Husband: Could you count them aloud for us?

Barista: You want me to count the ice cubes?

Husband and wife: Yes.

Barista (blinking): Really?

Husband and wife: Yes.

Barista (dropping cubes into a glass): One . . . two . . . three . . . four. (She looks up, stopping.) Is there a certain number you prefer? I can stop there.

Wife: No, we'll know when we see it.

Wade: I don't think you need the cubes.

Husband and wife (after stepping back to let the next customers move up to counter): Pardon me?

Wade: I said, I don't think you need the cubes.

Wife: And why is that?

Wade (in a whisper): Because you're both icy enough bitches as it is.

Wife (making a gagging sound): Well, I never.

Wade: Well, maybe you should, because you just can't walk into town and act like you own it. It's a small place filled with people who have very long memories and lifespans.

Husband (grabbing Wade by the shirt): Who the hell do you think you are?

Wade (looking around helplessly, thinking silently): *A reformed cynical urbanite who just rediscovered his city cynicism. Just when I thought I'd turned the corner, I ran into him again. And I think I missed the old guy.*

Husband: I should beat the shit out of you.

Wade: I'm gay. And I bite.

Husband and wife exit coffeehouse.

Cue applause.

End scene.

The Chain Fairy

can feel the cynical body snatchers returning, so, in order to clear my body of negativity, Gary asks me to do some of the summer things that we first did on vacation when we came here, things we believe can restore my youthful vigor and my belief that humanity is good and not simply here to annoy me.

For a day, Gary and I become tourists again: We buy fudge and stroll the streets of Saugatuck-Douglas, hitting every art gallery, home accessories store, quaint shop, and antique mall. We purchase enough cabin-themed tchotchkes to decorate Ralph Lauren's winter home in Aspen.

We then stroll the boardwalk that meanders along the river leading to Lake Michigan, look at the boats, and eat fudge. It's so sweet, it makes my teeth ache more than my cashew brittle.

And then we see the Saugatuck Chain Ferry, one of the last operating chain ferries in America. For a dollar, an attendant will hand-crank you across the Kalamazoo River along a chain that stretches underneath the channel. The ferry is white, ornate, and pure Americana.

It was one of the very first things Gary and I did the very first time we were here on vacation.

"Let's take the ferry, fairy," I say to Gary.

We board the little water trolley, which is attended by two kids who look as if they just shot a Pop-Tart commercial. For a few minutes, we are the only ones on board, and I look at Gary, and he looks at me, and I believe the world will once again be OK.

But then I hear slurping, and a family of six boards the ferry eating ice cream cones as big as their heads. The wife is wearing mom jeans, white sneakers, and a T-shirt that says CURVES, while the husband is wearing Tommy Bahama shorts, Oakley sunglasses, and a T-shirt that reads MY COMPANY WENT FROM "GOOD TO GREAT" AT THE 2006 RETREAT AT THE MARRIOTT!

The kids—even the baby in the stroller—are covered in ice cream, and the mom is trying to clean them off with dry Kleenex that keeps sticking to their faces, almost as if they have just shaved and badly cut themselves.

Dad proceeds to roll the stroller directly over my toe, which just happens to be fully exposed in my flip-flop.

"Ouch," I say.

He doesn't respond.

The wife looks at me, waiting, like all moms do, for me to smile at the baby in the stroller that has just given me a hammertoe for life.

I don't smile, because the baby looks like Ned Beatty.

And it's a girl.

I mean, the poor thing doesn't stand a chance in life.

The family proceeds to stand directly in front of Gary and me, enclosing us in a makeshift human prison cell.

And then the dad looks at me and Gary—not once, but twice—and then does this hammy double-take. I can read his mind:

Two men?

Two men in capris and tank tops!

Holy Sodom and Gomorrah, Batman!

He pulls his brood close, as though we're going to drag all four kids into the water and swim away.

Then the husband whispers something to his wife, and they both stare at us.

"They're giving us the look," I whisper to Gary.

"Snap! Crackle! Pop!" Gary replies, because he can't understand me.

And then the wife says something to the oldest girl, who's probably fourteen, and she gives me the look.

I know the look. I'm fluent in it. I've been getting the look since I wore ascots as a child. The look comes in a variety of forms: the clueless

look that grows into knowing; the amused look that comes from seeing something odd and unusual, like a unicorn crossing the street;
the "I love the gays!" look; the disgusted "you're going to hell" look; the
angry "I'm going to kill you" look; and this look the entire family has
just given me, the uncomfortable, "I've never seen anything like you
before in my subdivision of beige-sided ranch homes that are all exactly the same design except for an optional bay window in the living
room" look.

Gary is whistling and looking around the family at the big boats
motoring up and down the channel.

I decide to ignore the family and focus on this slice of summer
perfection.

"You should crank the ferry," Gary says. "The kids will let you.
Their arms are tired anyway. It would be fun."

I look at the big old crank, and I do want to do it. Anything
involving exercise and I'm all in, and it looks like a great shoulder
workout.

"You think?" I ask.

I start to stand, but I hear the husband ask the attendants, "Hey,
do you mind if I crank the ferry? I'd like to show 'em how a *real* man
does it."

Now, the assumption from everyone else on the ferry is that the man
is talking to his family, trying to be a funny straight guy, but he shoots
me the look again, and I know he's preempting my crank, that his
" 'em" means Gary and me.

"Oh, no he di-unt," I say to Gary, doing my best angry black
woman imitation.

"Snap! Crackle! Pop!" Gary says.

Thirty seconds into his crank, the man is exhausted, dripping wet.
I can actually see his nipples and fat, inverted belly button through
his thin "Good to Great" corporate T. He is blowing like an exhausted
racehorse and gives up. The Pop-Tart kids take over, and we mosey
the rest of the way across the river.

Once you cross to the other side, a tourist can do many things, including tour the historical museum, walk to the beach, or climb Mt.
Baldhead, the highest dune in town.

"Wanna head right back?" Gary asks. "That was nice."

"No, let's wander for a while," I say innocently. "We're tourists for a day, remember?"

Instead, I spend the next half hour shadowing the family like a hired assassin as they wander along the river and poke around the museum. And then we board the ferry when they board.

"Mind if I crank us back?" I ask the kid once everyone is seated, the gate is shut, and no one has the option to leave or object.

I bend over the giant hand crank, putting my back into it, and churn like an ephedrine-fueled hamster, my arms spinning, my hands a blur.

I actually throw a wake off the back of the ferry.

I am light-headed and faint when I finish but still manage to turn and give the dad the testosterone-laced "Who's the man now?" look.

The eldest girl is staring at me, transfixed, so I give her the "You better work!" look, which, considering her square jaw, sideburns, and Little League jersey, she'll know all too well in a few years.

And then, as I stand under a TIPS APPRECIATED sign while everyone exits, an elderly woman gives me a dollar.

"You earned that, young man," she says.

I Haven't Seen That at Old Navy

decide to dedicate myself to summer—focus on what I love most—which means dedicating myself to the beach.

My goal? To tan in order to achieve a shade somewhere between Bain de Soleil and Idi Amin.

There is nothing more enchanting or comforting than lying half-asleep on the beach and hearing muffled voices float on the wind, partly obscured by the waves and the sand. Lying here, still, the sun a blinding opiate, I catch pieces of conversations that float to me, some of which stick like windblown trash against a hurricane fence.

"He just Frenched me, right in the middle of Target. I was like, 'Umm, I'm looking at sandals. You *didn't* just do that, right?'"

"Oh, my God. His mother-in-law is here for three weeks! You've met her. It's like eating with Hannibal Lecter every night."

"Yeah. If you wanna go to the private beach, just pay five bucks. Over the dunes, there's hundreds of naked men. It's crazy, kind of like a sandy Mardi Gras."

With this, my ears perked, and I pulled a Scooby-Doo.

Hrumph?!

I had wondered why a nonstop army of men in thongs hauling backpacks had tromped by me, none even bothering with a second glance down, even though I was wearing a brown-and-orange Sauvage swimsuit that miraculously made me look like I had a butt. It was as though I had been laying out between Fatty Arbuckle and Ernest Borgnine.

But then I look over at Gary in his beach chair. He is passed out cold, his mouth open, and I forgot that I have placed a grape in his belly button and a potato chip on each nipple, giving him the look of a hairy mermaid.

I throw a small rock at his head to wake him, but he just swats the air.

"It's crazy," the voice that floats to me is saying. "My brother's gay, and he says it's like Fire Island used to be in the eighties."

Hrumph?!

Now, I know our area is mega-gay; in fact, it has one of the biggest gay resorts and bars in the Midwest, where, in the summer, loaded bears replace winter coyotes. And I know this beach—Oval Beach, one of the most gorgeous beaches in the U.S., long stretches of un-touched dunes overlooking an expanse of Lake Michigan—has a rather definitive line drawn in the sand (straights left of the boardwalk, gays right), but I didn't realize this beach also had a private, hidden gay area. I thought people were paying five dollars to drink alcohol or take their dogs to the private side.

I try to ignore the conversation and am just about to fall asleep, in fact, when sand flies into my mouth, and I hear what sounds like a kindergarten class screaming in my ear.

I pop open my eyes, and there is a minimum of twelve kids under the age of five or six running around—lake to beach, beach to lake— wailing like banshees. Three harried moms, looking as if they could care less if the kids barbecued seagulls or traded a sister for a Slushee as long as they got a day of sun and relaxation, occasionally look up and shake their heads.

The kids, for some reason, seem intent on hovering directly beside me and Gary. We have, mistakenly I now see, perched our possessions near the shoreline to catch the lake breeze. But we are in front of the boardwalk, in a kind of neutral sandy Swiss territory, where interlop-ers from the straight side feel comfortable entering.

The children seem absolutely riveted by the skintight brown-and-orange Sauvage swimsuit I am wearing and the ad hoc mermaid attire sported by Gary.

When I glare at them, they begin to scream and run, kicking sand back into our faces. The commotion finally wakes Gary, who wipes the drool from his mouth, eats his bikini top, and says, "Wassasassafrasmatas?"

"Breeders," I whisper. "Everywhere. It's like they all got sent here on vacay while Ty Pennington redecorates their houses."

Over the next half hour—while the wives read Jennifer Weiner and eat a hundred one-hundred-calorie snack packs of cookies and the husbands read James Patterson and sneak Corona out of their bags—their children level the earth like baby Godzillas.

One of the little girls has the nasty habit of screaming, "Mommmeeeeeeeeeeeeeeeeeeee!" at a pitch and volume typical for only Mariah Carey or airport runways, and one of the boys—destined to be me—keeps showing his butt to his little buddy and asking him to spank it with a sand shovel.

By this time, a fissure has formed in my cranium, and Hyde has punched in his time card to relieve Jekyll.

"Shut up. Shut up. Oh, my God, please just shut the hell up. I want my summer!"

I think I am saying this to myself, but it is coming out.

Loudly.

So loudly that one of the dads tries to lean forward threateningly in his beach chair while sucking in his gut and puffing out his chest, but his back hair gets stuck in the webbing.

"What do you want to do?" Gary asks.

The beach is jammed like a Hannah Montana concert. So I tell Gary about the conversation I've just overheard, and we head for the hills.

"But just to check things out," I say to Gary.

"No, just to lay out," he corrects.

Of course, gay beaches are always gay ghettos—the prettiest but most isolated spots on the beach—simply because while they offer the best views, they are too far for straight people to walk to in Crocs.

After twenty minutes of treading through the hot sand like pack mules—my backpack filled with towels and waters and lotions, Gary lugging Eckhart Tolle and his beach chair—we begin to see a few brightly colored umbrellas dotting the sand dunes above us.

We hike straight up the side of a dune and turn around to look: The view is spectacular. Boats—big and small—are anchored near the beach, and people are dancing and swimming and drinking. We follow a sandy trail up another hillside that leads to another breathtaking view: an expanse of minidunes that drops to a beautiful pine forest. Beyond that in the distance is a lagoon.

"It's gorgeous," Gary says. "Gay men always have the best taste, don't we?"

But by the time we get our bearings, we realize there are a lot of people back here. A lot of naked people back here.

In fact, we turn just in time to see, at the base of a small dune maybe twenty feet away, a man in a diaper trying to get a hand job from a senior citizen with crippling arthritis.

And then an older hippie—a man who resembles an octogenarian Dr. Johnny Fever from *WKRP*—mumbles, "Hot guys!" when he sees us, totters up to us quickly, and asks, "Do you wanna see my thingie?"

Before we can shout "No!" Johnny Fever has already pulled his swimsuit down to show us something that looks like a fetus that's been stored in formaldehyde.

"Sweet Jesus!" I scream.

And then a kindly older man with a shock of gray hair, a giant paunch, and a weenie the size of a button mushroom tells us, "You have to go farther back for the young ones. We old farts can't make it that far anymore."

I look at Gary. He looks at me. And we start walking—five minutes, ten minutes farther in the blazing sand, hundreds of nude men beckoning like a mirage.

And then I blow out my flip-flop.

"You can't wear flip-flops on a hike," Gary says.

"I didn't know we were going hiking. Damn it, these are my favorites. When will I ever find a flip-flop that matches the exact shade of my swimsuit again?"

"Gimme!" Gary says, fixing it.

We finally hike to the top of a virtual sand mountain, with hundreds of little peaks and valleys, tall dunes, and grass creating little curtained pockets from the rest of the world. We no sooner find a private pocket and begin laying out our towels and beach chairs, and reapplying lotion, than a disco ball drops from the crystal-blue sky and what looks like the male cast of *Gossip Girl* suddenly appears in front of us, flexing their muscles, completely nude.

"What brings a hot couple like you two back here?" one asks.

First of all, anyone who calls us "hot" is a winner in my book, no matter what he's wearing—or not wearing.

"Looking for some fun?" another asks.

"We're a thripple," says the last.

My Lord, I haven't seen this much three-way action in a town since my parents took me to see a singing group imitate the Andrews Sisters in Branson.

And then one piece of the thripple says, "We're in a relationship, but we like to add a little fun every now and then. Three plus . . . you know, two . . ."

He smiles at me, prettily but blankly.

I'm wondering if he can even do the arithmetic.

"Equals five?" I laugh.

No one gets it.

I'm wondering how you can be in a three-way relationship at the age of, what, twenty-two? Don't all those overlapping evening hours at Old Navy make it hard to connect with one another?

And then I think, *Hey, but maybe they can afford a washer-dryer together.* I was all alone and had to go to a Laundromat until I was twenty-five.

"You think we're hot?" I ask.

"Yeah, man!" one says.

"Really?" I ask again.

"Really, man," the one who looks like Chace Crawford says, and when I look up from my position on the blanket, he is hard, his penis inches from my face, like a really beautiful microphone.

Another of the *Gossip Girl* boys is making out with one of his two boyfriends.

Did this ever happen at Walden Pond? I think. *Did Thoreau have to confront this?*

What would Lucy do?

I can't think of anything this time, so I rely on my old pal cynicism. I simply picture this gorgeous trio folding T-shirts for $3.99, saying, "Thanks for shopping at Old Navy!" before heading back to their studio apartment nestled alongside the El tracks, eating ramen noodles for dinner and spending their nights on MySpace and Manhunt.

I have to admit their little show is occasionally moving but largely embarrassing—kind of like *Cats*—and when it's over, and they ask me what I think, and I respond, "At least straight people read," I finally realize that not only did I throw away Life Lesson Nine, but I'm actually proud to be a cynic.

Cynicism, in fact, is a great thing, the American bedrock, and probably the only thing that keeps me out of orgies and off a lithium drip.

Wade's Walden—5. Modern Society—4.

LESSON TEN

Redefine the Meaning of Life and My Relationship with Gary

I learned this, at least, by my experiment: that if one advances confidently in the direction of his dreams, and endeavors to live the life which he has imagined, he will meet with a success unexpected in common hours.

—Henry David Thoreau, *Walden*

Why Are You So Frosty?

G et up!"
    I hear these words, but they are emanating from the mouths of a trio of very attractive young men and directed at my flaccid penis. In fact, they are talking into it, as if it were a mic and they were auditioning for *American Idol*.

"Get up!"

I feel my body moving, shaking, quaking. *I'll show you,* I say to the men. *I'm not that old!*

"Get up!"

I open my eyes, and Gary is standing over me. It is still dark. Marge has her eyes covered with her paws.

"What time is it?" I ask.

"It's time for you to spend a day with me," he says.

"But I have to write."

Gary walks out of the bedroom.

I stumble out of bed because I know this is a sign of the apocalypse. My human tornado is out of bluster. The man I describe as a sidewalk sale of feelings is out of emotional merchandise.

This is bad.

Very bad.

I walk into the kitchen, where Gary is standing over the sink eating a giant bowl of cereal, a special combination of five different cereals that he mixes together to create "Gary's Granola," the end result containing enough fiber to make a gorilla go "Ooohhhweee!"

"Where are you going today?" I ask gingerly.

"Does it matter? You don't even care where I go or what I do anymore."

"Yes, I do!"

"Where was I yesterday?"

"In Michigan."

"Narrow it down, please."

"Somewhere in Michigan."

"See . . ."

"What is this about?" I ask.

"You have to ask," he says, "and that's really the saddest part."

"Give me ten minutes," I say.

An hour later, I'm ready, and I settle into the SUV next to Gary, who proceeds to drive an hour to the closest city north and then an hour to the closest city inland.

I watch him silently as he goes about his day as a salesman.

He looks like an alien in his perfectly ironed, perfectly boring slacks and button-down, on his cell, talking "business" with his boss in Chicago. He looks like a pod person as he disappears into one depressing office park after another, carrying his briefcase and samples. He looks more than defeated when he returns.

He looks dead.

Where is his humor? His goofiness? His passion for life?

At noon, he pulls into a Wendy's.

I don't eat fast food. So I sit in the car and stare at him.

"I have an expense account," he says. "We can't go to a four-star restaurant."

We order Frostys and take a seat in a hard booth, Muzak humming in the background.

Could this day possibly get any more pathetic?

Yes.

Suddenly, Gary begins to cry.

I don't know what to do, although I'd like to tell the man I see at the drive-through that perhaps if he passed on the extra bacon and cheese and the super-size fries, he might not need to use a sleep apnea machine.

"I . . . can't . . . do . . . this . . . any . . . more," Gary says in tearful gasps.

He sounds like a sprinkler.

"It's . . . not . . . me. Schlepping all over the state, trying to start a branch, trying to sell. I don't even know who I am anymore. I feel like all I've done is sell out."

He stops to blow his nose.

"We supposedly moved to start over, to find ourselves. But you're the only one who's really taken a leap. And now you're alone most of the time. And you seem OK with that."

I look into Gary's dark eyes. His thick double row of lashes, which look like spiders attached to his eyes, are dewy and damp.

I ask the question I don't want to ask.

"Are you happy?"

"Does it look like it?" he answers. "I just need to know if I'm part of the equation anymore. Do I fit in with your Life Lessons, Thoreau?"

"What are you talking about? Of course you do!"

"Do I? I feel like I'm just a prop in your play sometimes. I feel like you tell me every day, 'Just get out of here so I can write.' You never say it, but that's what you tell me every day with your silence. You seem fine with my misery as long as I keep making money, keep my benefits and retirement plan, keep our world at least somewhat stable, while you do what you want. Well, I'm tired of being the stable one! I can't be the stable one!"

He stops.

He is kind of yelling now.

OK, he's shouting, really, and people are staring.

I smile at all the diners as if there might be a surprise vote after lunch on who they think is the most attractive diner at Wendy's.

Gary is right, though.

Our relationship was once built on a strong foundation, a mutual understanding: I would be the emotionally and financially stable one, and Gary would nurture me and the home while injecting fun and excitement and unpredictability.

Right now, though, it seems as if we are both standing on quicksand.

My mother once told me that any time a relationship changes—for better or worse—it feels like it is suddenly built on quicksand. There is no solid earth anymore, only a moving undertow that seems dead set on consuming you before you can even make sense of it.

Gary and I were once a modern-day Ricky and Lucy.

Only our roles have reversed now.

"I just have to know that you need me in your life, in this journey," Gary says. "And I need to know that you're OK with me taking a leap, too, because I can't go on like this. I need to follow a dream. I moved for you, but now I need to move on for me."

What would Lucy do?

She would start bawling, of course, and reach over to hug Ricky. So I follow her lead.

We are a bad after-school special, I think, *hunched over our Frostys, sobbing.*

A teen from behind the counter at Wendy's walks over and asks us if our food is OK.

"I ordered a vanilla Frosty, but I got chocolate," I lie. "I didn't realize that until now."

The girl picks up my cup, shakes it, realizes it's empty, and then looks quizzically at me.

"I have underdeveloped taste buds," I say to her. "Little-known birth defect. Takes me a while to detect flavors. It's like being color-blind in the mouth."

"I'm so sorry," the girl says, rushing away with my cup.

Gary laughs.

I slurp my new Frosty quickly until my head freezes, thankful that I can't tell if the pain in my noggin has been caused by the cold or the financial head injury our next leap of faith will surely inflict.

I See the Light

While my dream has always been to write, Gary's has been to entertain.

He would be a great first lady.

But those openings are few and far between, it seems.

So Gary begins working weekends at a local B&B owned by our new friends from Chicago. They, too, have taken a leap, leaving their corporate jobs to follow their hearts and run an inn on the water.

Though Gary is now working seven days a week—having yet to leave his sales job—his spirit and buoyancy have returned. He greets guests at the inn, checks them in, and helps prepare the gourmet breakfasts.

He experiments in our kitchen at home in his off hours, honing the perfect chocolate chip cookie recipe, adding more fresh spinach to his spinach squares, making the topping just a bit crisper on his blueberry crisp.

Gary whistles while he works, like one of the Seven Dwarves.

"Your dwarf name would be Fabulosity," I tell him.

He laughs and wipes his hands on an apron that says I GOT YOUR LOW-CARB DIET RIGHT HERE! with an arrow pointing to his nether regions.

This is the man I fell in love with, the man I knew.

A few weeks later, I am rocking in a porch swing on our back deck, which we have recently enclosed with a pergola. The sunlight is filtering through the lattice, casting everything in odd squares of

"Get me a calculator . . . please," I muttered.

"Do you realize," I said, after a few minutes of punching on the calculator, "that by the time you pay this credit card bill—if you're even still alive—that each pair of your parachute pants will cost four hundred and eighteen dollars? Do you realize that you're still paying off stuff you bought at Oaktree and J. Riggins and His Place? These stores don't even exist anymore! You're the only one who ever bought anything there!"

"Oh, my God! I loved Oaktree," he said wistfully. "They had these sweaters with leather patches on the elbows . . . it was my smart look."

"You should've worn those more often then," I said. "How could you do this? You need to grow the fuck up."

I paid off Gary's credit card debt, thinking I was saving him, but I didn't realize he didn't need saving. He had turned his life around without me—quitting drinking, ending a succession of bad relationships, going back to school—and he could have done the rest on his own, too, paying off his debt, starting his own business, finding his dream job.

But I thought he needed saving. I thought he needed me to be his Ricky. I thought he needed to fit the nine-to-five American mold, just like I had done.

Misery certainly needed company in my world.

So Gary ended up taking a sales job that included a 401(k), health insurance, and paid vacation. He ditched his own dream of becoming an entrepreneur, of building cute little vacation cottages in the woods to rent out to weary urbanites, of entertaining and decorating and cooking.

The man who never sold out, sold out.

And the most odious part was that he did it for me.

He did what he thought I wanted him to do: grow up.

But all I really ever wanted was for him to grow.

I just never allowed either one of us to do it.

Gary and I are rocking on the porch swing. Twilight is fading.

Yes, in my previous life, I would have raged right now about him quitting his job and lectured and fretted and grabbed a calculator to figure lost income.

But I have thought too long about health care plans and 401(k)s and doing what everyone else wants and expects, and fitting into a way of life that doesn't really fit into our way of life.

I have now learned that there is never a wrong time to do something meaningful and courageous in life, something that makes you deeply and achingly happy. There is only a right time: a moment to hold your breath, close your eyes, and jump.

We both have less than four hundred months in our life's checking account, but—call me stupid—that, for once, seems more important than what remains in our account at Bank of America.

I wanted a Life Lesson, and I got one. We will put our question to the test—*Are we happy?*—and pray that a resounding *yes*! leads to success and fulfillment.

For now, however, all I can do is hold Gary.

And that seems to be the only thing that matters.

We must hold tight as we leap off life's bridge and fly through the air without any parachutes. I know this time, at least, we will be holding hands and leaping together.

Gary doesn't say he's scared about what he's just done. He doesn't need to. There is a quiver in his voice, which we both pretend is caused by the chill in the air.

So we rock, and rock, and rock, just like children, because, for once in our lives, it's perfectly fine to live in the moment, to be here in the twilight.

The Garden Ninja

In the midst of our leap, we receive some good news: It looks as if our house, which has been on the market for months—a mix of being overpriced and a downturn in the housing market—will finally sell. The strain of two mortgages will finally end.

So I return to St. Louis for the first time since we moved.

I want to give our house a look-see, a quick spruce-up and cleaning, before the sale. Really, I want a final good-bye. The first time I left—on that wickedly cold winter's morning—I had bawled, more out of the fact that I was terrified about what we were doing.

I now had a second chance to say good-bye.

Gary balked at returning. Gary becomes deeply attached to things—houses, shirts, watches, a birdhouse from his mother—and he was not ready to return here yet. He needed more time. Like a decade. But we didn't have that much time. Or we'd be broke.

"It was our first house," he told me.

The trouble, however, is the fact that it remains our first house. We haven't sold it yet. I am attached to the house, too, but the sensible part of me knows we have to sell it. Immediately. Two mortgages, two taxes, two insurances, and double bills for gas and electric are beginning to add up.

We step onto our big front porch and open the creaky wood front door of our ancient brown-shingled bungalow, the transom window rattling above, as usual. Our house smells empty, alone. There is nothing really, except for a sign-in sheet and business cards from agents sitting on our kitchen counter. I walk in and shut my eyes. I can hear our Christmas parties, our parents making dinners, Gary and me laughing, Marge barking, her nails clip-clopping on the wood floors.

I can hear . . . Gary sniffling.

"I miss this house," he says. "We made a mistake. I can hear the floors creak, the windows rattle."

I hug him.

"Listen," I say.

We can also hear the highway traffic, radios and TVs, police sirens and ambulances. I can smell burgers and fries from the neighborhood bar.

Things are the same, but different.

"Do you miss that?" I ask.

And then someone yells, "Yoo-hoo! Is someone here?"

We jump. We are not expecting anyone now.

It is an agent—not our agent—showing the house. She is a heavy-set woman with a silky scarf and that determined look you see in the Glamour Shots of real estate agents all across the United States.

Her client is a handsome, seemingly bored young man, who she tells us has been transferred to the city from the West Coast. He is tan and sports a big swoop of pretty hair along with a scowl.

"You're the owners?" the agent asks. "I didn't think anyone would be here. This place is sooooo . . . what's the word? . . . Intimate. The kitchens in the homes I sell are usually bigger than this whole place."

She laughs, and I want to punch her in the face. Her neck jiggles as she chortles and then pops loose, up and over her jacquard scarf, like a jack-in-the-box.

"I thought it would be cool, you know, to own a house," the man says. "I lived in a loft."

The woman laughs. And so does her neck. She has never lived in a loft. Or done anything out of the ordinary. She bought that scarf at Dress Barn. I'm sure she thinks eating at Applebee's is a big night out.

"Where did you two move?" the agent asks me.

"Michigan."

"Ooohhhh!" she says, surprised. "You didn't stay in the city? Michigan? Why Michigan? Are you running from the law? Isn't it still winter there?"

"Is Michigan near one of the Dakotas?" the tan man asks us.

"Let me know if you have any questions," I say. "We certainly don't want to be in your way."

I hate both of your guts, I mouth silently, *but buy this stupid house.*

Gary and I exit to our sunroom off the back of the house, a bright little square with a wood floor that Gary hand-painted. It overlooks the gardens Gary spent years cultivating.

The sunroom leads down an angled deck and into a small city backyard rimmed with perennial gardens. Our old redbud, still bent and gnarled like an old man, is blooming its spectacular pinkish blooms. We spent thousands of dollars to keep this tree alive, and it is still kicking. I pop open a window to air out the room, and then we head outside to walk in the gardens. Gary visits his plants, like old friends: There is a kerria bush Gary bought with his mom. Here is a lilac he transplanted from his grandmother's yard. Here are the peonies from my mom. Here is the oakleaf hydrangea, the first plant Gary and I picked out together.

This garden is still alive with memories. It is ready to awaken to the love of a new owner.

Gary kneels on the ground and rakes some dead leaves aside with his hands. Everything has come back to life now, and both of us already know—even though we have been gone—that the gardens, with a little work, will be spectacular. Just a little tender care is all that is needed, a little watering, a little pruning, a little love. The new homeowner will have a heavenly hideaway with just a touch of effort. Gary has created something special. We are passing along a beloved family gift.

"Oh, my God, I'd just gut this whole place. You have the money. Knock down this wall and that one, really open it up, and put in the granite counters and stainless appliances we all want."

This is the agent. We can hear the conversation through the window I have opened.

"What's up with all this granny tile anyway? It creeps me out."

This is the potential buyer. Laughing, in a snotty, nasal-toned way.

And then they are on the sunroom, Gary and I hiding—like fucking insane men—underneath.

"A garden?" says the buyer. "Jesus. I don't have time for a fuckin' garden. Didn't these guys work? Were they, like, Buddhists or something? I haven't had a plant since my mom gave me a ficus. It died in like a week, man."

The two keep talking, babbling above us, until all we can hear is "rehab," and "awesome contractor," and "just flip this house, you'll make a mint."

And then we hear the potential buyer say, "What'd be cool is to rip out these lame gardens, build a master suite and bath, and then concrete the rest of the backyard. And that dead tree in the corner needs to go."

Gary and I leap out into the yard like garden ninjas, and I realize too late—though I am the nongardener—that I am the one shouting. "We can't sell this house to you. It's a 1917 bungalow. It's a piece of history. It was built as a summer retreat from the city, when this was just farmland and open space. The wood floors are original; the rooms are supposed to be boxy. And the kitchen tiles are authentic. If you want granite and oversized, useless wastes of space, this woman will find you that. Guaranteed. In the suburbs. So get out. Please get out of our house!"

"Well, I never," the woman says.

"What the fuck ever, man," the guy says.

Gary and I drive to Home Depot, buy a shovel and a hundred little plastic buckets, and dig up nearly every remaining plant in Gary's garden. We take stones and seashells we collected on vacation, we take every burning bush, hydrangea, and peony, unearth a huge rose of Sharon and joe-pye weed. We fill the back of our Honda Element until it looks like the earth has vomited into the SUV. And then we hug our beloved, tough old redbud good-bye, say so long to our little house, and drive away. Forever.

We vowed never to tell anyone what we had done.

"Our house will sell now," Gary said on the drive back to Michigan, tears forming in his eyes. "It can sell now."

And it does, just a short time later.

Wade's Walden—6. Modern Society—4.

Part Three

The Final Test

I left the woods for as good a reason as I went there. Perhaps it seemed to me that I had several more lives to live, and could not spare any more time for that one.

—HENRY DAVID THOREAU, *Walden*

There are people who put their dreams in a little box and say, "Yes, I've got dreams, of course I've got dreams." Then they put the box away and bring it out once in a while to look in it, and yep, they're still there. These are great dreams, but they never even get out of the box. It takes an uncommon amount of guts to put your dreams on the line, to hold them up and say, "How good or how bad am I?" That's where courage comes in.

—ERMA BOMBECK

The Corn's as High as Wade's Blackened Eye

am driving down our two-lane country road, talking on my cell phone, grooving to ABBA while checking my hair in the rearview mirror.

I restack my bangs just in time to see my car catapulting toward the back of a tractor that is going maybe four miles per hour, considering there's a strong wind at its back.

I stick my head out the window, forsaking my hair.

Behind the wheel of the tractor is a farmer who is roughly 150 years old. He looks a lot like that farmer in *American Gothic,* except way less expressive. And the tractor looks like one of those tractors that farmers used when Eli Whitney patented the cotton gin.

I turn down *Mamma Mia!* enough to yell, "Hey!" at the farmer.

He doesn't respond, partly because he is too busy flipping a toothpick around and around in his mouth—front to back, back to front—with his tongue, and partly because the tractor is louder and more irritating than a Jonas Brothers concert.

So I honk and yell, "Hey! Move over!"

Nothing.

No country wave, no giving me the gesture that it's OK to pass.

I should not have taken this so-called shortcut.

I crank ABBA back up, wait until we crest a small hill along some farmland, and then rev my engine and swerve into the opposite lane.

When I am parallel with the farmer, I glance over at him and see that he is pointing in front of him with his index finger.

OK, it's not really a finger, it's a nub, the only remaining section of his digit after what I am sure was some hideous combine accident.

I cannot turn away from his nub. I am sickened yet mesmerized. In fact, I instantly picture myself with my very own nub, realizing I would be rendered helpless: I would not be able to insert my contacts; I would not be able to dab on moisturizer, bronzer, or under-eye concealer; I would not be able to sport an attitude ring; I would not be able to type the letters H, J, M, N, U, or Y on my laptop, making me no longer able to utilize the words *hominy, yum,* or *jumbo* in sentences, which I instantly decide would paralyze my creativity and render me mute.

I am still staring at his nub when it begins to jab forward spastically.

I turn just in time to see a potbellied pig sitting in the middle of the road.

But of course.

I have three options, none of them good.

I can swerve into the tractor, right into Farmer Brown, only to be extracted an hour later by the jaws of life, a writer who can't write because he's now a nubby torso.

I can make sausage patties out of helpless, tubby, pink Babe, who I swear is wearing a little bow tie.

Or I can veer my car directly into the cornfield beside me.

I grab my steering wheel and yank my car into the cornfield.

When it finally comes to a stop, stalks of corn smothering my window, I lay my throbbing noggin back on my headrest and wonder—for about the hundredth time since we moved—how I got here and why I've stayed.

I am riding the El around Chicago, in town for a few days of book signings and interviews. There are city people surrounding me, people with all their fingers, people who are reading books and listening to iPods, people wearing the latest Michigan Avenue fashions, people who hatefully ignore their fellow brethren, just like they're supposed to do.

There are no turkeys or pine trees or pigs or tractors.

Only endless buildings, and people, and restaurants, and stores.

I miss the city.

The selling of our home in St. Louis was like cutting my umbilical cord to the city, and that final snip sent me—like any baby—into a wailing hissy fit.

I was fine living in the country, fine learning my lessons . . . when I still had an out.

You see, I could have always pulled our house off the market. We could have always moved back to the city.

I had an option. A plan B. But now I don't have any options. And a gay man must always have options.

Standing in Sephora, I am overwhelmed with options, so I buy $300 worth of half-ounce moisturizers and firming agents and line erasers and hair paste to undo the damage of living through raccoon attacks and blizzards and ice fishing.

I have so many options in Kenneth Cole that a clerk first assigns a guard to keep an eye on me, and later, as I haul around four pairs of shoes, asks if I'd like for my lunch to be delivered while I continue shopping.

Gary and I still worry, quietly, to ourselves, that perhaps being in a city is vital to our overall emotional health.

Which is why we explore Chicago with a sense of giddiness, much like we did when we were young and had first moved to St. Louis.

Everything is fun and new again. The buzz energizes us.

No one is driving a rusting tractor on Michigan Avenue, and I don't think I saw a feed store next to Jimmy Choo.

We spend one day mauling the Michigan Mile, hitting Bloomingdale's, Neiman Marcus, Saks, Nordstrom, Gap, Prada.

After we shop, Gary and I hit the art museum and Millennium Park, stopping only long enough to wait in line—like any local or tourist must—for Garrett's popcorn.

We see a show one night and then do it all over again the next day. Except this time, like any gay man does between shopping, we begin to discuss real estate.

Perhaps a condo in Chicago's South Loop, where everything is seemingly at our fingertips: parks, shopping, museums. Although I was a St. Louis Rams season ticket holder, I think I might even be able to convert into a Bears fan due to the proximity of Soldier Field. (But *never* a Cubs fan.)

Or maybe the Lakeview neighborhood, which has everything: great restaurants, great flavor, a great gay vibe, and a great bookstore, Unabridged.

We eat dinner outside in Lakeview before waking early and running the lakeshore. And then—just to immerse myself completely in the city, to try on my Carrie Bradshaw urban outfit and see if it fits me as well as it did in the past—I buy copies of *The New York Times, Chicago Tribune,* and *Chicago Sun-Times* and head to a city coffee-house with my laptop to write for the afternoon before my book signing.

This time, I am a real writer in the city. I am Sarah Jessica Parker in slides and he-capris. I'm no longer a wannabe. I can reinvent myself. And doesn't *Sex and the City* sound way more fun than *Sex and the Country*?

I open the door of the coffeehouse, and everyone is animated, energized, and wearing black. They look edgy.

I feel like I have lost my edge. I feel like a worn blade on a pair of Dorothy Hamill ice skates.

I need to reclaim my sharpness.

But as soon as the door to the coffeehouse closes, I hear it. Or, rather, I don't hear it: the noise. The traffic. The cabs. The honking. The construction. The yelling.

And then the door swings open again, and it sounds like the world is ending. Then it shuts, and there is a second of stillness accompanied by vampirish darkness.

I look around, and people are hunkered over tiny café tables, with newspapers, and babies, and laptops, and iPods, everyone seeking a little piece of Sunday solace.

I order a coffee, try to read, and then try to write. But my head is still buzzing from the weekend, buzzing from the buzz. I cannot concentrate.

I turn up my iPod. I try to listen to Vivaldi, but I can't write when there's any music—even classical, even no lyrics. I can't write anymore with noise.

So I mute my iPod and realize that while people are trying to talk quietly in here, they are shouting, still shouting, thinking they always have to talk over the noise, over someone else. They are conditioned to do so.

An hour passes. Two hours. My cell rings. It's Gary.

"Where are you?" he asks, in a bit of a panic. "You need to get ready for your reading and signing."

I reach down to power off my Mac, and it's then that I realize the only words I've written—like a gay Dorothy—are "I miss home."

That evening, just before I am about to read to a nice crowd at a great old bookstore, I look into the audience, stare at the faces, into their eyes, something I like to do in order to gauge who's here, who's come to hear me, who I am reaching.

I can feel an audience's vibe.

Something catches my eye over the head of a well-dressed elderly woman wearing an outfit I just saw in a window at Chico's.

Directly above her head is a copy of *Walden,* shining—impossibly—like a beacon. There are hundreds, if not thousands, of books in this store, in front of me, and my eyes are drawn to this?

I smile.

I know my signs now, so I take this one with the same seriousness as if God Himself had vaporized into the empty folding chair next to the Chico's woman, tossed a book at my head—something mammoth, like *War and Peace* perhaps—and screamed, "Pay attention, dumb ass!"

So, for the second time in my life, I do.

An antiquated honk—more like an "A-ooo-ga!" than a toot—shakes me from my shock-induced coma, and I raise my head to see the tractor moseying on past me, the farmer giving me the country wave.

Now he waves? And when did farmers get so snarky?

I give myself a once-over, and then I hear a very faint knock on my car door.

"Mamma Mia! Here I go again . . ."

It's a man in a blue shirt. His mouth is moving, but I can hear no words. And then I realize: I am partially deaf from the wreck.

"Can you turn your music down, sir?"

I do.

"I saw what happened," he continues. "Are you OK?"

"I think so."

"Can you move?"

"I think so."

"You almost hit Sassafras."

"What?"

"Sassafras. The pig in the middle of the road? Gets loose all the time. Just loves people."

Am I really having this conversation?

"You need to slow it down in these parts, don'cha know? Are you visiting from the city?"

"No, sir. I live just down the road. I've lived here for a while now."

"Really?!"

He says this as if he heard gas had just dropped to a nickel a gallon.

"Do you need a tow?"

"Yeah. But I've got Triple A."

I get out of the car, stand and make sure my legs are still attached to my torso, and then make the call to AAA, thankful I don't have a nub, or I'd be dialing 5, 5, 5, over and over.

I check my reflection in the window to make sure I don't resemble the Phantom, and that's when I realize I look like a gay scarecrow.

The dichotomy—of me, here, standing in a cornfield wearing a skintight tank top, choker, and workout shorts—is still startling.

I was speeding because I was running late to my kickboxing class.

You can take the boy out of the city . . .

Yes, I have found a gym here. Yes, I have found a tanning company. Yes, I have found myself in the middle of a cornfield.

I have, quite literally, found the best and worst of both worlds here.

I pull a stalk of corn from under my windshield wiper and look at it closely. I have lived much of my life in the country and have never actually studied a stalk of corn.

I have heard my whole life—and never believed—that stalks of sweet corn hold only one ear. I always thought the stalks I drove by every day here in the country held like a hundred ears of corn and you could feed a small town in Iowa just off a single stalk.

Well, I'll be damned.

One ear.

While I'm waiting for my tow, I pick about ten ears and toss them in my car, which means I won't have to stop at the produce stand this week.

The tow truck driver finally pulls into the field—leaving smashed stalks of corn in his wake—and the first thing he says to me is, "Don't I plow your driveway in the winter?"

"Don't know," I say. "I've never actually seen your face. Want some corn? It's free."

"That's field corn," he tells me. "You can't eat that."

Yes, I am still the world's most unlikely Thoreau.

The truck tows me back onto the road—my car makes it out, like me, amazingly, unscathed, except for some scattered kernels and husks trapped under my windshield wipers—and I drive home and immediately head to the screen porch.

It's time to center myself.

I close my eyes, block out the world, and as I am reaching a point of complete calm, I hear what sounds like the quiet whoosh of snow. When I open my eyes, it looks like it is snowing.

In the middle of summer.

I smile. Since I recognize my signs now, I leave the screen porch, the door banging my exit, Marge following, and make my way into our woods, my place of worship, in search of cool and quiet.

In search of the snow.

I find it at the base of a few old, giant cottonwood trees and sprawl my body under them, wait patiently for a strong, warm summer wind to come and exhale its last breaths, a hot sigh that blows the cotton from the trees, which drifts down over me like summer snow.

I shut my eyes, and when I look up at the falling cotton, I fool myself and pretend it is winter, knowing it's just a few months until the resorters leave and the lakeshore is all mine.

Fall will come in all its rural brilliance, the sugar maples' leaves will turn Technicolor shades of red and gold and orange, and then the days will turn colder, shorter. The snow will begin to fall, and this time I will welcome the solitude to sled, to snowshoe, to write, to reclaim the woods and our little picture-perfect towns.

And then Gary and I will thumb our noses at winter, pack up Marge and all of our luggage, and head to Palm Springs in February, because while I love my life in the woods, the city is still part of me, just like the country was part of me when I lived in the city.

I can only take so much snow. I need sun. I need warmth. I need people. I need a highway or two.

I also need a tan, good shopping, and a twenty-screen cineplex with stadium seating. Even if it's just for a couple of months.

And I'm OK with that.

Am I still scared?

Yes.

Many days, I feel as if we are still free-falling from this giant leap in our lives, but most days I am thrilled to be in charge of my destiny. I firmly believe now that life must have risk, both calculated and irrational.

Did I create Wade's Walden?

Yes.

And no.

Let's call it a draw, shall we, like a hard-fought hockey game that ends in a tie, each opponent earning new respect from the other. Or, better yet, I am first runner-up in the Miss Michigan pageant, knowing the experience has made me a better person and that perhaps, just perhaps, I'll nab the crown the next year, or the next.

My life here—like everyone's life—is an ongoing duel between right and wrong, decisions made and decisions squandered, courage vs. inertia, dreams that you dream and dreams that you make come true.

But my ongoing duel—my city-country tango—seems to work well: I may wander our woods in women's jeans, shop for mole killer at the country store in giant Gucci sunglasses, and never be able to live off the land like Thoreau, but that doesn't mean I don't appreciate what's happening around me, what's happening inside me.

I have learned it's not about *reinventing* myself, it's about *becoming* who I always knew I could be.

Coyote Ugly

t's Thursday night.

    Garbage night.

I ain't afraid of no stinkin' raccoon.

That's because I now know how to protect myself: I bungee-cord the garbage can lid shut.

Yes, I have learned a lot during my time at Wade's Walden.

It is a warm night, and I haul our giant-wheeled trash bin up our long, winding gravel road in plaid flip-flops, plaid shorts, a tank top with some sort of lifeguard symbol on the front, and a choker with greeny-blue glass beads that match my eyes.

Of course, it's dark, and no one can see me. But that's beside the point.

I am me.

I will always be the world's most unlikely Thoreau.

But aren't we all? Isn't that the point in life, to fall, to fail, to stand up and move on, to find out who we really are before it's too late? I mean, how can we find our path if we don't know where we're going or why we're headed there?

I drop the trash off—wheeling the can the right way, or Lord knows they won't pick it up—look over, and roll my eyes at the illuminated trailer, which now features a fuchsia sheet as a dining room curtain.

Nice look. I must've missed that in the latest Pottery Barn catalog.

An owl hoots in a nearby sugar maple.

I ratchet my head upward. I can see the owl's giant eyes peering down at me.

And then something rushes by in the woods.

Or should I say some *things*.

I hear baying, barking, and my stomach drops. I spin around, going, "Whoa! Whoa! Whoa!" in the sort of voice Tim Gunn might use if he were mugged.

Suddenly, it is quiet again, and the clouds pass to reveal a full moon.

I look up. It is bright as day.

And then a group of coyotes yip—one, then another, almost like hyenas, until their voices merge into a choir formed in the depths of hell.

One of the many things I have learned in the country, especially from my camouflaged compadres at the country store, is that you don't want to mess with coyotes. I remember the boys saying that sirens and strobe lights tend to scare them, but, damn, I don't seem to be carrying any of those in my plaid J. Crew shorts tonight.

However, my rural brethren also said that yelling and throwing rocks and sticks can work, too.

You see, these are the things we talk about—instead of *Project Runway*—in the middle of nowhere when it's nine o'clock, a storm is approaching, and you need to buy a generator and a case of beer.

I pick up a handful of gravel, throw it into the night, and begin screaming, but nothing's changed since the first day I moved: No one can hear me holler out here in my holler, and anyway, I sound like a junior high school cheerleader who just got tickled by her boyfriend.

Then I see something that looks like a small collie scoot by on the edge of our land, and I feel my bladder convulse and then clench.

The number-one rule of thumb I have learned about coyotes is never to turn and run. Though coyotes are rarely a threat to people, they might view anything that flees as scared prey, like a small dog. And, Lord knows, a coyote could easily mistake me for a shih tzu.

The coyotes bay once more, and I think, *Screw this!* So I run, like Carl Lewis in the Olympic hundred-yard flip-flop dash, making it almost to the end of the driveway before I blow one out.

Damn you, Old Navy!

Somehow, I make it, breathless, into the darkened back entryway of our house and am able to bolt the patio door shut before I turn and trip over something furry and dense sitting in the middle of our floor.

I am on my knees, in pain, trying to remain motionless, still.

I rotate my head just enough to see a raccoon glaring at me.

I scream.

Something along the lines of "Oowadooiedibbledow!"

I can tell my knee is bleeding, but I'm hoping the urine I released moments earlier will serve as a natural antiseptic or antidote, like it does on stingray bites.

And then I hear little paws tripping along our floor, percussion to the bass of my pounding heart.

All of the animals in Michigan's woods have banded together to kill me. It's like they were trained and then released into our woods by Jerry Falwell.

Or perhaps this is the vengeful offspring of Burt. Like Son of Chucky.

The scratching is getting closer, so I reach for the Sephora artillery I still carry, no matter when or where.

And then something is licking me, on me, and I can feel hot breath on my face.

"Are you . . . ?"

I jab at the raccoon with my lip shimmer.

And then I squirt my spearmint breath spray.

Twice.

Because that's what I always do to ensure freshness.

Wait a second. Raccoons can talk?

"What the hell are you doing? Stop! Stop!"

It's Gary. He is coughing violently.

He grapples for the wall and finds the light switch.

He is rubbing his eyes, still coughing.

"I heard you scream, Thoreau. I wanted to see if you were OK."

And then I hear Marge reverse-sneezing.

"You tripped over one of the dog's stuffed animals, you idiot," Gary says.

I turn, and a fuzzy brown raccoon from PetSmart is smiling dopily at me.

"I'm sure you and Marge both have really nice breath now," I say.

"And seared retinas," he adds before managing a laugh and taking a seat by me on the floor. He briskly rubs his reddening cheek, where I jabbed him with my tube of Burt's Bees.

Sitting on our butts on the brick floor by our back patio door, we can see the moon hanging low in the sky.

"It's a beautiful night, isn't it?" I say.

"Mmmm," Gary sighs, sounding suddenly content. "It usually is out here."

The moon is huge, and it brightens the countryside. Through our open windows, I can smell the end-of-summer breeze, which is soft and a touch cool, the air filled with the smells of the lake and Gary's flowers and the grass and the aging knotty pine of Turkey Run.

I grab Gary's hand, and he puts his head on my shoulder. We are the kings of codependence.

"Are you happy?" I ask.

"Yes," he answers. "For the most part. I feel like I'm still finding myself, but I don't think that journey has an end, you know. I still hate living next to a trailer, and I wish this area would change more quickly, but I'm learning *want* and *need* are very different from *happy*."

He pats Marge on the head, and she kisses his face.

"How about you?" he asks. "Are you happy?"

"I think so. I'm learning it's OK to be. You know, I'm still cynical, I still need a little city in my country life, but . . ."

And here I stop because I sound like Dr. Phil.

"But, honestly, I feel like I can finally stop running. I feel like I'm finally home."

Gary sighs, chokes back a sob—we are *so* dramatic—and he puts his head back on my shoulder for a second.

"Hey. Can I ask you another question?"

Gary nods.

"What would you do if you could not fail?"

He looks at me and then at the moon. "Honestly? I'd open a rural retreat center for urbanites who need to detox. I'd build a few knotty pine cottages—just like Turkey Run—on our property and forbid guests to bring cell phones and laptops. I'd make them great, healthy breakfasts and offer yoga on the beach, meditation, exercise, hiking, kayaking. I'd give them what we have, if only for a few days. I think the world needs to relax, people need to laugh, people need to de-stress. Our world is missing *this*."

"I want you to have that," I say. "You *will* have that. I want you to live your dream, too."

"Oh, and I'd learn to dance. Two gay men with four left feet should learn to dance. I mean, Midwestern white people are so repressed with how they view their bodies," Gary continues. I made the mistake, I realize too late, of asking him an open-ended question. True-false or multiple choice always works best. "And I want to travel, maybe live in a foreign country someday."

I picture all of this and see us getting voted off *Dancing with the Stars* before sequestering ourselves in a whitewashed villa in Greece, and then trying to smuggle Marge into Mexico and ending up in a stifling Tijuana jail with dirt floors washing men's bodies with banana leaves.

I decide all options seem fine and dandy.

"What about you, Thoreau?" Gary asks. "What would you do if you could not fail?"

"Exactly what I'm doing now. I want to write the rest of my life. Memoirs. Real life is so much more bizarre and interesting than fiction, isn't it? Especially when we're involved."

And then, somewhere in the woods, very close by, the coyotes yip, Marge begins to bay, and we stand and sprint around our cottage, shutting all the curtains and bolting all the doors.

"What are we doing?" I finally ask. "We're *inside*."

"Don't be an idiot," Gary says, jumping into bed and pulling the comforter up to his chin. "I mean, if Marge can open a door with her snout, don't you think starving country coyotes could open a door with theirs? *Hello!*"

"Are you telling me," I say, because I can never let a stupid conversation go, "that you think a coyote has the mental and nostril dexterity to unlatch the lock on our front door, then turn the knob clockwise, enter our home, open our bedroom door, make it to the bathroom—where, by then, we would be hiding—and slide open a pocket door before ripping us apart?"

"Yes! Exactly! You finally get it!" he says. "But you wanna know the worst part? No one would hear us. We'd just yell ourselves silly while we got mangled. I mean, at least in the city someone would hear me scream."

And I've got to hand it to him this time: He's 100 percent right.

I kick off my flip-flops and shorts and snuggle into bed next to Gary, Marge jumping in last to spoon my empty side.

In the distance, the coyotes howl.

The moon illuminates the shadows of windblown pines and sugar maples dancing beyond our curtains like Zumba instructors, and before we begin to drift off in our little corner of the country—two city boys still trying to make their way in the woods, in this world—I whisper the bedtime saying we've become so fond of repeating:

"Good night, Ricky," I say.

"Good night, Lucy," Gary replies.

Acknowledgments

The following folks deserve oodles of thanks, more than these few lines can truly deliver.

My parents: You should have your own reality show. I'd love to see the girls from *The Hills* come spend a year with you in the Ozarks. Truly, I love you more than you'll ever know. And, Mom, you will make it through this, got it? I need you.

Gary: You are a brave man to let me write about your life without editing; you are a crazy man for believing in me so wholeheartedly, which is frightening and completely undeserved; and, most of all, you are a kind, compassionate, beautiful man, which is why I love you.

Wendy Sherman: You say, "Write," and I write. And then you make incredible things happen. But I could not write every day about my life without feeling such trust and without knowing there is such belief in my work.

Julia Pastore: You are talented, patient, and unwavering. You make every sentence stronger, every book better. You believe, too. And that makes me believe.

Shaye Areheart: Thanks for your continuing enthusiasm and support.

Melanie DeNardo: I mean, come on, she loves my stuff. And she knows her stuff. And she tries to accomplish the impossible. I should know; I was a PR guy who couldn't hack it any longer.

Everyone at Harmony and Crown: Thank you for your hard work, expertise, support, and enthusiasm.

Carol Fitzgerald: You are a human tornado, and your enthusiasm sweeps me to a better place.

To Saugatuck-Douglas: Thanks for welcoming another unconventional artist into your artists' community.

I would also like to thank and credit a number of source materials, references, and authors that not only provided background research on Thoreau but, in a few instances, also stated my thoughts and feelings better than I could: Jonathan Levin, who wrote the introduction to the Barnes & Noble Classics edition of *Walden and Civil Disobedience*, provided more illumination than all of Gary's night-lights combined. The quote in my opening essay—"To find myself, to find my modern-day Walden Pond, by stripping away superfluous luxuries and living a plainer, simpler life"—is really his words, simplified. In addition, his introduction provided terrific background and insight for the essay "Wade's Walden," as well as into Thoreau the man and *Walden* the book; I thank him and his more highly developed intellect profusely.

I also quoted from Cindy McGroarty's April 11, 2005, *Newtopia Magazine* article "Yankee Independence: Henry David Thoreau and the Birth of American Counterculture" in the essay "My Church," and her thoughts helped me understand Thoreau's view of and struggle with organized religion more clearly.

In addition, I used numerous online sources, such as *Encyclopaedia Britannica* and Wikipedia, to provide background and research.

And, finally, to Henry David Thoreau: Thanks for wandering into the woods so that others could follow and reconnect to those things that matter most in life.

About the Author

Wade Rouse is the critically acclaimed author of *America's Boy: A Memoir* and *Confessions of a Prep School Mommy Handler: A Memoir.* His essays have appeared in numerous publications and collections, including *The Customer Is Always Wrong: The Retail Chronicles.* A graduate of Drury University and Northwestern University, he lives in Michigan, where—between blizzards and beach weather—he is busy writing his next memoir and inventing a pair of waders that are stylish, functional, and feature a slight heel.

Visit Wade's website at www.WadeRouse.com.